PURSUED BY A BEAR

DAVID HOWARTH

Pursued by a Bear

AN AUTOBIOGRAPHY

COLLINS
8 Grafton Street, London W1
1986

William Collins Sons & Co. Ltd
London · Glasgow · Sydney · Auckland
Toronto · Johannesburg

BRITISH LIBRARY CATALOGUING IN PUBLICATION DATA

Howarth, David, *1912*–
Pursued by a bear: an autobiography.
1. Howarth, David, *1912*– – Biography
2. Authors, English – 20th century – Biography
I. Title
941.082'.092'4   PR6058.089/

First published 1986
Copyright © David Howarth 1986

ISBN 0-00-217525-8

Photoset in Linotron Sabon by
Rowland Phototypesetting Ltd
Bury St Edmunds, Suffolk
Printed and Bound in Great Britain by
T.J. Press (Padstow) Ltd, Padstow, Cornwall

CONTENTS

ILLUSTRATIONS

ONE

But what's it all for?

Usually, the title of a book or of a chapter is the last bit of it that I write. I am not much good at titles. But I owe this chapter title to a massive lady who climbed the Acropolis of Athens on a summer afternoon, steaming at the armpits. I was sitting in the shade at the top, trying to look cool and learned.

'Dave,' she shouted, fanning herself with the *New York Herald Tribune*, and of course I listened. But it was not me she was calling; it was a small gnarled man in a Panama hat.

'Dave,' she repeated, and nodded her head at the Parthenon. 'You know all the answers. So what's it all for?'

'Why, I told you, honey,' he said. 'It's a temple.'

'Sure, I can see it's a temple. I'm not stupid. But I mean, what's it all *for*?' But Dave was not listening, he was watching a bright blue butterfly, and making half-hearted lunges as if he hoped to catch it in his hat.

'Well, for God's sake,' she said hopelessly to the world at large, 'we come all this way to see a temple, and all he can look at is a goddam butterfly.' Nobody answered. I ought to have tried, but I had been busy asking myself the same question, not only about the ancient temple but about life in general, and my own in particular. What's it all *for*? I was no nearer to an answer than Dave; further perhaps, because he – confronted by that enormous man-made miracle – had the sense to watch the small miracle that was not man-made, and seemed to be satisfied with wonder.

It was years ago, and now I am getting old but still no nearer to an answer. If I were, I would be a genius or a preacher, but I am neither.

*

It's a mistake, I know, to start a simple story with pretentious ideas, half-baked. But it is really rather hard on civilized humans that each of them should know he is an insoluble enigma; it muddles so many things they do. That is what I was thinking as I sat on those stones, worn by millions of feet in thousands of years – and what I have often thought before and since in other, less hallowed places. It worried the ancient Greeks precisely as it worries the people who programme computers; and in between them, philosophers and priests and poets have put the problem into words but never arrived at a satisfactory answer – or none that satisfies the rather meagre brain I am equipped with. 'Our little life is rounded with a sleep'; or, as Swinburne put it more exactly, 'a watch or a vision between a sleep and a sleep'. For there are two sleeps, one before I was born and the other after I am dead. Unable to think of either with any clarity, we guess they are the same, with life as a dream or a short awakening between them. I am much nearer now to the second than the first: seventy years from the first, and perhaps five years, or even five minutes, from the second. It does not worry me that I did not exist in 1905, so why should I worry that I shall not exist in 1995? I do not need to imagine life after death, any more than I can imagine life before birth. It has been fun to wake up in the twentieth century, but not in the least important: in history, it is clearly the normal state of affairs that I should be either unborn and unthought of, or dead and forgotten. I am rather sorry that the most interesting decade of the century is probably still to come, and I shall miss it – the time when computers develop an artificial intelligence far ahead of ours.

Yet in the dream, or in the short awakening, things happen. You have adventures, exciting or comic, which seem to be unique; you share experience with your fellow humans, you begin to learn, you fall in love, you deceive yourself with an image of yourself – until you can hardly believe that in all those years you have never done anything that would amuse or interest anyone else, that you have never learned anything worth passing on. Perhaps it is foolish conceit, and if so I am ashamed of it, but the longer you survive, the stronger the feeling becomes. Hence autobiography.

And there is one difference between the two sleeps; not an

inherent difference perhaps – nobody can possibly know – but a difference in the way I look at them, caused by that other mystery, the passage of time. I can only guess what will be happening ten years after I die, but I can read or be told what was happening ten years before I was born. So I have glimpses of the very surprising series of chances which led in the end to the secret moment when my parents joined to conceive me and provided the mixture of genes that made the creature I call 'me' and other people call 'him'. Look at it that way, and being conceived is more an end than a beginning, and the story of anyone's life ought to go back far beyond it. I am going to start in 1814.

Before I dig back so far, I must just introduce two small boys a hundred and one years later: Londoners, five and three years old, in the middle of the First World War, probably in sailor suits, tidily starched and pressed in the manner only old-fashioned nannies achieved. I recognize the older one as my brother, but I do not recognize the younger one as me. I suppose this is a difficulty everyone has in seeing himself when he was very small. One always sees everyone else, even one's brother, from outside, but one grows to see oneself uniquely from inside. That is what I cannot do with that overpolished child. He is hardly awake from his timeless sleep. All I know about him is secondhand: he was unnaturally solemn, so solemn that a friend of his parents called Harry Bashford, when the child was not much over one, bet him five shillings he would be a bishop before he was thirty. It was not such long odds as it sounds – the family had always been prolific in producing bishops. I don't remember meeting Harry Bashford again for fifty years, but he lost the bet and on the very day of my thirtieth birthday he sent me a cheque for five shillings.

So I see the brothers doing things long before I can see that one of them was me. They go for decorous walks every day in parks with their nanny, firmly holding on to a pram that contains an even smaller sister, sometimes going as far as Holland Park or Kensington Gardens, though that means crossing the main street of Notting Hill Gate, menaced by motor buses. In retrospect, it always looks like autumn. They can see their own breath; the pavements are slippery with wet leaves from the plane trees;

sometimes there is dirty snow, or the pea-soup fog that London was famous for. Those fogs really were the greenish yellow of pea soup; you could scarcely see your hand in front of your face, the lamps of carts and carriages loomed up a yard away, and even nannies lost their way home.

The brothers met other similar children with other nannies in the parks, but they did not like them much. People they regularly met and liked were crossing sweepers, who must have been desperately poor. Their job was to sweep up the horses' droppings on crossroads, so that even ladies in their long skirts could cross the road. When they had nothing to sweep, which must have been most of the time, they sat on wooden boxes which contained their brooms and shovels and their lunch. I do not know if anyone employed them. Probably they existed on pennies from passers-by. Anyhow, the brothers gave them pennies, I hope without an air of condescension, and were sometimes given an orange from the box.

Other people who got pennies were organ-grinders, but seldom face to face. If an organ struck up its tune outside the house, you wrapped up a penny in a bit of paper and threw it out of the window, and then watched through the nursery window-bars to see the organ-grinder hunt for it in the gutter and touch his cap. Very superior people affected to despise the organs, and sent out a servant with 'sixpence to go to the next street'. The brothers did not approve of that, and I think they were right. Before radio or gramophones, the organs at least were cheerful.

The family lived at 24 Lansdowne Crescent, one of those tall, thin London houses with six storeys from the basement, where the servants worked, to the attics where they slept. I doubt if anyone now has the whole of such an inconvenient house; they are turned into apartments or bedsitters. But you did not have to be rich to have one then, with a nanny, a cook and three maids. The family was not rich, but hard-working and middle-class: their father had a civilian job in the Admiralty, and so did their mother in wartime. Of course the children were privileged, and of course there was a shocking gap between rich and poor. But the brothers were too small to know about privilege, and would have been instantly sat upon by their elders if they had shown any sign of being snobs. Nannies were the only people allowed to be snobs: with their vocations, they had to be. But a good nanny was the centre of her family, loving and loved. People brought up by them often loved them more than they loved their parents. It was not unfilial, just that one saw them more. They were the people who were always there, with comfort when it was needed. It made children more vulnerable. Inevitably, nannies sometimes left, and when they did it was as awful as a death. When our favourite nanny left to get married, I got under a table which had a cloth hanging down all round, and in the privacy of that sort of tent I howled and sniffed for hours. To get *married*? Why in the world did she want to get married? Weren't we all happy together? Everyone left me there, wisely I expect, until I recovered and stopped; but I was never quite the same again. I had glimpsed how cruel and strange the world could be.

Lansdowne Crescent was on the very edge of the respectable part of Kensington, where it degenerated to the slums around the tracks of the Great Western Railway. It still is. The brothers were never taken down the hill towards the tracks, and they did not know slums existed. But a favourite walk led past the end of the street market of Portobello Road. The nannies made them clutch the pram more tightly, and hustled them past. Heaven knows what dangers they imagined lurking down there: the Lower Classes perhaps, who might be dirty or even use rude words. To the boys it was fascinating, the shouts of the traders and the wild shadows of acetylene flares on windy winter days, and they longed to plunge in and join it.

The brothers must have gone that way on the first day I clearly remember. A grandmother had taken them for their walk (sometimes even nannies had half a day off) and they went to a toy shop called The Dolls' Hospital. It was quite a long way on very short legs. It was not autumn for once; when they came out of the shop there was bright blue sky above, and looking up they all saw a crowd of silvery aircraft. That grandmother was famous for inappropriate comments. 'Look, children,' she said, 'there go our brave defenders.' Whereupon there was a racket of bombs and gunfire, and puff-balls of anti-aircraft fire surrounded the planes; for they were not our brave defenders at all, they were German, and it was the first ever daylight air raid on London.

We made for home. But my brother had a sort of tricycle called Quicksilver, which he propelled by pulling and pushing a hand-lever, and Quicksilver was not quick, he was dismally slow, and slower still if you tried to push him. Our grandmother was harassed, and no wonder, not so much perhaps by the bombs, which were small in those days, as by the hot jagged lumps of anti-aircraft shells which were falling all around and by our snail's progress, and she seized Quicksilver and hurled him into somebody's front garden.

That was what woke me from primordial sleep — not the aircraft, which were pretty, or the bombs, which were quite exciting, but the sudden awful demise of Quicksilver. (I dare say somebody rescued him, or the bits of him, afterwards, but I thought he had gone for ever.) That taught me that war was a serious affair, and that I had enemies, although I had not meant them any harm — two lessons I have never had time to forget. I know it was trivial, and I know hosts of children since then have learned the same lesson in far more shocking ways. Even then, there were hosts whose fathers disappeared and never came back, and other hosts (but not English) whose homes became battlefields. I was lucky. But I see myself quite clearly, for the first time, as part of those events; I became a person that day. The two brothers became not 'they' but 'we'.

I did not mean to write much about my brother: he would not thank me for writing his biography. But the more I think about childhood, the more do I remember that he shared it all with me. He was always there, always two years ahead of me and invariably a helpful, kind and patient boss. Until we went to school, I don't think we felt the need for any other friends. I have known him longer than anyone else, and he has always been the same, in spite of all sorts of provocation. There ought to be an ode to elder brothers.

Our mother was a Paget, and Pagets have been distinguished in English history since the time of Henry VIII. Now and again when I was young I had vague ideas of aristocratic ancestors. In particular, I hoped I was descended from Lord Uxbridge, who was a Paget and commanded Wellington's cavalry at Waterloo; it was he who produced that enchanting if legendary bit of dialogue when he was riding beside the Duke at the end of the battle and was hit in the leg:

His Lordship: By God, sir, I've lost a leg.

His Grace: By God, sir, so you have.

— and then was carried four miles to the village of Waterloo by four soldiers holding the corners of a blanket, and had the shattered leg sawn off on somebody's dining table without the slightest change in his pulse-rate, although the surgeons' saws were getting blunt by that time in the day.

He was a martial hero all right, but he was not my ancestor at all. I learned later that there are at least two families of Pagets, the grand Pagets and the poor Pagets. We are the poor Pagets. In 1815, when Lord Uxbridge was leading his famous charge and losing the best part of his cavalry by mistake, my own direct ancestor was Samuel Paget, a peaceful ships' chandler and a minor ship-owner in the small North Sea port of Yarmouth. His wife Betsey was a homely, apple-cheeked person, and their son James, who was my great-grandfather, had been born the year before. I doubt if Lord Uxbridge would have deigned to speak to Samuel had they ever met; he was not even a minor country gentleman, he was a tradesman whose father had been a small-time smuggler, and snobbery then was outrageous. But Samuel was quite a grand person in his own little world of Yarmouth. He was elected mayor, and built a dignified house for himself and his family on the quayside.

In fact, the people of Yarmouth took hardly any notice of the battle of Waterloo. They had had such a stupendous party the year before when Buonaparte, as they called him, was imprisoned in Elba, that another would have been an anticlimax. On that occasion, in April 1814, they had set up a row of tables half a mile long on the Yarmouth quay, and 8023 people sat down together to dine on beef, plum puddings and beer, while the bands of the local militia marched up and down playing 'martial and other airs'. The first table was opposite Samuel Paget's house, and he and Betsey presided at it. She had roasted a rump of beef and boiled a hundred and fifty pounds of pudding. He had provided the plates and jugs and spoons, the bread and the barrel of beer, and sixty clay pipes and half-ounces of tobacco. After dinner, fifteen toasts were drunk, each on a gun signal from one of his ships, and there was the biggest bonfire anyone had ever seen. It was a bucolic affair, but as well organized as any state occasion and probably much more fun; and Paget, as everyone called him (even his wife), was one of the leaders of the town who ran it all.

Later in life, he had a disaster. He is said to have been the only Englishman who ever went bankrupt running a brewery. Now, that seems a rather endearing and comic achievement, and typically Paget – the Pagets are not often businessmen. But at the time it was a long-drawn-out tragedy. Nobody blamed Paget for it; it seems he just brewed his beer too well and sold it too cheaply. But also, he financed the whole thing with mortgages the trade could never carry. Bit by bit, he had to sell everything: first the chandlery and the ships he owned and had named after members of his family; then the brewery itself; then the big house on the quay; and finally, all the family's treasures inside it. None of it raised anything like as much money as he expected, and he was still in debt when he died, though he never seemed to understand he was.

The Pagets were always good at producing large families, closely united, proud of their own peculiar customs, and perhaps a bit too prone to mutual admiration. Samuel's was the largest of all, but it was dogged by tragedies. Betsey had seventeen children in twenty-five years. The first, a daughter, lived to be over eighty, but eight died as children. Three more, all sons, died in their twenties or early thirties leaving only the youngest, who was another daughter, and four surviving sons. One of those four, whom all the others thought eccentric, was the only one who deserted Yarmouth and the family circle. He went to Peru, had three wives and nine children, and ran up debts of his own. Another became a schoolteacher and then a vicar. Luckily, the other two were brilliant. George became Professor of Physic at Cambridge University and was knighted, and James, my great-grandfather, became the leading surgeon of his time, Surgeon Extraordinary (whatever that was) to Queen Victoria, and a baronet. As young men, in order to salvage the old man's credit, they both raised money by insuring their lives and borrowing on the insurance. When they began to earn, they both chose to live in poverty, putting all their savings into paying the brewery's debts. Fourteen years after Samuel died James was still doing it, and quoting the maxim 'Owe no man anything but love.' He was engaged, but put off getting married for six years because the debts came first. When at last he won through to Victorian fame and prosperity, he set about building a distinguished family of his own in a mansion in Harewood Place, which is still on the edge of the fashionable medical district of London. His children are the first of the Pagets I remember, in their old age. The youngest son Stephen was my grandfather; he followed his father and became a surgeon.

All in all, the Pagets were certainly people with a character of their own, and I can see bits of them all in myself, and in my brother and cousins. One prominent bit is the Paget nose. All Samuel's sons had it, and all of us, even half-Pagets, have it now: large, with an air of commanding nobility but far from ornamental, a kind of mixture of Red Indian, the Duke of Wellington and Roman emperor. The girls have it too, but mercifully a modified version. My own daughters have it, to their grief, although they are only a quarter Paget; and my brother once met a stranger in a train and both of them instantly recognized the other as a Paget by his nose. The stranger turned out to be the baronet of his time. It must be a powerful gene that has preserved this patrician hooter through five generations, and more subtle aspects of Paget character also linger in us all. Whatever else we are, we are all unmistakably Pagets.

The one I most hope I resemble is my grandfather Stephen. He was not the most brilliant of Sir James's six children (two of the sons became bishops, and one a King's Counsel), nor the most eccentric. The prize for eccentric charm must go to his sister Mary Maud, who was known to us all as Aunt Midge. She was a first-class pianist. In her middle age she went totally blind, but carried on playing the piano. She never married, and was far from a beauty: she had the long Paget face and an outstanding Paget nose, and she wore a curly wig. Yet she was so full of life that even when she was stone blind and in her fifties, men kept falling in love with her; it was said the farthest outposts of the Empire were full of Aunt Midge's rejected suitors, trying to forget. She founded a club in the slums of North Kensington and ran it for years, and her house, not far from ours, was always full of destitute people who came for help and advice, mixed up with a bevy of young artists. She once invited the latter to redecorate the house. As she could not see what they were doing, they painted every banister on the stairs a different colour, which delighted her when she was told, and for the hall they chose a wallpaper with lines on it. The lines were supposed to be vertical, but they stuck it on sideways, so that it made a vast sheet of musical manuscript paper. Her guests were firmly invited to compose a few bars, inscribe them on the wall and sign them, and enshrined in one corner was the contribution of Sir Edward Elgar.

Our grandfather Stephen was a saintly man who never went to church; he said he felt nearer to God in the woods and fields. Perhaps it was a mistake to follow his famous father in surgery. He always said he was a failure, although for years and years he had consulting rooms and a house, a whole house, in Harley Street, the centre of the medical profession, which most surgeons would think the ultimate peak of success. In fact he must have been a very good surgeon, but he never made much money because he was too diffident. Our grandmother, hard up for housekeeping money, used to search in his pockets and find fat cheques he had not cashed because he felt he had not deserved them; often when he had a very rich patient he would recommend other surgeons who he said were more likely to effect a cure. When he did take on rich patients of course they paid him well, and gave him immensely heavy silver tea-sets; but he took on poor ones too, operated with equally meticulous skill and charged them nothing at all. On the contrary, he would find out who their dependants were and where they lived, and ask his wife to support them and look after them until the patient was well and able to earn his living again. So the couple acquired hundreds of destitute friends, and cherished them with perfectly Christian devotion. They called it helping lame dogs over stiles, and it was one of the principal interests of their lives. It was also where the money went.

These two were very dependent on each other. Whenever they were apart they wrote to each other twice a day. I have a scrapbook his wife kept on her honeymoon. Stephen took her to Switzerland, and lost their luggage on the way. He also took her on long walks in the mountains before breakfast. She did not enjoy them much, but realized they were the sort of thing she would have to get used to. So was his other-worldliness about money. They had twin babies, boys, who were stillborn, and after that two daughters, my mother and my aunt, but that was all – a small family for Pagets.

He gave up his practice altogether when he was only fifty or so, partly through his chronic diffidence and partly his chronic ill health: he had tuberculosis, and had to have thirteen major operations – an ordeal for a surgeon, one imagines. He took to writing books, some medical tomes and some collections of philosophical essays 'for the young people' – especially for his own daughters and for my brother, who was his first grandson and named Stephen after him. He was almost as bad at titles as I am. One of the collections was called *I Sometimes Think*, which was a gift to rude reviewers – 'It is good to know that Mr Paget sometimes thinks.' They were not best-sellers, but they were gentle and wise and are very well worth reading seventy years later – not least for the dedications. Not for the printed dedications – one of those said simply 'These essays are not worth dedicating to anybody' – but for the dedications to his wife that he wrote in longhand on the fly-leaves. Some of these were in verse, and this is the first half of one, dated Christmas Day 1910, which is especially like him:

> Oh thin and high-flown little book,
> So like the man who wrote you;
> Think not the busy world will look
> Inside you, read, or quote you.
>
> But go to her who, all these years,
> Has always made the best of me,
> Keeping me straight through doubts and fears,
> And all the stupid rest of me.
>
> Tell her I wonder if, and why,
> And where, and when, and wherefore;
> And how it is that I am I,
> And what the stars are there for.

And so on, diffident and loving.

All this may make him sound rather a prig, but he was not. His brothers the bishops published books of their sermons, but he never preached; he was far too humble. 'Nature never preaches to us,' he wrote in an essay on Wonder, and he simply set an example of tolerance and kindness, without ever putting it into words. It was said he never spoke unkindly of anyone.

His example had its most lasting effect through the musical parties they had every Sunday night. Most of the regular guests at these parties were young – his daughters' generation – and of course they made their own music: some of it was very good, my grandfather said, and did not add that some of it was bad.

These younger people, all in their early twenties, had far more freedom that one might expect of the Edwardian era. Once they had met, they did not only meet on Sundays. They went to theatres and dances together, gave charity concerts for the benefit of the poor, and spent their holidays, young men and girls, unchaperoned, canoeing on rivers and staying the nights in pubs. In the end, most of them married each other, and most of my parents' life-long friends first met at those musical evenings. For this was where my father came in. He could sing.

The Howarths came from even humbler origins than the Pagets. The first one we know of was an attendant at the public baths in Manchester at the end of the eighteenth century: surprising that there were any public baths, or any other sorts of baths in Manchester then. But he had a clever son, Henry, who went into the Church and shrewdly married into a family of bishops, so making a total of five bishops in my ancestry – or is it six? – which must be well above the normal quota. (That marriage also brought me an ancestor I know nothing about except his name. It was Habakkuk Postle.) So Henry quickly rose in his vocation and became rector of St George's, Hanover Square, which was and still is well known in London for fashionable weddings. That may have been when the Pagets and Howarths first met, two generations back from my parents. St George's is only a couple of hundred yards from Sir James's grand house in Harewood Place. It was his parish church.

The Howarths had a disaster too, even more dramatic than

the Pagets'. The Rev. Henry had several daughters but only one son, and when he was very young the son married a girl called Mary Macfarlane, who was only nineteen – my other grandfather and grandmother.

I have a weak spot for the Macfarlanes because (though they were always fighting like any Scottish highland clan) they do not seem to have been very good at it, and were always getting beaten up by the warlike Campbells. They had a fastness on a loch called Loch Sloy, in the mountains above Loch Lomond, and 'Loch Sloy' was their battle cry: a forlorn battle cry these days, because Loch Sloy has become a hydro-electric plant supplying Glasgow. Mary's father, I have been told, was The Macfarlane, the head of the clan, and she herself was a beautiful girl. So it must have been a gala wedding – not that any of them was fashionable, but St George's was used to gala weddings, and the rector's only son would surely have deserved one with his lovely bride.

Six months later, grandfather ran away to Argentina and never came back, leaving his teenage wife pregnant with the baby who became my father.

The story was that he had lost all the family's money on the Stock Exchange. I have always imagined he did something more; even then, you did not run away and stay away for ever just because you had lost your money, or even your family's money. Had he committed a crime which nobody mentioned? Were the police after him? Was The Macfarlane furious? The family clammed up on the subject and I was never told, and nobody now is alive who would remember. He must have lived in Argentina for about forty years, and I have often wondered if he started another family. When I was in Buenos Aires a few years ago, I looked up Howarth in the telephone book, but there were none. That doesn't prove anything. He might have had a good reason to change his name, or his descendants, if he had any, might not live in Buenos Aires, or have telephones. I like the idea of having whole families of Argentinian cousins I have never heard of. Not that I have much sympathy for him. It must have been a resounding scandal in the parish of St George's, and whatever else he did he seems to have treated his wife and his father badly. Better really to have gone to prison if he had to.

But she, left alone and penniless with her baby, decided to

make the best of things, and succeeded amazingly well. The only respectable occupation for what was called 'a Lady in Reduced Circumstances' was to be a governess, and she struggled at that for a while. But soon she did very much better. She somehow became a protegée of Lord Northcliffe, the newspaper baron, and he made her the first editor of the *Daily Mirror*, which he founded as a ladies' daily paper: hence its name. It was a failure. It seemed ladies did not want a daily paper. So he turned it into an ordinary daily, which it still is, and he made Mary editor of the women's page of the well-established *Daily Mail*. There she remained, a great success, the first lady journalist in Fleet Street, until she retired. I do not know how she did it: sheer competence, I suppose, and toughness in that masculine world, and a becoming modesty, and an indestructible sense of humour. Nobody who knew her in her old age would have said she was very competent, but I think that was because of her sense of humour: she really liked to be laughed at, and often pretended to be sillier than she was. Nor do I know how long she kept her beauty. There are no portraits of her between nineteen and sixty-five, when my brother is said to have said she was 'emornously stout'.

While she was working, my father was brought up by a series of maiden aunts, which is often disaster for an only child. He was sent to Westminster School, where he soon developed a hearty dislike for the classics master, the Reverend Herbert Nall. Unluckily for everyone, the Rev. Nall fell in love with Mary. I am sure he was not the only man who did, but she clung to the memory of her vanished husband and refused to divorce him, or legally presume he was dead. But the Rev. Nall, later known as Uncle Herbert or Uncle Rabbit, was a stayer. He waited for her for at least twenty years, trying patiently to please her disapproving son by taking him fishing in Norway, and driving them all to Switzerland in the motor cars he owned from the earliest years of the century, which was no small adventure then.

Uncle Herbert was a tragic figure really. In about 1908, Mary heard that her husband was dead, and she agreed to marry Herbert at last. She was nearly sixty, and so was he. Soon after that my mother and father married too, my brother and I were born, and the marriage Herbert had awaited for so long turned to ashes. Mary was much more fond of her son than she was of this new husband, and she doted on us two little boys. The house where they lived (in the village of Ayot St Peter, north of London) became for him, the old bachelor, a sort of nightmarish nursery, and I remember that he very seldom emerged from his dark little study except for lunch, and endured each noisy and messy meal with his head in his hands and one hand covering his eyes. He always wore mittens, and nobody managed to love him.

So those were the ancestors who made me what I am, or what I was before experience changed me. But I am still puzzled about it all, the whole business of getting born. Philosophers explain it, at least to themselves, and Christian friends tell me it was the plan of God. But I cannot see any plan in it. Am I to think every accident of these ancestors' lives – for example that my great grandfather lived while so many of his brothers died – was decreed so that I should be born, instead of somebody else? It defies my idea of reason. To take the most obvious case, what if Grandfather Paget had not had musical evenings, or if my father had not been able to sing or had not had romantic blue eyes? He would have married somebody else, and so would my mother, and both would have had children perhaps – but not me. What happened to all those unborn children, each a sleeping but potentially self-conscious individual? So far as I can see, it is pure chance that I ever existed or seemed to exist, and the same goes for everyone else. Why should that worry anyone?

TWO

Mewling and Puking

Ayot became our second home. In spite of Uncle Herbert's wraith-like presence, it was a perfect house to grow up in, though madly inconvenient for grown-ups to live in. It had a cobbled stable yard with brick buildings on three sides, which might have been Tudor. The house itself was separate, joined on by a long, glass-covered passage; it had once been two cottages but somebody had extended it with four large Regency rooms and an elegant staircase. Our grandmother's study, which she hardly ever used, was in the cottage part, and so was Uncle Herbert's, which he used all the time. Their floors were two or three feet below ground level and their ceilings were low, so the door to the upper floor of the cottages, where we slept, was halfway up the Regency staircase. The stone-flagged kitchen, the servants' bedroom and a barren room grandiosely called the servants' hall were all in the stable part, so every meal had to be carried on trays down three stone steps, along the frigid passage, down four more steps, up five and across the hall to the dining-room. The whole house, twenty rooms or so, had no heating except the kitchen range, a small fireplace in the main rooms, seldom lit, and what was called a bogey stove at the bottom of the stairs. All of them burned coal. No wonder Uncle Herbert wore his mittens: we were brought up to break the ice on the water we washed our faces in. Unless we were ill, when we had a fire in the nursery grate. All my life since then, I don't remember anything more sybaritic than being very slightly ill and going to sleep with a flickering fire, stoked by an anxious nanny.

And the garden: it was very large and formal, ruled by a gardener of infinite patience called Elsie who lived cosily with Mrs Elsie, like Beatrix Potter characters, in a cottage behind a high laurel hedge. Not only Elsie but everything else at Ayot brings Beatrix Potter back to me. Until the other day, I thought she belonged to an earlier generation, and I was amazed to learn she was still writing her stories, and drawing her pictures of those immortals – Tom Kitten, Squirrel Nutkin, Peter Rabbit, Jemima Puddleduck, Jeremy Fisher and all the rest – while I was reading them. I must have had them hot from the press, probably the *Daily Mail*'s review copies. They were so real I thought they all lived at Ayot; not in the garden except Jeremy Fisher, who was a frog (you could see him any time in the tank in the greenhouse), but just outside the brick walls on the village green, where a very ancient lady called Fanny Gaylor (straight out of Beatrix Potter herself) kept the post office and sold stamps and humbugs and worked the telephone exchange unless she was busy. If she was, nobody in Ayot could make a telephone call and that was that.

The garden grew grapes and asparagus, and you could eat plums and peaches warm from the sun, but its main use was as a railway marshalling yard, and later for slow bicycle races. As a railway, it was fitted with signals at the stations and junctions, which my brother operated; I usually had to be the engine which pulled some sort of train and dutifully stopped, hissing impatiently, when the signals were against it. I liked the slow bicycle races better, and I would still have a go at one if I were encouraged, though I would certainly crash. The whole idea was to take as long as you could, without falling off or putting a foot down, to cross the yard, wobble out through the archway, negotiate some delicate work on the narrow brick paths in the rose garden (difficult there to avoid the pond), and continue round Elsie in the potting shed, in and out of the greenhouse under the grapevine, round the house and back to the starting line.

The railways were really our father's idea. He was devoted to steam engines and indoctrinated my brother, and me to a lesser degree. Between us we had hundreds of postcards and cigarette cards of engines, and an elaborate model railway too: it was screwed to our bedroom floor, and made that floor undustable. Luckily we also had a real railway, which we treated as almost our own: the Luton and Dunstable Branch of the Great Northern. It was axed years ago, but it had a station at Ayot then, half a mile down the lane beyond the forge, operated by a kind stationmaster called Mr Wood. It was a single-track line with a passing place at Ayot, and Mr Wood let us change the signals, which took all our four arms (the points were too heavy for us), and punch the tickets of selected passengers, and even put halfpennies on the track when we heard the train coming: the engine flattened them beautifully to twice their size. I can still smell Ayot station: a mixture of hot steam, creosote from the wooden platform, and Fry's chocolate bars from the penny-in-the-slot machine. We loved Mr Wood, and sometimes asked him to tea. Our grandmother's afternoon tea was formal, a forgotten ceremony now, with a silver service on the drawing-room table, cucumber sandwiches, anchovy toast, scones and butter and jam and cakes, and shallow bone china cups. Mr Wood had a bushy moustache, and it fascinated us when he pressed the moustache with his forefinger and sucked, and got an extra mouthful of tea out of it. We were too well brought up to giggle. Instead, we found a moustache cup for him: a Victorian invention with a ledge which kept the drinker's moustache out of the drink. I hope it made him feel at ease. He deserved to.

Our father's greatest enthusiasm was intellectual. It was making up railway timetables. We drew maps of large islands and gave them railway systems. The main town was always called Port Face-ache; it had a market day on Thursdays and a ferry on Saturdays, with extra trains to suit them. Some tracks were double and some single, there were hills up and down, which changed the speed of the trains; there were expresses, stopping trains, freight trains and summer excursions. It really needed brain-power to avoid fatal accidents by running trains down single tracks in opposite directions, and to finish the day with all the trains in the right places and facing the right way: only local trains could go backwards. My mind boggled much sooner than my brother's or my father's, and I often went to bed and left them working it out by candle-light.

I think I was the only person who even pretended to be interested in what Uncle Herbert was doing, all that time while he lurked in his study. He was a man with hobbies. He began, before my day, with carpentry, and in the small apartment in the stable yard called the chauffeur's rooms (though there was never

a chauffeur) I discovered a superb collection of abandoned car-
penter's tools. Then it was sewing, on an old Singer sewing
machine. He sewed shirts and pyjamas for everyone. Unluckily,
he always used the same sort of material, and it had such a
barbed-wire texture that nobody would ever wear his careful
offerings. He finished up with salmon. That was more than a
hobby, he really was a world expert on salmon and sea trout.
He not only caught them, but all those months and years in his
study he measured their scales under a microscope, and he wrote
enormous books about them. I went in sometimes and peered
down the microscope, which pleased him as much as he could
be pleased. If you know how, you can tell a salmon's life-history
from its scales, and he gave me a slide of a scale of his champion
salmon of all. I think it proved the salmon had spawned five
times, and I was too ashamed to tell him when I lost it.

Another permanent hobby, and somehow out of character,
was his cars. The war of 1914 put a stop to his epic drives to
Switzerland, but when it ended in 1918 he still had his car, a
Humber. But the first one I remember clearly was an American
contraption called an Overland. Our grandmother sometimes
insisted he should take us all for rides. Like all cars then, it was
an open four-seater, and she sat in the back, wearing a dust-coat
and a hat with a motoring veil over it. He always drove at
seventeen miles an hour – touch eighteen, and that Overland
made protesting noises somewhere in its machinery. Still, it
seemed a great speed, and whenever he went round a corner his
wife would sing out from the back 'Oh, what a beautiful swerve',
and we all took up the cry, like a flock of parrots. That made
Uncle Herbert grind his teeth, of course – and he really could
grind his teeth – and stamp on the accelerator until at last the
speed crept up again towards eighteen and the works protested.
Downhill, on the way home, though, he sometimes managed to
force it up into the twenties, and then the cry from the back seat
would be 'He smells his stable!'

Yet there was never a quarrel. All my childhood, I never heard
an angry word, at Ayot or anywhere else (except my own,
perhaps). Uncle Herbert never argued, never spoke up for himself,
never lost his temper; he just suffered in total silence. But he must
have suffered. His life had gone wrong, and we were all so horrid

27

to him. I could hardly bear to think of him now if he had ended in misery; but he did not. He made a friend in the salmon world, who lived in Edinburgh, and the friend had a youngish wife; call her Elizabeth. These two, it seems, admired Uncle Herbert and gave him the respect and affection any old man needs, which we had always denied him; and he rebelled. He took to setting off from Ayot in his car in the mornings, and arriving in Edinburgh the same evening. This was coming on for the 1930s, and he had an up-to-date car, an Austin, but he must have been a new man and driven like the devil: over 300 miles, and no motorways then – the Great North Road, the A1, wound its devious way like any English road and went right through the middle of every town. These sudden expeditions made our grandmother wild. She spoke of Elizabeth as 'That Woman', and thought or pretended Uncle Herbert was having an illicit last-minute affair. Nothing is less likely: he was a handsome old man, but he was well on in his seventies, when most men are supposed to have given up things like that. I imagine he found affection, perhaps the first in his life, and repaid it with gratitude and love, but I don't think for a moment it was anything but strictly respectable.

We got our come-uppance in the end. Our grandmother died in 1938 to the grief of us all. Uncle Herbert brought Elizabeth to the funeral, his final sin in the eyes of the family. The house at Ayot was sold, and all our grandmother's property went to him. I doubt if she meant it to. Perhaps she had not made a will, or perhaps she had made one when she married him and never got round to changing it. I was told he left it all to Elizabeth. Anyhow, we never got anything except some books and bits of furniture as souvenirs. Served us right.

Our grandmother was the centre of everything at Ayot, except the railways. We called her Gaga – a silly name which I still confess with hesitation. Of course we did not know its connotation of senility, it was simply another of my brother's early mistakes, his first attempt to say Granny. It is a pity parents cherish their first-born's mistakes, but we all do it. I do not think she was 'emornously stout', just stout enough to be comforting.

She must have spent most of her life on the *Daily Mail* writing about fashions and cosmetics, but when she retired she took no interest at all in clothes, especially her own. She could make a hat last ten years, and when it finally fell to bits she did not buy a new one, just resurrected another from the discards of previous decades and patched it up. She never looked dressed in her clothes, rather bundled up in them like a parcel. Mostly they were brown jumpers she knitted and darned herself, and shapeless skirts, and an equally shapeless overcoat, also brown, with a belt round it which emphasized her bulges. As for cosmetics, I think the only thing she used was oatmeal. It was supposed to soften the water, and she kept a big glass jar of it on the washstand in her bedroom. We ate it, but the jar was always full. To us, her appearance was utterly endearing. We could never have loved a tidy lady so much.

She read to us whenever we had nothing to do, starting with Beatrix Potter and working up through *Bulldog Drummond* and the *Railway Magazine* to the most unsuitable modern novels — nothing even slightly educational, though she had an erudite library. She did jigsaw puzzles too, and played endless games of ludo and halma, and never showed any sign of being bored with our company. She always wanted us to win the games, and we usually did, because she pretended she could not understand them. Ever since, I have been a dead loss at competitive sports and games. I always want the opposition to win, which ruins most games unless one can do it as subtly as she did.

The only other thing I see her doing is knitting, mostly clothes for us, beginning I suppose with romper suits and certainly ending with manly Fair Isle sweaters, which the Prince of Wales made fashionable. In my vision, she sits in an upright armchair beside the fireplace in the drawing-room, with an oil lamp on the mantelpiece behind her. This must be a later recollection, because she has a wireless set and a Scotty dog which sits on her lap mixed up with the knitting. At the same time every evening in those days the BBC played 'God Save The King', and she thought it her patriotic duty to stand to attention. It always seemed to take her by surprise, but not the dog. At the first drum-roll it knew what was coming: sighing and grumbling, it scrambled off her lap with strands of wool round its legs. She tried to gather everything up, but never succeeded. One by one, the multi-coloured balls of wool escaped and rolled across the floor, each leaving its trail behind it. Then, pushing herself up by the arms of the chair (I do it now myself) she lost her grip on the body of the knitting, and the needles. As often as not, she managed to be at attention just as the anthem ended, but then there was the wreckage of the knitting to tidy up.

This sounds as if we laughed at her, but we never did: she laughed at herself, and we laughed with her.

Her policy of pretending to be foolish – she was far from foolish – made her get people's names wrong. Sometimes she used nicknames. All the vicars of Ayot – and there must have been a series of them – were called the Reverend Patch: not the Reverend Mr Patch, which might have sounded respectful, but just the Rev. Patch. We had a young acquaintance called Graham, and she always called him Hannibal.

'But why Hannibal?'

'It's his name.'

'No it's not, his name's Graham.'

'Graham? What nonsense. Who calls him Graham? He's Hannibal.'

Things too: the brass candlesticks we all took up to bed were called Miss Cambilam.

'Why Miss?'

'Well, they're not married, are they? Who ever heard of a married candlestick?'

I would not be surprised if she was the first to call Uncle Herbert Uncle Rabbit. His study was just like a rabbit-hole, and when he crept out of it, blinking and a little bewildered in the sunlight, he was very much like a large grey rabbit peering around for enemies who might pounce.

When we went to boarding school, each in his turn when he was nine, Gaga played a new role. (We never made her nickname public.) The first school was at Horsham in Sussex, the second at Tonbridge in Kent, both a long day's journey there and back from Ayot by train, but she came to visit us two or three times a term, carrying her enormous handbag with the knitting in it, and her bundled-up umbrella, and festooned with heavy parcels of food as if we had been prisoners of war. I came off second best in the parcels. At some time I must have told her I liked seed cake, which is a very plain cake with caraway seeds in it. I suppose I said it to be polite; I did not like it at all, but for years the heaviest thing in my parcel was a huge seed cake. All the same, the parcels were very welcome and made us popular. And after the first shock, she was welcome too. She cured us once and for all of the fear all little boys have at boarding school, that their parents will come and see them and disgrace them by wearing the wrong clothes or talking too much. But Gaga was so outrageous in her battered hat and her belted coat that she soon became famous in both schools. My brother bore the brunt of her early appearances, and by the time I arrived two years behind him he was proud of her eccentricity. So was I. Nobody else had a visitor anything like her.

And in the holidays we still spent half our time at Ayot, which was always blissful, even when we were too big to be trains. She often took us to theatres too, some strange entertainments for a boy hardly in his teens. I dutifully fell for the stars of the musicals, especially Jessie Matthews. But the one I remember was a thin brown girl in a murder play, ingeniously set behind the scenes of a musical so that one got the best of both worlds, a murder and a line of chorus girls. I never told anyone about this near-naked nymph and I never knew her name, but I never forgot her. If she is still alive, she must be over eighty now, which is sad.

People might have said our grandmother spoilt us, but children are never spoilt by love and kindness. With tact and discretion too, luck, and an element of strictness, it may teach them to love, which of course is the most important lesson of all.

THREE

Morning Face

I hardly knew my father until I was middle-aged and he was old. Even my mother told me, late in her life, that he had never been an easy man to know. I think the cause of that, and of most of his troubles, was his upbringing by his maiden aunts – the father, still alive, whom he never met, and at school the awful trauma of Uncle Herbert. It made him, in contrast to my mother, an intensely unsociable person, always a loner, never able to have a close relationship with anyone, even with her. So far as I know, he had only one intimate, an Oxford university friend named John Reynolds who unhappily died rather young. He was the only person outside the family circle he called by his christian name. All the rest of his friends or acquaintances were academics, doctors or professors of branches of science, all known to him by their surnames. He never seemed to think any other sort of person could be a friend, and he had no use whatever for girls, not even his daughter, our only sister. He hardly spoke to her.

His own subject was Geography, and when he was young I guess he wanted to be an explorer, or a mountaineer, or a blue-water sailor. But he lacked the push for any of those vocations and before he knew where he was he was trapped, with a wife and three children, into a life of commuting, like hundreds of thousands of middle-class Englishmen.

For soon after the end of the war, in 1919, we moved from Kensington to Sevenoaks in Kent, then a small market town, but now a suburb. At the same time he got a new job, as secretary of the British Association for the Advancement of Science, and he stayed there for twenty-five years. The British Ass, as it was more handily called, had a very small office in the attics of Burlington House in Piccadilly – himself and two male clerks –

in the ambience of the Royal Society and the Royal Academy, and he commuted there from Sevenoaks six days a week. It was that job that put him on the edge of the academic world but never quite within it. After some years he was elected a member of the Athenaeum, the most intellectual of London clubs, which pleased him greatly, and for about twenty years he walked down Lower Regent Street at one o'clock, ate his abstemious lunch alone in those rather forbidding surroundings, and walked up again.

My first conscious feeling of sympathy for him was not until I was ten or eleven. In Sevenoaks he rented a large late Victorian house up a long steep hill, and one summer evening I happened to meet him just as he reached the top. He looked exhausted, grey-faced, his mouth hanging open to get his breath, his London hat, suit and briefcase tragic. It came to me as a shock that we had been playing around all day and he had been labouring at something he didn't want to do to support us all. I felt I ought to have run down the hill and met him at the station and carried the briefcase; but a gesture like that, I knew, would only have embarrassed him and neither of us would have known what to say. As it was, we did not even say hello.

I don't know why he married. My mother told me he made the fateful proposal when they were both running down a scree on the lower slopes of the Matterhorn (she must have been invited on one of Uncle Herbert's last expeditions). I imagine he chose that moment in the half-hope that she would not hear, or at least to give her a chance to pretend she did not hear. But she did, and after the wait that etiquette demanded she said yes – because, she told me, he had such romantic blue eyes. People often marry for even less reason, but the blue eyes misled her. The warmth of a romantic relationship was quite beyond him. So far as I know he was never unkind to her, except to the extent of being irritable, and that was mostly at breakfast and mostly directed at me: 'It is my wish that in future you will not come down late looking like a boiled owl.' In many marriages people would settle for less. But in another of her talks with me when she was old and he long dead, she referred to her sex-life – 'which as you can imagine, dear, was practically non-existent'.

I had never tried to imagine it; that would have seemed impertinent. But looking back now as far as I can, which was about the time we moved to Sevenoaks when I was seven, I know they did not share a bedroom. I never saw him kiss her: perhaps he never did, or never after their honeymoon. The only gesture he had, presumably of affection, was to touch the tip of her nose with the tip of his little finger. She did not seem to be enthralled by that.

I think that was his basic lack in life. He was completely bored by sex. From her hints in old age (only hints, she was never disloyal to him), I would guess he felt sex was a distasteful, undignified performance, unfortunately necessary in producing children, and that he only endured it just often enough to cause us to be born, and never for pleasure or as an expression of love. That is a sad shortcoming in anyone, but again it was not his fault, it was another result of his upbringing by those aunts. He might have become homosexual, but he probably never heard of homosexuality, or thought of it if he did as a rare disease that affected a few other people – people like Oscar Wilde, but not ordinary, healthy people.

When I was about twelve, he suddenly took an interest in me, and for months he insisted on bathing me. I hated it, I was a prudish little boy and I had been bathing myself for years. But I think now he was only plucking up courage to try to tell me the Facts of Life. One night he achieved it when he was drying me.

'Does that thing of yours often get hard?' he asked me.

'Sometimes,' I said. I thought he might have seen it.

'And does any stuff come out of it?'

'No,' I said. It did, but I wouldn't have told him or anyone else if ink or strawberry ice-cream had come out of it.

'Well,' he said, 'remember, whenever you have a bath you must be careful to dry between your legs.' And he decorously handed me the towel to do so.

I still don't know what he meant. Perhaps I ought to, but that was the beginning, the literal whole and the absolute end of my sex education.

Things are different now. My stepdaughter came home from her primary school one day when she was seven, took her thumb out of her mouth, stopped twiddling her hair and said, 'Mum, we had a fillum today. When they gets they's erections, why does

34

some stick up and some stick out?' Everything else was crystal clear to her, but her mother did not know the answer. Nor do I.

Like most fathers, ours always wanted my brother and me to be interested in the things that interested him. First it was trains and timetables; in another phase he took us on bicycle tours, four or five days at a time, to look at the architecture of village churches. Later when he took us on holiday it was the dregs of the ambitions he had never fulfilled: exploring, deep-sea sailing and mountaineering. But the ambitions had shrunk. We went to mountains, but only the gentlest mountains in Scotland or Wales that anyone could walk up. As for salt water, he hired houseboats, ancient pensioned-off yachts lying safely at anchor in harbours, with rowing boats for getting ashore. We had houseboats during various summers in Chichester harbour, Salcombe harbour in Devon, and Loch Lomond in Scotland. He succeeded up to a point in handing on his interests. Heather on hills still brings back a holiday atmosphere to me, and both of us took up his ambitions and followed them much farther towards fulfilment than he had. Not that either of us became an explorer, but when we took off separately on our own we both went to faraway places off the beaten track. I was luckier than my brother because my thirty-five years as an author led me to deserts, tropical jungles and the Arctic sea-ice, and many odd places between. At sea, we both cruised widely under sail. And both of us took to more adventurous mountains.

Sometimes we could share it with our father, or bits of it. When I was living in the Shetland Islands, as I did for eleven years, he came to stay and I had only to provide a small boat and a small boy to manage it for him, and he was perfectly happy pursuing sea-trout. I don't think he caught any trout but the small boys did, and that pleased him just as much. And my brother, who is a gourmet, drove him on tours of France. That was not easy because my father distrusted French food, and while my brother was wading through the *menu gastronomique*, he would eat nothing but omelettes. But one of the meals they ate became quite a legend.

He had always refused to drink, because he said he didn't like the taste of alcohol. Consequently, when we were small, there was never a drop of drink in the house. When my brother went to Oxford and was just beginning a life-long discriminating love affair with wines and spirits, he said they must at least have a glass of sherry at home to offer their guests at dinner parties. My mother, perhaps, needed no persuasion: grandfather's musical evenings had not been dry, and in later life she was never without her sherry. Our father was talked into it but would not so much as sniff it himself. However, at that memorable meal in France, a crêpe with a fancy name was on the menu and he said he would try it: he liked pancakes. It turned out to be ten pancakes, each one flambéed in a different liqueur, and he ate the lot and loved it.

I think he watched our modest adventures with envy, though he did not say so. I know he remained a sadly frustrated man all his life, frustrated by shortcomings which were not his fault but the fault of his upbringing. When at last he retired, very late (even his retirement was frustrated by the Second World War), he wanted to go and live in a cottage overlooking a sea loch on the far west coast of Scotland. But he knew very well it was not a practical plan. My mother could not have stood it: she was far too devoted to her friends, and would have thought it unbearably lonely, and he would not have dreamed of doing it without her. One day when it was pouring with rain I found him looking forlornly out of his bedroom window at a very large puddle in the drive. 'I suppose,' he said, 'that's the largest sheet of water I shall ever live on the shore of.'

Mamma and Papa: my brother and I chose to call them that as a reaction against the childish Mummy and Daddy: it seemed pleasantly old-world and it suited them better. Mamma was a much more open and instantly likeable person than Papa, and much more accessible to us; yet strangely, my recollection of her is almost a blank before she was quite an old lady. The fact is that we were seldom at home. When we were small, our time was divided between London, or Sevenoaks, and Ayot, and she had to compete for our thoughts and affection with Gaga and the nannies, and did not seem to mind if they won. And soon after the move to Sevenoaks we were both sent to boarding school.

A public school in England, of course, means an expensive private boarding school: a free day school, which is really public, is a state school. I confess I don't know why anyone who has been to all the trouble and expense of having children should want to hand them over entirely to schoolteachers and send them away for eight or nine months every year, right through the most interesting and exciting part of their growing up. I did not do it with any of mine, but most English parents do, or did, if they could afford it, and there are endless arguments about it. Many people who were sent to these famous schools wonder how they survived to think of themselves as civilized, and I am one of them.

It was not that we did not enjoy it. I enjoyed it all, after the first year which was deliberately made a misery, nominally through ancient tradition, but really to satisfy the sadism latent in so many boys. That year was full of degrading nonsensical rules and minor tortures. One was to be made to hit the back of your own hand with a stiff hairbrush until it was covered with spots of blood, and then to whirl your arm round so that the blood-spots hit the ceiling. The ceiling of the tiny dungeon where the new boys lived was covered with the blood of earlier generations. In addition everyone in that year was the private fag of a prefect of seventeen, to clean his shoes, perhaps to wash his smelly feet, to carry his books to school, and do any other chore he was too lazy to do himself; and all fags, all their spare time, had to lurk in their dungeon waiting for a shout of 'Boy!', upon which they all had to run in a flock to the prefect who shouted, ready to do what he demanded. You did not learn much in that year except how to keep out of trouble, which is perhaps a valuable lesson, and you came through it only because you knew that next year there would be an influx of even younger boys, and you could look down on them.

After that, life became a matter of defying school rules. Many of them were so silly that it was a pleasure to break them, and you became increasingly expert at it. But sometimes you tried and failed, and the penalty was to be beaten. I was always getting beaten. The beating was done by the housemaster or a prefect – it depended what sort of rule you had broken – and the weapon was a very thin flexible cane with a curved handle like a walking stick, specially made for the job by some fiendish supplier of scholastic equipment. It hurt like hell. It did not draw much blood, but raised red weals across your bottom exactly the shape and size of the cane; proud people displayed them afterwards. I cannot think why nobody ever rebelled and just refused to bend over the table.

I have no quarrel with the Spartan life, except that many parents thought they were paying for something much more. What I do regret is the way these schools shut us into a world of their own creation, and cut us off from reality. Politically, socially, artistically and sexually we remained uneducated: we were taught exactly nothing at all, unless we tried to teach each other.

Politics: we were not allowed to have a radio, although they existed, or to buy a newspaper except on Sundays, when the few who could afford it invested in the *News of the World*, the most salacious Sunday of the age. The general strike, the most profound social upheaval of the century so far, happened when I was at school and I did not know it had happened at all until I went home for the holidays. Only one boy I knew expressed political views: he said he was a Fascist.

And society: nine tenths of our fellow-citizens were banned from our acquaintance, not by rule but by custom. Anybody with an off-beat accent, all tradesmen, craftsmen, labourers or artisans, anybody who had not been to a public school, was beneath us. Even the day-boys, who were few, were looked down on as oicks, because their fathers were thought to be shopkeepers, and we did not make friends with them.

As for sex, we never saw, knew or spoke to a girl of any kind: they were all among the untouchables. Some boys get through the years from thirteen to eighteen without apparently thinking of sex at all; others are obsessed by it. Those who were obsessed had to work it out on the prettier boys: there was nobody else. The school seethed with gossip of these liaisons. A few were frankly carnal: most were ethereal, and their only hoped-for climax was a glance exchanged, with luck even a smile, or at the very extreme a secret hug. Boys fell in love, truly in love, with other boys they saw only across the aisle in chapel and had little hope of ever seeing anywhere else.

I am sure it did no permanent harm to anybody, but it did

indirectly do some temporary harm. The public schools went on year after year producing boys who were homosexual because they had never known anything else. Most of them grew out of it: there were no more genuine homosexuals among them than among any others. But when they did grow up, and if they took to girls, they were inclined to be gauche and clumsy and ignorant of what to say to a girl, how to interest or please her, how a feminine brain or body worked. I know my own daughters despised public school boys, who were away most of the year and incompetent when they were not.

Men who are made to feel incompetent often over-react to prove how virile they are, and my guess would be that in the long run the public school morality, if you could call it morality, tended to create male chauvinist pigs, not gays. Perhaps that was what was needed a hundred years ago for running the Empire, when those schools enjoyed their finest hour, but nobody could have planned such a devious way of doing it.

As for me (since this is my story), I recovered fairly quickly from that lop-sided training, but with nothing effective to put in its place. After three blissful years at Cambridge, where again there were no girls, or none who impinged on my consciousness, I lived alone in a flat in London, where there were plenty. But by then my ideas of social behaviour came straight out of P. G. Wodehouse, whose heroes (addicts will agree) were always falling in love at first sight, and the instant they had done so proposed marriage to the desirable creature, defying ferocious aunts. Whenever I met eager beddable girls I scared them into panic flight by proposing to marry them. That was not what they wanted at all, and it was not what I wanted either, but I thought it was what I was supposed to do. The mistake was fatal to my plans.

The reason why I chose to go to Cambridge instead of Oxford was absurd, like most of the decisions of my life. My father and brother had both been to Oxford, and my father would have liked me to go there too. But at my first school – the preparatory school before the public school – there was a new young science master called Bill Oakley. I think he was only a teenager himself, but he was a most inspiring teacher. His example made me decide when I was eleven to be a physicist and mathematician, and I stuck to that aim throughout my education: for ten solid years I absorbed maths and physics and not much else. Cambridge then had the most famous physics laboratory in the world, the Cavendish, where under Lord Rutherford most of the early work was done on nuclear physics. So I thought Cambridge was the only place that could teach me. It was all nonsense, of course; I never had the makings of a first-class physicist, and any university could have taught me all I was able to learn. Still, it gave me a healthy pride just to walk into the Cavendish, though I never so much as saw Lord Rutherford.

However, I quite often met Sir J. J. Thomson, the doyen of the previous generation of physicists and the first man to 'split the atom'. He was Master of Trinity College, and my father entered me for Trinity not so much because J.J. was a physicist as because his wife was a distant Paget cousin. They were charming and courteous to undergraduates, but dinner in the Master's Lodge was always a daunting privilege. J.J. was, or seemed, a very old man by then, but he could lead a conversation on any subject known to man. It was the first time I had ever tried to breathe in the real stratosphere of high-table talk, and I learned very soon that my own brain was second-class equipment. Not only was his conversation fascinating; so were his teeth. The upper set seemed to be hinged. When he talked, he lowered them and spoke through the gap above. When he took time to eat he pushed them up with a loud decisive click and ate through the gap below.

He could have been the original absent-minded professor. Walking through the town, he was a traffic hazard: he would stop and stare at anything that caught his eye, with his mind light years away in some erudite problem. Once he stopped at a lurid cinema poster, rocking backwards and forwards on his heels, his hands behind him clasping his stick, gazing up at the half-naked lady in front of him, but quite unaware of her or of the queue of cars or the crowd that was gathering round him. When the problem in his mind was solved, he said 'Humph' very loudly and walked on, taking no notice of anyone. It was said – I don't know on whose authority – that he once met his wife going the opposite way along King's Parade, and when she spoke to him he looked scandalized and edged past her thinking she was a 'lady of the streets' who was trying to pick him up. He may never have known who I was but I admired him greatly, and he taught me something important: not physics, but some degree of humility.

I was a long way from being clever, but I was not the most stupid of undergraduates. Now you have to be very clever to get into Oxford or Cambridge, but then all you needed was a father who could pay £300 a year, and Cambridge was cluttered with rich young men, some noble, who never went to a lecture and never did any work but spent all their days riding horses with horsey women, and their nights causing minor riots in the streets and blowing their hunting horns in the courts. They congregated in Trinity. It must have been difficult to live there for three years, as they did, without being influenced at all by the place. Trinity was founded by King Henry VIII, and its Great Court must surely be the most elegant, beautiful and breath-taking campus in the world: its Tudor Great Gate, where an impeccable top-hatted head porter presides (he once refused Gaga entrance with a memorable phrase because she was carrying her Scotty dog: 'I assure you, madam; they'd as lief see a lion in the courts'); the vast ancient hall where the priceless Holbein portrait of the founder watches you jovially while you dine; the library in an adjoining court, a masterpiece of Sir Christopher Wren; and the river behind it where young men propel punts with either grace or disaster – every inch of it is a distillation of centuries of learning. But if you chose, you could spend your years there without taking any notice of it, and still end with some sort of degree.

I did better than that, but not very well. I did not work enough because I went there straight from school and nobody had taught me the most important scholastic lesson, how to work by myself – and later because my brain simply boggled, especially in maths: beyond a certain point in higher maths, I just could not understand any more, and I gave up trying. Nobody pushed me, or not very hard. Instead, I took to roof-climbing, a peculiarly Cambridge sport. I achieved the circuit of the roofs of Trinity Great Court without getting caught by the porters, but not the most difficult and dangerous historic ascents: the spire of the Roman Catholic church, or the horrifying exposed climb of King's College Chapel, where custom demanded you should lash unfurled umbrellas or leave chamber pots upside down on the highest pinnacles.

Roof-climbing led, of course, to rock climbing, but only in the vacations because the countryside round Cambridge is flat; and rock climbing led to motor bikes, to get to the mountains. My first motor bike cost me £3 and was called a Grigg. I have never heard of another Grigg, and I suspect Mr Grigg was a man who made one motor bike in his back yard in the early 1920s and never made another. My friends called it the Monarch of the Glen because it had wide spreading handlebars like the antlers of Landseer's stags, but it was a perilous apparatus with a flat-out speed of 27 m.p.h., an acetylene headlamp and a belt drive which often flew off and lay coiled in the road like a snake. It also had a saddle with springs sticking out, which wore away the whole of the seat of my pants. There was a crisis of public decorum when it cast its belt in the High Street of a north-country town on a Saturday night, and I had to get off and bend down to rescue the belt and then fit it on again. Still, I rode the Monarch to the Isle of Skye on the west coast of Scotland, which has the best rock climbing in Britain, and rode it home and sold it again for £3. I loved the animal, but it had a mind of its own, sometimes surprisingly kind but often malevolent. Then I graduated to a Matchless, which cost £6; I rode it in the famous trials of that era, London to Land's End and London to Edinburgh, but I didn't love it.

Our parents never fussed us, which was just as well because I was learning to think the only worthwhile sports are not competitive, but are more or less dangerous. Sometimes their tolerance was amazing. My father bought his first car when I was eleven, a new round-nosed Morris Cowley. My brother could drive it at once (he was always an expert driver) and he very soon taught me too. They must have let me apply for a driving licence years before I was old enough by law: when he was sixteen and I was fourteen we drove the family to Scotland. That was not dangerous, but rock climbing and motor cycling were, and so was long-range cruising, which we both took to later.

Danger is enjoyable, I learned, when it lies in your own hands to overcome it, and to overcome your own fear. If your survival depends on somebody else, it is no fun at all. Rock climbing is perhaps an exception; sometimes on the climbs that were classed as 'severe', or some that were merely 'difficult', I knew I could not do it myself and was very glad to be on the rope below a leader I knew and trusted. Motor cycling is not the same fun now, because you depend on so many other lunatics on the roads. Cruising, to my mind, remains the perfect sport, at its best single-handed or with a family who perfectly trust you to know all about it and do not know much themselves. Like mountaineering, it has moments of unparalleled peace among its problems, and most of its dangers are imaginary.

There is far too much emphasis now on the value and sanctity of life. Of course you should be careful of other people's lives, whoever they are; of course you should not kill animals for fun, or tread on insects. But your own life is your own, and you do not enjoy it fully if you never risk it. My own younger children have been taught at school never to take any risks. It thwarts them. For a long time, they were scared to eat butter because it might give them heart disease, and they demanded margarine full of polyunsaturated fats, though they knew no more than I do what those are. Their school would have had them spend their lives in fear of dying. But your life is for living, and I think you should be free to end it when you are ready, and so learn to look forward to its ending with equanimity. I have wanted several times to die, once or twice when life was very unpleasant, and more often when it was perfect. I think I only once told anyone else. My wife and I were sailing alone in Greece (this was thirty years later) and we anchored one evening in a deserted bay. When the sails were down and the anchor chain had rattled out in that warm pellucid water and she put the first glass of ouzo in my hand, the purest of peace descended. The smell of herbs drifted out from the shore, the silence was enhanced by the sound of goat-bells from two converging flocks on the hills.

'I'd like to die,' I said.

She knew I meant it, and of course that I wouldn't do it then and there.

'I don't think there could be a better time,' she said. 'Except that there's squid for supper.'

So we began to compose the sort of obituary notices people put in the papers: 'HOWARTH, DAVID. Peacefully, at a goat-herds' convention near Galaxhidi . . .' And I went on living, but more in gratitude for such a wife than for the squid.

43

FOUR

The BBC

When I came down from Cambridge with my degree (not a very good one) in physics and maths I had to get a job, and I got one designing circuits for John Logie Baird, the inventor of television, at a salary of £3 a week, on which I managed to live in London and run a car, but not to eat very much.

Baird was very unlucky, like many inventors. When I joined him, he was entirely under the thumb of financiers, and he seemed a puzzled and worried man. He wandered rather vaguely round his workshops and sometimes peered at what his assistants were doing. Nobody took much notice of anything he said. What he had invented was the idea of turning a moving picture into a signal by scanning it; in other words, by dividing it into lines and transmitting each line in sequence. But you cannot patent an idea, only the means of achieving it, and the only means he had thought of was a revolving disk with small holes in it in a spiral. As the disk whizzed round, each hole in it traced a different line on the picture, and the light that shone through them could, in theory, be used to modulate a radio wave and a similar machine at the receiving end. So far as I remember, the disk was about two feet across, and it gave a picture about two inches by three: a very rough picture, because there were only thirty-two holes in the disk and therefore thirty-two lines on the picture. But it worked. I think he transmitted a recognizable picture of the finish of the Derby by land-line to London in 1931, and I think I was there for the very first transmission of a moving picture by radio, which must have been in 1932. It was an opera singer, the transmitter was at the Crystal Palace in south-east London, and we received it in the workshop near Covent Garden. We had no idea, of course, of the monstrous social force we were trying to bring to birth, but it was a moment of triumph. It proved it could be done.

Very soon after that, the rival giant EMI came up with the cathode ray tube, which did the same thing and did it very much better, with ten times as many lines, and with the revolutionary plan of using a band of much higher radio frequencies. EMI scooped the pool, and Baird's disk was abandoned. I had designed some novel circuits, but they were never used, and he never made the fortune that had come so close.

Between the moment of triumph and the moment of disaster, I had left – not because I had foreseen what was going to happen, but simply because the BBC offered me £4 a week to do a job that needed no technical knowledge whatever. For the extra pound I abandoned my ten years' expensive education, and I never used physics or mathematics again. It was a waste. All the same, I am grateful to that very young teacher Bill Oakley for starting me going that way. I am glad I still have some lingering notion how physics works and what mathematics is about. It has not been useful knowledge to me, but knowledge does not have to be useful.

Thus I joined the BBC when I was twenty-one years old and the BBC itself was eight or nine. It was an excellent, cosy little organization, so small that you could know everyone except the engineers in distant transmitters. It was concerned only with sound of course: regular television was still in the future. It had just moved into Broadcasting House, which seemed one of the wonders of the world with its studios in a central tower and insulated by offices all round them, so that no suspicion of a noise from the world outside could get in (except to the concert hall in the basement where you could hear the trains on the Bakerloo line far underneath). It was all ruled by Sir John Reith, the Director General, who was something between a headmaster and a medieval Jehovah. You very seldom saw him, and I was astonished late one night when I was in the staff canteen and he came in all alone and ordered his egg and chips and asked me if he could sit at my table. He was affable, and I was tongue-tied. Normally, if he wanted to speak to somebody he did not use the internal dial telephone like a mortal, he caused the outside telephone to ring three times. The effect on junior members of the staff was as if the Last Trump had sounded: I suppose he meant it to be. Everyone took their feet off the desks and guiltily leapt to attention.

Personally, I think the BBC still has the standard of excellence he imposed, or most of it, in spite of being huge: it still has his passionate regard for truth and good manners, now in a ruder and more mendacious world – just as the foyer of Broadcasting House still has the optimistic motto he inscribed over half a century ago, 'Nation Shall Speak Peace Unto Nation'. He could not have been bettered as the first Director General of such a novel enterprise. Some people laughed at his puritan, Scottish Calvinist outlook. I did myself. But the BBC has often needed a positive guide through the infinite maze of power-hungry pressure groups, some sort of mast to nail its colours to. The same sort of people may hate to admit it, but a lingering recollection of Reith is still this guide.

It had one defect in those early days, and I expect it still has: what I think is called Parkinson's Law. If you were told to start up a new department, the department automatically grew, because the bigger it grew the more you were paid and the quicker you won the accolade of an office with a coloured carpet instead of the standard grey. I joined a department like that: sound recording, which was quite new. It was not an engineering department, or a programme department, it was Administration. I remained second in command of it, but rather quickly understood it was quite unnecessary. All it really had to do was receive requests from programme departments for sound recording and pass them on, on a different form, to the engineering department that made the recordings. Before long, there were nearly thirty of us doing or supervising this useless chore.

The only other positive thing we did was to play the recordings in the programmes and we did become expert at that, if only because nobody else had ever tried. This was long before tape recording, which you can edit with scissors. (There was indeed a sort of tape recorder, called a Blattnerphone, but its tapes were steel and a reel was most of three feet across and so heavy that only a strong man could lift it on and off the machine. The tapes were also much too expensive to cut, and needed a welder to join them when they broke.) We therefore used discs, and editing a disc has its problems. I designed a sliding pick-up arm which you could pre-set and lower on any groove you chose; the BBC still uses the identical gadget, and when I see one in a modern studio I enjoy telling the modern staff I invented it. They look at me with awe as a relic of an earlier civilization.

It worked, but it had its limitations. A single groove on a disc lasted nearly a second and it needed a knack, and some luck, to anticipate your cue by a second, lower the pick-up on the previous groove and fade up the chosen bit of the record at the split-second it was needed. We had a row of six turntables, and sometimes for reminiscent programmes we did feats of juggling which pleased us enormously, like playing extracts of a hundred discs, each on its cue, in sixty minutes.

For some time, though, nobody was allowed to broadcast a recording without explaining that it was one; Sir John felt it would seem like deceiving the listeners. That Reithian rule was relaxed for the King's annual Christmas Day broadcast. King George VI, unlike his father or his brother, had a stammer. It fell to us – me and two other adroit and even younger men, Kenneth Todd and Arthur Philips – to record the King and edit out the stammers. It was delicate work, and with the element of luck we could never be sure of removing every hesitation and repetition every time; so we re-recorded it. From the finished product nobody could ever tell he stammered at all, and nobody ever explained it was a recording.

The most amusing gadgets we administered were Mobile Recording Units. Now, when you can carry a tape recorder in your pocket, it is odd to remember that the first unit was in a converted laundry van, and the second, the perfected product of the engineering division, filled the whole of a seven-ton truck, carried a crew of four and had a speed limit of twenty miles an hour (or was it thirty? Anyhow, it was frustratingly slow). One of us always had to go with these mammoths on their expeditions for no reason at all except that our department had to grow. So for each recording, however simple, there were three engineers, a driver, usually two programme people, a producer, a speaker, and one of us. There was nothing for us to do except hold the microphone and give the starting cue to the engineers, as if the producer could not have done that himself.

One of these expeditions, memorable for me, was the funeral of the composer Frederick Delius in 1935 at Limpsfield in Surrey. There was no programme man with us because the recording was requested by News, who were a programme department but no more permitted to speak than we were: they wrote the news, and it was read for them by an announcer. (The story that under Reith announcers always wore evening dress is a legend: they did only if they had to receive a distinguished speaker who might turn up in evening dress himself.) So that day, for once, I was all on my own. It was a job I took on eagerly, because Delius had been one of my earliest musical loves, if not the first of all.

I sometimes wish I had been a composer, not a writer: so many words are superfluous, and so many emotions have no words. But I am not a musician at all, only a member of those English concert audiences who (as the conductor Sir Thomas Beecham said) do not know much about music but like the noise it makes. On the back of the sleeve of one of my Delius records there is a quotation: 'The sorrow that lies at the heart of all mortal joys, the bitterness at the core of all great sweetness.' That is appropriate: his music is purer poetry than a poem in words.

Nevertheless, I must try to say why I specially like the music of Delius, because that is the point of this story. I do not think I knew any of his major works when I went to his funeral, except 'Sea Drift', which is a setting for baritone, choir and orchestra of a poem by Walt Whitman. What I knew, and what most amateurs know, are his shorter orchestral pieces. 'Brigg Fair' is one of them, a setting of a Lincolnshire folk song, and the titles of the others tell the character of them all: 'In a Summer Garden', 'Summer Night on the River', 'A Song before Sunrise', 'On Hearing the First Cuckoo in Spring', 'A Song of Summer'. But the music is not descriptive, it is evocative, and these are the images it brings – summer, warm nights, calm flowing water, peace, gentleness, contentment; and one must also add love and companionship, because it never suggests a melancholy solitude. Youth is another ingredient; at least, so it seems to me. Perhaps that is only because I heard it when I was very young. Delius was

over forty when he wrote the first of it, and he was a desperately
sick old man when he wrote 'A Song of Summer'.

I have not often been to Limpsfield since the funeral, but
last winter I took my granddaughters there, because my Paget
grandparents are also buried in the churchyard and my daughter
thought it might give the children a feeling of family history. I
could not find their grave, but I found the other at once: I
remembered exactly where it was. It has a headstone now with
two names on it and nothing more – no claim of fame or hope
of immortality – Frederick Delius and Jelka Delius, his wife.
There are yew trees in the churchyard which look immensely old.
Last midwinter they were dank and mournful but the funeral
was in May, and they were glowing in the early summer sun,
with a blackbird singing in them. The date of Jelka's death is
marked on the stone as 28 May 1935. I must have been there on
25 or 26 May, because she died two or three days afterwards.
He had died nearly a year before, and that was one of the strange
things about that funeral.

We English claim Delius as a great English composer (we do
not have too many) and so he was, in so far as he was born in
Bradford in the industrial north of England in 1862. But to tell
the truth, both his parents were German and he lived almost all
his life in France. He died in France, but said he wanted to be
buried in a country churchyard in the south of England. The
request surprised everyone, because he had no special connection
with the south of England, and none at all, as far back as anyone
remembered, with the Church of England. But that was certainly
what he said, so after long arguments with French officials his
body was brought to England and the ceremony at Limpsfield
was arranged.

There is a lot to be said for having a funeral a year after
somebody dies. A corpse is a thing to get rid of, as quickly and
neatly as possible. A year later, when the sharp edge of grief
had worn away, friends could meet for a funeral, in church or
anywhere else, without creating a public ordeal for the people
who loved him best and miss him most. The funeral at Limpsfield
was solemn but it was far from gloomy; in fact, on that perfect
summer day, it was a perfect expression of the dead man's music.
There was a crowd of musicians. Sir Thomas Beecham, an old

friend and admirer, had brought down a section of the London Philharmonic Orchestra and they played the summery music in the church. I suppose nobody but a composer could have quite the same privilege of communicating with his own friends at his own funeral. Afterwards, Beecham made an oration by the grave, and it was then that the blackbird sang.

Although so many of Delius's friends were there, his wife was not. She had come over from France, but on the journey she had caught pneumonia.

They had been married for over thirty years. By all accounts, it was a marriage which reached heights of happiness and survived through canyons of despair. Jelka was an art student in Paris in the 1890s when they met. He was ten years older than she, a tall, thin, romantic Englishman who lived alone and seemed to her to be aristocratic, although as a matter of fact his father was a wool merchant. She fell in love with him quickly, both with him and with his songs, which she sang to his accompaniment. But Delius was a feckless young man. Jelka was not his only girl-friend and he had no inclination for married life. So she settled down to wait for him, and waited seven years.

Soon after they met, she persuaded him to take her boating on the river in the village of Grez-sur-Loing, which is about sixty kilometres out of Paris, and they landed in an old deserted garden enclosed by a church, a ruined castle and a rambling empty house. She knew it was there; she had painted in it several times before. But if it was a stratagem to take him there, it was only half successful. He was charmed by the garden's ancient peace, and said it was the sort of place he would like to work. But he did not ask her to marry him.

Then the house and its garden were offered for sale. Neither Jelka nor Delius had any money, but she persuaded her mother to buy it; and when they married at last, in 1903, the house and garden became their home, and except for the years of the 1914 war they lived there ever after.

Their resources were small, and their prospects even smaller. Delius had written a respectable quantity of music but it had seldom been published and hardly ever performed. But as it happened, he was on the verge of success. In the first few years of his marriage, his music began to catch on, and in those years he wrote most of the work which is best remembered today. In 1914 success deserted him, not through any fault of his own but because the war had started and music in Europe had practically ceased. For the same reason he and Jelka had to leave their home and move to London, and as both of them were of German origin the years they lived in London must have been miserable. After the end of the war, before the musical world had come to life again, he experienced a personal disaster even more complete. In 1921 he fell ill. For three years Jelka took him from place to place in Europe, in a desperate search for a cure. Sometimes their hopes were raised, but by 1925 he was totally paralyzed and blind. She took him back to the house at Grez-sur-Loing, knowing he was incurable and would always be helpless, although his mind remained as clear as ever; and there in the garden where she had taken him when she was first in love, and in the house where his genius had flowered so briefly, she nursed him for nine years until he died.

I did not know any of this history when I went to Limpsfield. I took my records back to London and broadcast bits of them in the news that night, and that was that. But the next day, or the next but one, my telephone rang three times: the Director General. It had never happened to me before, and I jumped up in awe and wondered what I had done or failed to do.

'Howarth, sir.'

'Did you record the funeral of Delius?'

'Yes, sir.'

'Then please take the records to this address. Mrs Delius is ill, and I am told she might like to hear them.' And he gave me the address in Kensington. It was a nursing home.

That regal command made no allowance for technical difficulties. The only portable gear we had for playing our records was a wind-up acoustic gramophone which very quickly wore them out. Also, the recording I had made of the music in the church was nothing like concert standard: the acoustics were difficult, I had only one microphone, and I had never tried before to record an orchestra. So before I set off, I went to the gramophone library and borrowed the commercial records of my own favourite bits of Delius: among them, the 'First Cuckoo' and 'In a Summer Garden'. I was very young, twenty-three I suppose and young for my age; I knew very little of life, and nothing at all of death; so I just thought that if Mrs Delius was ill it might cheer her up to hear some of her husband's music, and I did not think in time that I might be meddling with deeper emotions.

The room in the nursing home was darkened. A woman took me in, and stayed while I was there. I thought she was a relation or friend of Jelka Delius, not a nurse. I put my gramophone on a table by the bed; and I hardly dared look at the spare, drawn, motionless face on the pillow, because I had begun to understand – though I do not think anyone told me – that she was dying. I played 'The First Cuckoo', which I had recorded in the church, and then Sir Thomas's oration. You could hear the blackbird. At the end of it, she turned her head towards me where I stood in the half-darkness, and she smiled and said 'Dear Tommy'. That was the only time she spoke.

When that was finished, I whispered to the woman who was waiting: 'Do you think she would like to hear more music?'

'Yes, I think she would,' the woman said, and I put on one of the records I had borrowed. It was 'In a Summer Garden'.

I do not know the technical words to describe that piece of music, but there again are all the images I have tried to put into words: love, youth, tranquillity, content; and superimposed on them, the gaiety of bright flowers, birdsong, and sunlight reflected on ripples of running water. The work ends in a shimmering series of chords so soft and so remote that the music seems almost not to move and not to end, but only to dissolve as trees and flowers dissolve in dusk when night falls on a garden. When the last of those chords was ended, the woman said, 'I do not think she can hear any more,' and I looked again at the face on the pillow. The eyes were closed, and it was perfectly still.

I read in the papers that she was dead; but it was not until many years later that I learned a little more about the music I had played her, and understood how reckless my choice had been. That was after the Second World War, when orchestral concerts began again in London, and I heard 'In a Summer Garden' at the Albert Hall. Somebody lent me the score, and I saw for the first time the inscription that Delius had written on it. Even now I do not know what emotion I brought to that elderly lady in the last few conscious moments of her life: a happy recollection, or a regret for love and youth long faded which is almost unbearable to imagine. 'In a Summer Garden' was written soon after Delius married her, before the misery of the war and the agony of his paralysis. The garden it was designed to evoke was their garden at Grez-sur-Loing. At the top of the score he had written, 'To my wife Jelka', and had added two lines from Rosetti:

All are my blooms, and all sweet blooms of love
To thee I gave while spring and summer sang.

FIVE

The Night the Palace Caught Fire

All my life, I have had work that completely absorbed me; I have never been aimless or bored. I only realize now, when so many young men I know have no job at all, and not much prospect of ever having one, what a privilege that has been – as great a privilege as keeping out of hospital, which I have also done so far. For seven years it was broadcasting that took all my attention. Only the war uprooted me from that. In itself, it is not a bad thing to be uprooted: like a greenhouse plant, everyone needs re-potting once in a while.

A constant threat of it is unpleasant, though. Throughout those seven BBC years none of my friends expected to live very long, nor did I. It was not a fear, but a reasonable deduction. In the previous war, a whole generation equal in age to ours had been wiped out. Every village still had its war memorial, every year there was a sentimental Day of Remembrance, and everyone knew it was going to happen again. I was lucky to have a father alive: a very large proportion of my friends did not. Broadcasting made it more real. We could hear the Nazi rallies, their brainwashed war-cries – *'Sieg Heil! Sieg Heil!'* – and their ranting leader, and we could see them marching, robots, not yet on television but in the newsreels. A powerful, efficient race of neighbours had lost their reason and gone berserk and we knew they were gunning for the French and the Jews, and then for us.

I can't say it oppressed us terribly, but it did make a philosophical difference. Personally, I thought the best of life would be over anyway by the time I was thirty, and I did not very much want to live longer and be middle-aged: or so I persuaded myself. Very few of us tried to do anything to stop it: that was up to the politicians, and we were so certain they were making a hopeless incompetent mess of it that there seemed to be nothing we could do. We did not want in the least to be heroes: heroism might be a German fashion but it was certainly not a British one just then. There were a few dedicated conscientious objectors, but the great majority of us just assumed that when it started we would have to try to fight back and would lose; nobody yet had tried to persuade us we might win. When finally it did start I was twenty-seven, nicely ripe for cannon-fodder, and all the time I was a young man I had been waiting, far from bravely but not unhappily, for someone to tell me I had to go and get killed.

In September 1936 something unexpected happened in the BBC. A friend said, 'I hear there's a new man in News.' We were strolling along a corridor in Broadcasting House, pretending to be BBC executives, whose gait in those corridors was once described as 'purposeful but ineffective'. What he said was an understatement. The new man was Richard Dimbleby. A gale of fresh air was about to blow through the News Room: indeed, a new era of broadcasting was about to begin, and a special new era for me.

After Richard died in 1965 his son Jonathan, who was writing his biography, came down to Sussex to see me because, he said, he believed I was his father's closest friend. I thought for a moment, and then said 'Yes, I was' – and not without pride. I do not know who had told Jonathan: perhaps his mother Dilys, or his elder brother David, or Richard himself. I did not need to add, because he knew, that our active friendship had been short; only four years after we met the war sent Richard in one direction and me in another. (I called him Dick; I don't quite know why except that his family did, and I remember him as Dick. Richard was always his official name. Everyone else used it, so I had better stick to it now.)

My own younger children have hardly heard of him; broadcasting, or television now, is the quickest, almost the only creator of fame, but also the most ephemeral. So I will explain.

He was a year younger than I, twenty-three when he joined the BBC. He had been a journalist since he left school, and at that moment was the editor of the *Advertiser's Weekly* and the youngest editor, he claimed, in Fleet Street. He had had the nerve to write to the BBC News Editor pointing out that broadcast news was accurate and reliable but deadly dull: and indeed it was, it all came from agencies and always began with the formula 'Here is the news, copyright by Reuters, Press Association and Exchange Telegraph.' He proposed a way of making it more exciting, and offered in modest words to come and do it himself. A letter like that from anyone else would have had a freezing reply, if any; but Richard always got away with things, by sheer charm and an enthusiasm that was as catching as measles, and a few weeks later he was on the staff.

There he found he was up against brick walls. His basic idea was that the BBC should have its own observers, specifically himself, who would be ready like newspaper correspondents, day or night, to go to the scene of any news, write and broadcast their own reports and bring eye-witnesses to the nearest regional studio and interview them there – or much better still, take a recording van and record the whole thing on the spot. This sort of thing, he pointed out, would be very important when the war began. But the BBC, for all its excellence, was simply not organized for anything so brash and spontaneous. Everything happened by filling in forms. Members of the staff hardly ever broadcast themselves, except the anonymous announcers and a very few sports commentators. Every spoken word was scripted – again excepting sport – and not only scripted but taken down in shorthand and filed afterwards as a 'P. as B.', a Programme as Broadcast, presumably in case of litigation. Recording vans were booked months in advance. Richard's ideas defied all these conventions, and nobody senior would listen.

It is self-evident that he succeeded. By the end of the war his was the best-known voice in Britain, and after the war when television began again his portly figure and a face that can only be called cherubic became as well-known as the voice. When he died prematurely of cancer, he was without question the best-loved and most expert broadcaster there had ever been. He was a self-made man, but his funeral was in Westminster Abbey. Earl Mountbatten wrote that Richard had millions more friends than he could ever have known, and the then Director General, Sir Hugh Greene, wrote of him as 'a patient, gentle, courteous, confident, compassionate, loyal and brave friend'. Thence my pride.

Surrounded by the brick walls of opposition when he began, Richard set himself to undermine them by starting a sort of underground movement of young and junior men. He recruited me right away, because I was more or less in charge of the movements of the recording vans, and because he discovered I was prone, like him, to wild enthusiasms, if I was given a lead. What he wanted was to be able to ring up any time, day or night, and dash off with a recording van wherever there was news. The whole idea delighted me: I was fed up with the inanition of sound recording. There were six or eight other people too, recording engineers or administrators, who had the sort of temperament it needed, and if they were married had wives like Richard's who could put up with it. We could not always do it; often, both vans were booked by more sober-minded programme departments. But if we conceivably could we did, and we all began to enjoy these rather lunatic expeditions much more than the sober ones – partly because they were exciting, and largely because it was Richard. He was a fat man even then, but a man of stupendous stamina and energy – and yet of sympathy. He always understood technical difficulties if they were real, and if they were not he blasted them to bits. Nobody could resist him long. 'No use asking permission,' he would say on the telephone in the middle of the night. 'They'll all be tucked up and asleep. And if they were awake, they'd say no. Let's get the story first, and argue afterwards.' It worked, up to a point. No senior person, he proved, cared what we did, provided we did it with decorum and were back at our desks in time for the nine-to-five job for which we were paid – a pittance, I might add. Richard was getting £7 a week, and so was I by then. But we did not care – or not much.

We happily worked all the time, until we simply could not stay awake any longer. Richard lived out in the western suburbs, and I do not know how he contrived to be perfectly happily married, as he was. His wife Dilys had been a journalist herself, and was splendidly sympathetic. As for me, I was always accessible because I had no such romantic ties and lived in a flat in Carnaby Street. That was before Carnaby Street became one of the sights of London for its trendy boutiques. It was an ordinary Soho back street, and full of interest. I lived over a baker's shop in a permanent delicious smell of hot French bread and croissants.

My neighbour upstairs had delirium tremens and in his worst attacks, which came when he ran out of booze, he was haunted by BBC announcers, whom he said he could hear in the air. He hated them, and sitting up with him at night in case he tried to kill himself, I hoped he would never discover I almost was one. Opposite, on the other side of the road, were two nightclubs or brothels, the Sphinx and the Florence Mills. The two buildings were joined inside, and when the police raided the Sphinx, as they did almost weekly, all the clients of both came rushing out of the Florence Mills; and vice versa. Sometimes it got too exciting, and girls were pushed out of windows. A flat in Soho was thought a blessing by my friends who had girl-friends, and some of them had keys; so coming home dog-tired, I was likely to find other people in my bed. I secretly envied them, but I slept on the floor and left them there. With my P. G. Wodehouse morality I had no idea how to get a girl into bed, and only the vaguest idea what to do if I got her there. For me, the merit of Carnaby Street was that it was only five minutes' walk, or three minutes' run, from Broadcasting House.

I had another asset too, a vintage sports car. It was an Invicta, with a perfectly beautiful polished aluminium six-cylinder engine, and that was my love. I had spent months (before I knew Richard) building new sports bodywork on it. I never quite finished (it is one of my weaknesses not to finish things) but I knew every nut and bolt of it – which I still think is the only way to enjoy a car – and I used it for the recording expeditions. I have a most vivid mental picture of tearing up the Great North Road at night (like a character from Dornford Yates: 'The great Rolls thundered across Europe, bats dashing their brains out on the windshield') while Richard slept with his head on my lap underneath the steering wheel and the recording van came trundling miles behind. It had a sad end, that car. During the war, while I was away, there was a patriotic outcry for aluminium for making Spitfires or something. Most people sacrificed their saucepans, but my mother also gave my beautiful car to a scrap dealer.

Richard always worried that we might miss some superb bit of news because we had no organization to back us up. Newspapers always have an editorial staff on duty, but between about nine in the evening, when the BBC News Room went home, and lunchtime the next day, we had nobody to tell us what was going on. So he arranged privately with Reuters that they would telephone him or me at home, on alternate nights, if anything newsworthy happened. It did not last long. Reuters night men never quite got the idea that we were tied to a lorry, and for a week or two he – and Dilys, no doubt – not to mention me, were woken up five or six times a night by items like Threatened Drought in Siberia, or Serious Unrest in the Kalahari. Then he let the arrangement lapse, as privately as it began, and when we went to sleep, which was rare enough, we stayed asleep.

The cumbrousness of the recording vans was his millstone. There was a strong naval influence in the Engineering Division then and everything had to be built like a battleship, ten times as strong and reliable as anyone else would have made it. Above all, the quality of sound always had to be as near perfection as the technique of the era allowed. That was why our best recording van weighed seven tons: it was good enough, in good hands, to record a symphony. But Richard's belief was the opposite: for news work, sound quality did not matter if speech was comprehensible. In fact, a bit of a deviation from studio quality might add to its sense of urgency and drama. Both of us knew a perfectly adequate recording channel could be carried on the back seat of an ordinary car, which we could drive ourselves. That was what he longed for: or to be exact, not an ordinary car, but something fast and glamorous, say a Lagonda, with an illuminated sign on the front, 'BBC NEWS' – something that everyone would recognize and expect to see wherever anything happened. But senior people in the BBC would firmly have said that gentlemen did not do things like that. For a long time we plotted (he loved plots) to have a simple recorder built in secret, and take it in the back of my Invicta and broadcast its discs without telling anyone how we had done it. Surely, we thought, if we could do it three or four times before we were found out, people would have to admit it was possible and the engineers would be shamed into doing it officially. The snag was, we could never afford it. It was a dilemma. One half of us admired and valued the BBC's high standards, the other half longed to put a bomb under it and propel it into innovation.

All the same, we managed to cover a surprising amount of

news with the recording vans. Very slowly, Richard's ideas of news presentation began to be accepted in the BBC, and listeners liked them. We went to ship launches, shipwrecks, mining disasters, floods – the strange sort of things that are counted as news in Fleet Street. I did not always go on his expeditions. I was still second in command of sound recording, marginally too senior to disappear without warning, office work was always catching up with me, my boss showed signs of rebelling, and there was plenty of competition from even younger members of the department. I reluctantly had to leave most of it to them. But I was there for what I might loosely call Richard's apotheosis. That was the night the Crystal Palace burned down.

It might have been made for us. The first news came on the agency tapes about six o'clock, just after the final editions of the evening papers. The story was ours alone till the morning – if we could get it.

Few people are blasé enough to resist a good fire, and that was a perfect fire. The Crystal Palace was built in Hyde Park, under the aegis of the Prince Consort, for the Great Exhibition of 1851, a huge arch of iron and glass which covered twenty acres. When the Exhibition was over nobody could bear to scrap the building, so they took it to pieces and rebuilt it on a less expensive site on top of a hill at Sydenham in the south-east suburbs. There it stood for eighty-five years until the night it made a mighty bonfire. It was not much use to anyone; it presumably belonged to the government, who could well afford to lose it – and, above all, nobody got hurt.

I couldn't find Richard when the news came in; he was not in Broadcasting House, so I left messages for him everywhere, rang the engineer in charge of the laundry van, who simply said 'We'll be there', and drove off in the Invicta, taking a senior man in News who had nothing to do with the problem but who wanted to come and watch.

Richard and I had been thorough. Among other things, we had worked out and explored the quickest ways out of London, at various times of day, to anywhere in the country. There were surprisingly few of them, seven I think, and Sydenham was on one of them. So it was easy. I knew the short cuts. There were police checks where traffic was being diverted, but Richard had got us press passes by then, and they waved us through. As we got closer, the streets were full of fire engines, all going hell for leather in the same direction, and I joined them, flashing through the red traffic lights, a driver's dream. It must have been 6.45 when I got there and parked the car outside a café in the main road opposite the building, which was already blazing magnificently. The laundry van came in by the same ruse, attaching itself to the fire brigade. And so did Richard. I don't know how he got there, but there he suddenly was, and I had never been more glad to see him.

There were scores of fire engines already, and more were coming in all the time, but with his journalistic instinct and skill he almost instantly found the Commander of the London Fire Brigade himself ('David, his name's Firebrace, isn't life perfect?') – not only found him but insisted he had to take him inside the building and, escorted by that dignitary, he vanished through its front gates. I went round to the back as a stand-by with a lesser fireman, just in case Richard never came out again – which did not look unlikely. We all knew what to do without telling each other: be ready to record before eight o'clock, to get the disks back to Broadcasting House in time for the nine o'clock news.

There was a strong wind blowing, and the back was the lee of the building. In the eddy behind it, there was a space that was reasonably safe: overhead was a vast arch of burning embers. I don't think anyone had thought the Crystal Palace could burn, built as it was of iron and glass, and I still do not know exactly why it did. It may have had a wooden floor, and the ironwork certainly had a century of paint, and putty holding the glass; as soon as one end fell in it all made a huge wind-tunnel with a draught through it like a furnace. It was quite impossible to get in from the back, as I had hoped. On that side, there was a row of glass corridors leading down to the gardens, and out of each a river of molten glass was flowing, and solidifying like lava when it cooled. Further in, iron girders were drooping and folding like sticks of spaghetti dipped in a boiling saucepan, and further out, in the garden, the trees were beginning to crackle. I got out again pretty quick, and ran back to the café and the laundry van, and there was Richard, deliriously happy, black and minus his eyebrows, scribbling his script.

Typically, he knew the whole history of the place by then, the vital statistics of it, who had designed it (Sir Joseph Paxton) and above all what the Fire Brigade was doing. They had sent out a first class call, or whatever they called it, which meant that every fire engine in London was there – and that was a sight worth seeing – and more had been called in from all over the home counties to look after the rest of the city. I don't think they were trying by then to save the building – that was going to burn until it had burnt itself out: what they were there for was to save the shops and houses all around.

But we did not record. By eight o'clock it was obvious that if we cut disks we could not get them away and back to Broadcasting House in time for the news. It would take all night. To start with, my car and the van were both surrounded by a web of hoses all over the road, lying on top of each other, some flat and some throbbing with water. Nobody could unravel them, and we certainly could not drive over them. Commander Firebrace was tolerant but he put his foot down at that. And beyond them, the main roads were full of fire engines and policemen and unnecessary ambulances, and the side roads already black and blocked by crowds of people watching. The only answer came to all of us at once. Richard, or it may have been me, timidly asked the senior engineer, 'Could you hook up your amplifiers to a telephone line?'

'Don't see why not,' he said, 'if you'll carry the can. Nothing else for it, is there?'

By a stroke of luck, a BBC man much senior to us had turned up to see the fun, the respected S. J. de Lotbinière, Head of Outside Broadcasts. Normally, his outside broadcast lines were corrected and balanced, far from ordinary telephone lines. He had no gear with him, and no engineers, but we had. We put it to him.

'Nobody's ever done it, so far as I know,' he said. 'But if there was ever a time to try, it's now. If you need me, I'll share the blame.'

So we invaded the café and rang Broadcasting House, and somebody told the Post Office to keep that line open whatever happened. Then the engineers pulled the telephone off the wall and connected the amplifier, mixer and microphones. It was about 8.40: twenty minutes to go. The excitement seemed even to spread to the Control Room at Broadcasting House, normally the most phlegmatic of places, where philosophic calm was the rule and engineers logged the slightest deviation from normality. I think someone had rung the Chief Engineer of the BBC himself; I don't know what he said, but it wasn't No. They could hear us. The quality, they said, was not good, but they supposed we knew what we were doing. One of us had an ordinary radio receiver (it may have belonged to the café) so we could hear our cue, and they must have fixed a long lead on it, because I could hear the programme on headphones. I stood in the open with one microphone for background sound and Richard with another was in the café doorway where it was rather quieter. The engineers inside the café were mixing the two. There were several minutes before and after nine o'clock when we could not talk to anyone because our only line, with luck, was going on the air. We had had no time to test anything. It was either going to work, triumphantly or, more likely, fail disastrously.

I could hear the announcer drone on, the usual dreary introduction to the news – and then it came, as I remember, in the most sceptical, doubtful and uncertain terms – 'We hope to take you over to the Crystal Palace itself, where Our Observer has been watching.' And in the headphones I heard the shouts, the fire engine bells and the deep bass roar of the flames from the microphone I was holding. I signalled Richard, and he started. We were on. It was ecstatic.

That was far and away the most exciting and dramatic news broadcast there had ever been. We knew it was, and felt it proved everything Richard had been preaching so long; but we could not know that night what the High Command would think, because our line was only working one way. The immediate effect was something we had not expected, or had not worried about. There had been crowds before, but the broadcast brought out most of south London. People who tried to come by car were turned back miles away, but a million or so must have lived within walking distance, and walk they did. A broadcaster does not often see his audience, but there they were in multitudes, blocking every street, crowding every park, standing on roof tops and craning out of upstairs windows. That did not please the police or the Fire Brigade, but it was a wonderful evening out for everyone else.

We did another broadcast that night in the final news at 10.15. It might have been second best, but at about ten o'clock there was a crisis. Richard, of course, was always true to BBC tradition; he never exaggerated, expressed his own opinion, or relied on hearsay. But he was never averse to drama if it came his way. 'Urgent message from the Chief of the London Fire Brigade,' he began. 'Anerley Hill is dangerous.' Anerley Hill is the steep main road running down from the west end of the Palace. Nobody remembers exactly the words he used. 'There are fears that the west tower at the top of the hill may fall. It has a water tank on top with 100,000 gallons of water in it (he knew the exact figure) and if it falls a huge wave of water is going to pour down the hill. Please clear Anerley Hill at once. Get on to the higher ground to the west, or get into houses and go upstairs. I can see the tower from here, and hundreds of firemen playing their hoses on the base of it, but it's smoking or steaming right up to the top. So I repeat the urgent message – please get off Anerley Hill.'

The danger was real, but in the event the firemen saved the tower. Indeed both towers – there was one at each end of the building – are still there nearly half a century later, with a huge space in between where the Crystal Palace was.

Listeners loved it, and within the BBC all sorts of improbable people congratulated us next day. Opposition to what we were doing faded, and never came back. It was accepted that when something important happened, Richard would be there.

He was there, for instance, and so was I, when Neville Chamberlain flew back from Munich and came out of the aircraft waving a bit of paper Hitler had signed and made the most famous misstatement of any Prime Minister, 'I think it is peace in our time.' For a moment, it seemed the threat we had lived with so long was lifted; but only for a moment. We were half-way back to London with our disk when somebody said, 'Do you believe it? What's Hitler's signature worth?' And the threat of death descended again, made heavier by the thought that the Nazi leaders had made a fool of our Prime Minister, and even then, we imagined, were laughing at the old man's gullibility.

Very soon after that, we made our first foray abroad, to Germany. Hitler's most immediate demand had been for the part of Czechoslovakia called the Sudetenland. Chamberlain had agreed, and proposed an international force should go there to see that the transfer was orderly. The Germans said we could go too, and so did the BBC, which surprised us even more. For broadcasting, that trip was a total failure. We never got to the Sudetenland, and the International Force never even got to Germany. Hitler had never intended it should, and had only agreed to keep Chamberlain quiet.

So the most memorable thing was the pomposity of Nazi officials, which brought out all the naughtiness of Richard's character. We were met at the frontier at Aachen by a deputation in huge Mercedes cars, led by a young Aryan called Schmidt-Hansen from the Ministry of Propaganda. Richard swept into Aachen in a Mercedes, dispensing Nazi salutes and Heil Hitlers like a visiting monarch. Who else with his physique, and at that delicate moment of history, would have insisted the man from the Ministry should teach him to goose-step? He did, and goose-stepped grotesquely through the hotel foyer. I expected a dungeon for him, or a firing squad, but some of the assembled Nazis in their assorted uniforms looked almost as if they would have smiled, if they had dared to see the joke.

On the other hand, Schmidt-Hansen wore a professional smile all the time, and never saw a joke at all – or at least, not our sort of joke. He wore civilian clothes, which made him doubly sinister. It soon became hideously clear that his orders, poor fellow, were never to let us out of his sight unless we were safely in bed. He took us to Hamburg, where the International Force was supposed to land. Every day, we told him we were not interested in the International Force, we wanted to be in Sudetenland, not Hamburg, but every day he relayed a new excuse from his Ministry. I don't know if he knew the truth: that the International Force, on Hitler's orders, was anchored somewhere out in the North Sea, that it was never coming, and that we were never going to Sudetenland without it.

We had a frustrating week or two. We felt that we and the BBC – never mind England or the rest of the world – had been deliberately swindled, and the only man we could take it out on was Schmidt-Hansen. I am not sure whether to be sorry: he represented something very barbarous. Our only weapon was to laugh at him; it was years since anyone in Germany had mocked the Nazi regime. While we waited Richard wanted, of course, to see the famous red light district of St Pauli. Schmidt-Hansen rashly said it was not there any more, the Führer had 'tidied up all that sort of thing'. To which the obvious answer was that if it wasn't there, there was no harm in seeing where it had been. Schmidt-Hansen had to take us there, and drive us around in his Mercedes. St Pauli seemed to be flourishing. Richard shouted with glee whenever we passed a conspicuous whore: 'Look, Schmidt-Hansen, look! There's another the Führer forgot to tidy up.' Even I got our escort's wintry smile when two utterly unattractive women were nuzzling my ears, one each, and I asked him the German for 'Please don't bite'.

Like any tourist, Richard conducted the Bavarian brass band in a beer hall, and he got them playing the British marching song from the previous war, 'It's a long long way to Tipperary'. A Norwegian from another table came and shook hands with us all, including Schmidt-Hansen, and thanked Richard for his courage in playing a song like that.

It was not a question of courage, just of exasperation. The climax came, I think, when we found that Schmidt-Hansen rang his Ministry in Berlin every evening and reported what we had been doing that day, which we thought was absurd and offensive. Richard somehow discovered the number he rang, and the name of the man he spoke to, and one evening we contrived to give him such a substantial hangover that he could not make his call. Richard rang the Ministry instead and said he thought he had better tell them Schmidt-Hansen was very sick, but we were behaving ourselves.

Very soon after that, our Nazi escorted us back to Aachen and politely said goodbye; and we saw his odious smile switch off as he turned away.

The BBC did not pay you for extra work, but you could save up whole extra days and add them to your summer holiday. I never had less than five weeks, and I spent them going as far away from London as I could and being alone. You cannot be an explorer in five weeks without any money to spare, and that was before one thought of going by air; but I had an idea which gave an illusion of exploring. I used to get a large-scale map of some bit of deserted country, usually in Norway, and choose a name on it – perhaps an obscure little lake, as far as could be from any road or house – and I set off to find it, pretty confident that nobody had been there before except perhaps local hunters, and the man long ago who made the map. Nowadays that might lead to disappointment, like the explorer who hacked his way week after week through what he thought was virgin South American jungle and came out in the backyard of a Hilton hotel; or the other who crossed the Empty Quarter of Arabia in mortal peril on camel-back, climbed a very large dune, heard the unmistakable voice of Bing Crosby and saw below him an American oil prospector's camp with air-conditioned caravans, throbbing generators and pop music on the radio. But in the 1930s it usually succeeded, and once I did much better than I expected.

In the steamer going up the coast of Norway I met a Norwegian army major who said he was on his way to make the very first map of the interior of Finmark, the most northerly province of all. We bought each other a beer and he asked me to go with him. Somewhere far north, we collected two young soldiers appointed to be his assistants, and later, on a solitary wooden jetty at the head of a fjord, a Lapp with a horse, whose job was to bring up stores from the coast to wherever the major was camped. He was the only man there when we landed, and he had waited for us a month.

People in the Arctic do not live by the clock. In winter when it is dark all day they sleep most of the time, and in summer when the sun goes round and round in the sky and does not set, they work all night. No span of time less than the seasons mattered to the major; when the sun dipped below the horizon, he would know it was autumn and time to go home. Meanwhile, he and his two soldiers usually worked for thirty-six hours or so, trudging from one hilltop to the next with their gear, then came back to camp and slept for ten hours, then got up for another ten hours and cooked and fished, then had another long sleep before the next thirty-six hours of surveying. I lazed around, sleeping if I was sleepy, baking bread if I was hungry and waging a war I could never win against mosquitoes. I have always been happy doing nothing.

After several weeks, we all lost count of days – until one night or day the Lapp brought a newspaper with our stores. It had a date I had thought was still safely in the future. Working it out, we decided that day was a Thursday, and I had to be back at my desk in Broadcasting House at 9.30 on Monday morning. The only hope was to walk south-east to a river called the Tana, which was the frontier of Finland, and follow the river down to a road which crossed it by a ferry, and catch a bus through Finland and a train through Sweden and Denmark.

It was an interesting walk to the Tana, with a compass but no map. The high plateau of Finmark has not one recognizable landmark; in summer, it is full of small lakes you have to walk round, and aimless streams you have to wade or swim, and huge shuddering bogs you may or may not be able to cross by jumping from tuft to tuft of grass. It was much harder than I expected to walk a compass course. Still, once I had started there was nothing to do but go on; I could never have found the camp again if I went back. So on I went, pondering what my boss would say if I turned up a week late and told him I had been stuck in an arctic bog, or if I didn't turn up at all. I walked without stopping while the sun went round in the sky from midnight to midnight – it must have been sixty miles or so – before I saw a river so wide it must be the Tana; and on it the blessed sight of a Lapp fishing in a canoe, who happily took me another fifty or sixty miles down the river, and provided for the journey a whole smoked salmon and nothing else. I made it to London with time to spare for a bath. That was the sort of holiday I enjoyed.

When Richard and I got back from Germany, I was restless. I loved the excitement of news work, and the feeling of being at the centre of things, and above all working with Richard. But he was safely launched on his career, he did not need any longer whatever help I had been able to give him. I had an illusion I had some brains and ought to be using them. So I got myself moved to the Talks Department. That was only a few floors up in Broadcasting House, but it was another world, calm, scholarly and leisured. You were paid to think.

68

There were seven men and one woman, all older than I was, and at the weekly meetings each of us had to propose ideas for talks or series of talks. If they were approved, the next part of the job was to find the leading experts on the subject and commission scripts; and then, almost always, to re-write the experts' scripts from beginning to end. The trouble was they all wrote (unless they had often broadcast before) in what they thought was elegant literary English. Their sentences were long and tortuous, full of grammatical inversions and subordinate clauses. Nobody who heard them, once only, on a loudspeaker, could ever have grasped what they were trying to say.

Many of course, being experts, were not at all pleased to have their work re-done by an upstart of twenty-five, and I found I had to be perfectly clear in my own mind why I had made each change. I began to learn something which, at a later stage, became most important to me: the elements of style in English prose. I hope I have never forgotten those early self-taught lessons. At any rate, I still take enormous pleasure in being as lucid as I can, and in polishing every sentence I write. I know this is something I shall come back to later in this story, probably at enormous length, so I will not write about it now.

The story leads to Ireland. I liked Talks, but I still felt claustrophobic in London. It is far too big: oppressive when you live in the middle, like Carnaby Street, to think it would take you an hour in any direction to get out of the place. So I got myself appointed as Talks man in Belfast.

Northern Ireland was peaceful then, but intensely political, and the BBC's Talks man was everybody's target. It was rare to meet anyone who did not want to get in to the studio and preach his own opinion; so I had to steer a rather delicate course. My most popular talks, though, were nothing to do with politics, they were discussions between a doctor and a housewife on how to feed yourself on a shilling a week (five new pence to the young). A terrible lot of people were so poor that this was a common problem. The doctor talked about healthy diets, and the housewife about recipes; and what they came down to was herrings (which were very cheap), tea (because the Irish insist on tea) and bread and margarine. They were both very good talkers, like most of the Irish, and had no need of my pedantic lectures;

and the doctor, I always understood, was a leader of the IRA. One day I scored an all-time first by having lunch in a pub with the IRA doctor, and dinner the same evening with Lord Craigavon the Governor-general.

But it was life away from work that woke a different part of me, which had been latent all that time. I rented a very small primitive cottage called the Porter Lodge near the hamlet of Ballymoran on the shore of Strangford Lough, and I lived there alone a long way from anywhere. Also I hired a derelict yacht that was hauled up on the beach. I found it was rotten from end to end, but that did not put me off, and I got it into the water in one piece and often went sailing. It was just as well I never went out of the lough and into the open sea. It would certainly have fallen to bits and sunk. This, I decided, was the real me. And indeed I have never lived in a city since then, and seldom far from a boat, unless you count being billeted in Arras in northern France for part of the war. I was perfectly happy and contented, but I knew it could not last.

I was not out of touch with Richard. Before I left, we had done two things. First, we had both taken a day off to christen his first son David. David is distinguished himself on television now, and I should think he would hate to be reminded that I was his godfather, or – though I am not sure this was so – that he was even named after me. I was a very bad godfather. It was not entirely my fault: I meant well. But what with the war and other distractions I did not see him again for years and years and – as always happens with other people's children – he was always much bigger and older than I thought he was. I believe (I may have embroidered this story) that on one birthday I calculated he must be at his first school, and sent him a boy-sized cricket bat, and got a charming letter back from Paris: 'Thank you so much for the bat. I am at university here, the Sorbonne, for a year, but it will be very useful when I come home.'

The other thing Richard and I did was even more far-reaching. He had been told that when the war started he would be the first of all radio war correspondents. He had asked for me to go with him, and the hierarchy had agreed. He promised to ring me just before the balloon went up, and I should come back to London at once. And so he did, two days before war was declared.

Expecting it, I had had a suitcase in my office for weeks. There was no time to go back to the Porter Lodge. I gave my car to my secretary – not the Invicta, a duller and more respectable one – and asked her to tell the owners of the cottage I would come back for my furniture one day. That night, I was on the boat for England, and it was five years before I went back for the furniture.

SIX

War Correspondent

When that war had ended, I wrote four books about episodes in it which I had been more or less concerned with. Then I stopped and turned to other subjects, because I thought it should all be forgotten. Now, on the verge of writing about it again, I have to get one thing off my mind: to say to people who do not remember it, as I have often said before, that everyone's recollections of it are selective and more or less mistaken, including mine. War should be remembered only with shame, as the most wicked of failures of human wisdom. But forgetfulness is a mercy. It hides the things too awful for memory to bear, or human conscience to admit, and leaves only, of all the crime and horror, a few stories that seemed either comforting or funny.

I thought in 1939 that the war we had to fight would come nearer than any other recent war to being morally excusable, and I still think it did. It was not a patriotic war but a war against a political and philosophical system which itself, we believed, was so immoral that it had to be opposed, even with the immorality of war. Nothing can make war either moral or logical. It turns morality inside out: killing and cruelty are its virtues. And as for its logic, the man you are expected to murder, the man you see in your gunsight, is not your real enemy, but probably a fellow-man as scared and bewildered as you are. At best, war can only be the lesser of two evils, but that was what it seemed in 1939. War was hideous, but a world ruled in triumph by Nazism would have been worse.

We did not know all about Nazism then, but at the end, when Belsen and Auschwitz were revealed and we learned that six million men and women had been 'liquidated', we felt we had been right. One cannot imagine cruelty and crime on such a scale, and among all the reports from concentration camps, one triviality has always stuck in my mind: an open tea-chest three quarters full of thousands on thousands of wedding rings.

This is not to say that wars have always been evil. Many men have a primitive instinct to fight, and in the old days wars satisfied that instinct. By and large, they were fought by armies of men who had the instinct, and peaceable people could leave the armies or navies to fight it out. But in recent history, the dangers of war have grown out of all proportion to the instinct. Whole nations of men were dragged into the First World War, whether they had any warlike instinct or not. They marched to war with women cheering them on, bands playing and flags flying, more or less buoyed up by the illusion that physical courage was a masculine virtue. The Second World War shook that illusion, at least for the British and presumably for the Germans, and should have shattered it for ever. Bombing of cities by both sides brought everybody into it, and proved that martial courage was not a male prerogative at all; women had just as much, and even the very young and the very old. Men who had made a brave gesture of joining the army found themselves living year after year in perfect safety in training camps in the depths of the countryside, but knowing that their families, wives and children, old mothers and fathers and grandparents, were facing all the rigours of war at home in the cities, and facing them with the courage that hitherto had been an army's pride. It was a strange reversal of roles, so far unique.

Personally, I was very seldom so frightened in war as when I was home on leave. I did nothing brave myself, but I knew very well some men of astonishing bravery, including one – a Norwegian – who won more British medals for it than anyone else has ever had. But I would not say that any of them were braver than my own mother and father, who were both in their sixties and calmly counted the hundreds of bombs that left holes in their garden and the neighbouring fields. You cannot measure things like that or compare them.

Nevertheless, people who lived through that war do not remember on the whole the enormity of the crime committed in their name. Even those who lived month after month under aerial bombing and saw their own cities reduced to rubble, and knew their own bombers were doing the same to foreign cities, do not see the thing as a whole. They tend to remember not hundreds of thousands of bombs, but one bomb in particular, or perhaps one night of bombing: everyone then had his own bomb story, which bored everyone he told it to. Many had a private bereavement, a private pain, or a private object of devastating pity, and of course they remember that most clearly of all. But if they were luckier, they remember with pleasure the friendship; because sharing a common enemy and a common danger does certainly make people more friendly to each other. And strangely, they remember the things that struck them as funny. War is prolific in comedy, especially the comedy of errors made by one's seniors, the sort of error the army graphically calls a cock-up. The more humble one's own rank, the more seniors one possesses, and high posts in war can be occupied by bone-headed people. So the more junior one was, the more one's recollection was filled by the frequent cock-ups.

I admit, with this elaborate apology, that my own recollections of those five years of life are as misleading as anyone else's; but I hope they contain a few bits and pieces of a mirror of the truth about war.

I was back in the middle of things at the moment it began – in the News Room in Broadcasting House when the Prime Minister broadcast that our ultimatum to the German Government had expired and we were at war with Germany. We knew what he was going to say, of course. What we did not expect was to hear the wails of the air raid sirens a few minutes later. We all trooped down to the basement carrying our gasmasks according to orders, and grumbling angrily that the Germans must have launched their bomber fleet before war had been declared. Nothing happened, and we were still grumbling when the all clear sounded. Long after, I learned that a solitary light aircraft had come from somewhere abroad, flown up the Thames estuary and landed peacefully. The alarm was the first cock-up of the war: not an important one, but a warning of plenty to come.

Richard was as well prepared as anyone and much better than most. He had got what we wanted by then, an ordinary car with a disc recording machine on the back seat: not a glamorous

Lagonda, it was true, only a plain but new and serviceable Humber. But we could drive it ourselves. A week before, he had driven it to Paris, with the recording gear and some pots of camouflage paint, and left it there in an underground garage he thought was bomb-proof. Three of us were appointed to man it: Richard, a recording engineer named Harvey Sarney, and me. We hardly knew Sarney, he was appointed by the Engineering Division, but he turned out a first-rate colleague: a very large and quiet man who was never unwilling, never complained. An engineer was always a third party in these affairs, and I don't think we ever discussed our more outlandish plans with him. But he was always there when they surfaced, unruffled and efficient, and in the course of time he willingly broke every rule in whatever bible guided BBC engineers, doing things and taking risks far beyond the duties of a recording engineer.

It was the first war in which a public broadcasting system had existed, and I think everyone in the BBC was aware the Corporation had an unknown job to do which was going to be uniquely important. We three were specially aware of it. In later stages of the war, the BBC had dozens of war correspondents, but we were the first radio war correspondents there had ever been: the most direct link between troops in the field and their families at home, and the only source of news more immediate than the daily papers. What we did, and especially what Richard said, was going to have a deep effect on people's minds in that crisis of human history. In retrospect our responsibility looks daunting, but at the time it did not worry us in the least. It was an opportunity we had only dreamed of.

We went down Regent Street and ordered ourselves the complete outfits of army officers, and the BBC picked up the bill – everything from caps to socks and shoes, the Sam Browne belts, the kind of greatcoat called a British Warm, even the swagger sticks; I soon lost my swagger stick, and still have no idea what it was for. The only things we did not have were swords and badges of rank; instead of the latter, there were embroidered labels on the epaulettes: British War Correspondent. Some army official told Richard we ranked with majors, which pleased him, and innocent soldiers saluted us; but we were non-combatant, and if we had any military authority it was negligible.

Before we left England for France, where the British Expeditionary Force was expected to be first in action, we had to appear in Broadcasting House in our gear. They wanted us to have our photograph taken, allegedly saying goodbye to the News Editor R. T. Clark. The picture was on the cover of the *Radio Times* and I saw a copy not long ago. We looked quite ludicrously young and shiny. But most of the goodbyes were very real. Senior executives shook our hands with tears in their eyes. They expected we would be the first to die for broadcasting and the BBC. We fully expected it too, but there were worse things to die for; and I at least (I can't speak for the others) was glad we were not expected to kill anyone else.

Of course when we got to France, there was no war at all. This was the beginning of what came to be called the Phoney War, which lasted all that winter. The Humber was safe in its underground garage, we sloshed the camouflage paint all over its gleaming back and chromium in a pattern we hoped would deceive the enemy, and we fulfilled a minor ambition by having a sign painted 'BBC' to go on the front of it. Then we drove unimpeded by anyone to Arras in north-east France, a dismal city in the most dismal part of Europe, which we had been told in strictest secrecy was the British headquarters. On the outskirts of Arras we asked a policeman the way to GHQ, and he told us without hesitation. So much for official secrets.

Of course we were doomed to learn all about military censorship. Most of it was commonsense necessity, but it sometimes reached heights of fantasy. The prime secret of all was where the British army was. Any Frenchman knew perfectly well where it was and was perfectly happy to tell you: on the frontier of France and Belgium, and more a hundred miles from any German. You cannot hide a stationary army in a foreign country; and since France had plenty of spies, it followed that any German who cared knew equally well where it was. Only the British were not entrusted with this secret.

By and by the army censors learned to trust us, to the extent that they let us do live broadcasts from this unmentionable zone. On these occasions, a major of Intelligence sat opposite us, with a Colt revolver which he sometimes put ostentatiously on the table. Richard always longed to start cheerfully, 'Well, here we are in Arras' – just to see what the major's orders were: to shoot him dead? Or blow the microphone to bits? Or possibly, since he was responsible, to blow his own brains out? Our nearest escape was on Christmas Day – a day that for many reasons I shall never forget. By then, for lack of a war to report, we were doing things like general knowledge quizzes live, between teams of soldiers at our end and their families in London. That day, just after their Christmas dinner, our team was to say the least festive. I had invented the questions Richard would ask their families, and made them harmless. But the questions London asked us grew more and more alarming, and we were horrified when we heard them ask 'What name of a French town did Mary Tudor say would be found in her heart?' Answer, the unutterable name of Calais. The censor's hand moved perceptibly towards his gun, but so imbued with secrecy were the soldiers that, drunk or sober, they all said they didn't know.

When we first reached Arras nothing whatever was happening, at least, nothing that could be called news. A few newspaper correspondents had arrived before us, and the army was creating an organization to look after their needs – such an organization, based on press telegrams, as there had been in the 1914 war, or for that matter in the Boer War or the Crimean War. We found the newsmen disconsolate, being escorted round deadly villages on the frontier, and each evening telephoning the day's official bulletin through to Fleet Street. Our needs and our resources were different, and the organization had to be stretched to meet them. For one thing, we had our own transport; for another, through Richard's foresight we were accredited to the French army, not only the British. Finally, as members of the BBC we had access to all the facilities of the French radio, including their high-quality landlines back to England. That was why the censors had to learn to trust us. That they did was largely through Richard's power of persuasion – he could charm even a man so august as the Director of Military Intelligence – and partly because the whole army became fascinated with the idea of performing and talking to home on the 'wireless'.

However, all war correspondents, or groups of them, had to have a Conducting Officer – an ex-regular soldier, more or less retired – to see that they behaved. Ours was named Captain the

Honourable Harry Tufton. Harry Tufton was a tremendous asset. His rank was not high, but his title and his easy cavalry manner gave him influence in the army. He was a humorous, critical and intelligent soldier, and a gourmet, and on his own admission he was immensely rich. We also felt rich, for the first time in our lives, because the BBC had a fixed allowance for anyone working abroad for a long continuous period, and it was the same whatever your rank: £2 a day. That just about doubled our pay. It did not put us anywhere near Harry Tufton's class, but the important thing is not to be rich but to feel rich. He had a big estate somewhere near Windsor, and I asked him once if he kept a flat in London too. 'No,' he said, in a classic reply, 'I keep a suite in the Ritz. It's cheaper in the end, you know.' For some reason he despised the Ritz in Paris. The only place in Paris he could bear to stay was the Hotel Crillon in the Place de la Concorde, conveniently round the corner from Maxim's. He did come slumming with us to the extent of agreeing one could eat at cheaper places than Maxim's, but whenever we were in Paris, which was whenever we could think of an excuse, we dossed down between the Crillon's ravishing linen sheets and sent our disgusting underclothes to the hotel laundry. My wife and I walked past the doors of that hotel the other day, and knew we were too poor to look inside.

We began in that autumn of 1939 by earnestly hunting for a battle. It was obvious the British were not about to fight one; there was nobody around for them to fight. But a battle was what we had expected, and what people at home had expected us to report. It was very hard indeed to believe that war had been declared and nobody anywhere on land was fighting it. With our French army passes and the blessing of the French War Ministry we were free to travel anywhere in France, and this we did, searching for somebody somewhere who was fighting.

The French believed they were safe behind the stupendous fortification they called the Maginot Line. We went there and made a programme about it. It was probably impregnable, as they thought, with vast underground barracks and armouries blasted out of rock, and lifts up vertical shafts to the gun emplacements above, which rose from the ground by hydraulic power like giant mushrooms. But like most lines, it had two ends.

One was on the Rhine and the other in the Ardennes, where Luxembourg and Belgium intervened between France and Germany; and of course when they were ready in the following spring, the Germans just came round the northern end of it, and it was useless.

Meanwhile, it was fully manned but silent. On top of it and beyond it to the east there was a no-man's-land where both sides had ordinary outposts. It was rather eerie up there, early on an autumnal morning, with the Maginot Line behind you. There was not a sound, either warlike or peaceful. Richard wrote a description which we recorded in a wood that was occupied by the French in the daytime and the Germans at night. You could see the German soldiers a couple of fields away. Everyone was on the look-out for trip wires or booby traps, but there were none. Both sides cooked in the wood, or at least made coffee; when we were there, the Germans' fires were still warm, and the Frenchmen blew on the embers and revived them and put their own kettles on. They hauled guns into place each morning, and hauled them away at dusk. We begged them to fire a gun, just one gun so that we could record it, but they absolutely refused. 'We fire a gun at them,' they said, 'they fire two at us. Then four, and war begins. Those are not our orders.' And again, 'I pray you, Monsieur, don't go beyond that bush. They can see you there, and they might do something. It depends who they have on duty.' Even seeing this scene, it was hard to believe it was real. It would be even harder, we thought, to make anyone else believe it, and we feared in the backs of our minds that the BBC would think we had been avoiding battle, not looking for it.

So we explored the whole of the Franco-German frontier. We drove up the Rhine, where you could look across at the German villages and countryside a couple of hundred yards away. No doubt there were fortifications, but we could not see them. It all looked as quiet as usual. People over there were still driving about in their Volkswagens; men and women were working in the vineyards. We wondered if perhaps the whole war was waiting for the grape harvest; it seemed as likely an explanation as any.

*

So to Strasbourg. Strasbourg was unique: a major city, completely undamaged and completely deserted. It was all in the field of fire of German guns from the other side of the river, its river frontage indeed within rifle range, and it had been evacuated the moment war was declared; everybody had fled, whether in panic or under orders I do not know – it looked like both – yet the Germans had never fired a single round at it. The people had only taken time to lock up their shops and offices, factories and homes, and they had never been allowed to go back there since, even for a day's visit. No human was there except a few patrols of soldiers or gendarmes on the look-out for looters. There were dogs and cats, gone wild or lying dead where the patrols had shot them. Cars were parked or abandoned haphazard on the sidewalks. It resembled nothing in life, except at first glance the biggest and most ambitious of film sets, the actors and technicians all gone. You could have expected to walk round the back and find it was made of canvas.

But it was the details that impressed me most and are still clearest in my memory. The café tables and chairs still stood on the sidewalks; some had tablecloths, cups and glasses, pecked clean by sparrows and trampled by pigeons' feet. Inside, the tables were laid for a breakfast of six weeks before, the wizened rolls of bread, the butter and milk grown over with mould. Here and there a crumpled napkin had been thrown down, among the droppings of rats, as if by a customer who had abandoned his breakfast in the middle.

And the shops. No windows were broken, but all were dirty and streaked by rain. Peering through the grime, you saw the window displays. Excepting the mouldering ruins of fruiterers, the most shocking – because the most human – were the expensive dress shops, the elegant fashions that had attracted ladies in the last summer of peace, now covered with dust and draped with spiders' webs; most shocking of all, perhaps, a display of bridal gowns for weddings that had never happened. Their veils were eaten by mice and stained by damp. The faces of the lay figures they were draped on should have been skulls.

Down on the river, we found the road bridge which joined the place to Germany still intact, but with a gun emplacement at

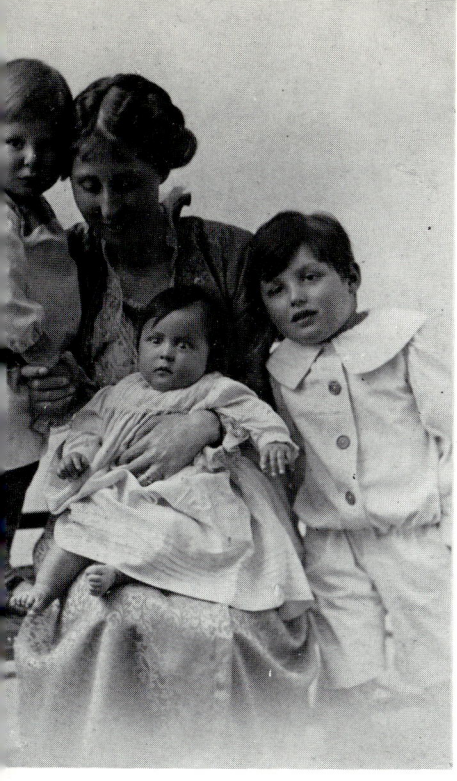

Ayot: early steam engine
told to wait in the sidings.

My mother with (from
right to left) my brother,
my sister and me.

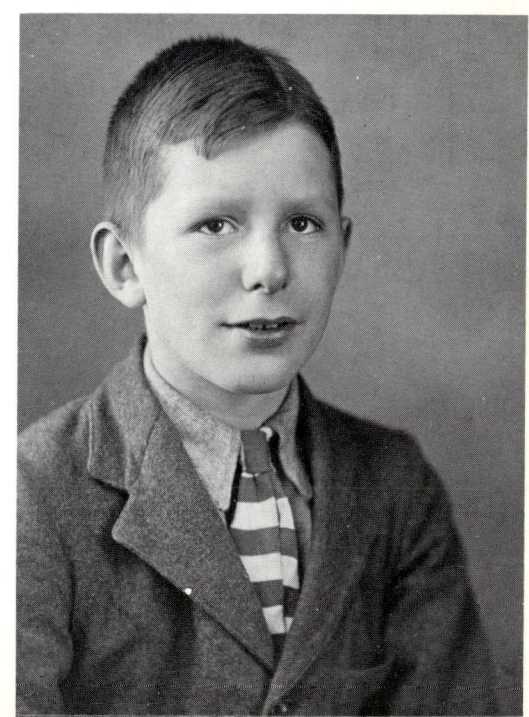

Big moment: the first school tie.

Above: With Richard Dimbleby at the time of Munich, greeted on the German frontier by Schmidt-Hansen.

Above right: 'Looking absurdly young and shiny' – Richard, me and Harvey Sarney with R. T. Clark, the News Editor.

Right: Richard and the Bavarian band.

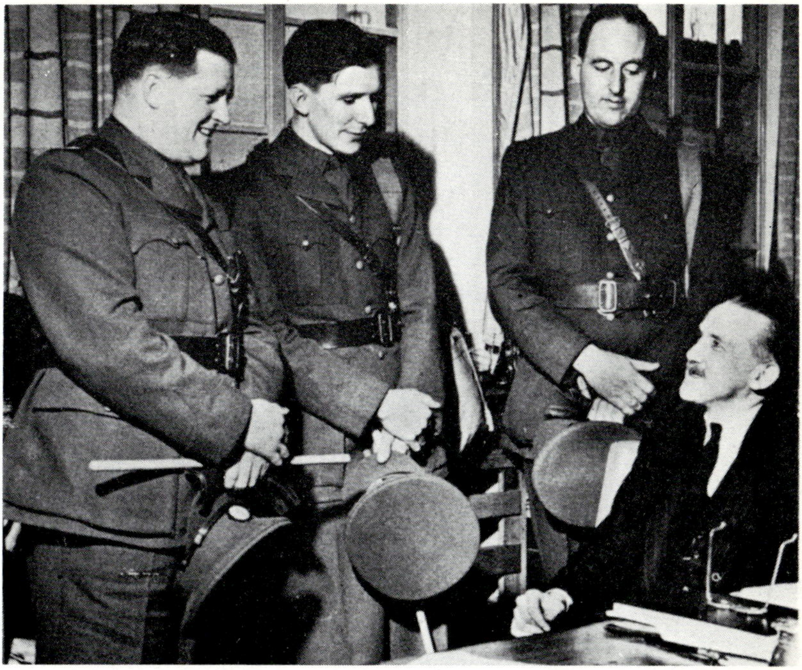

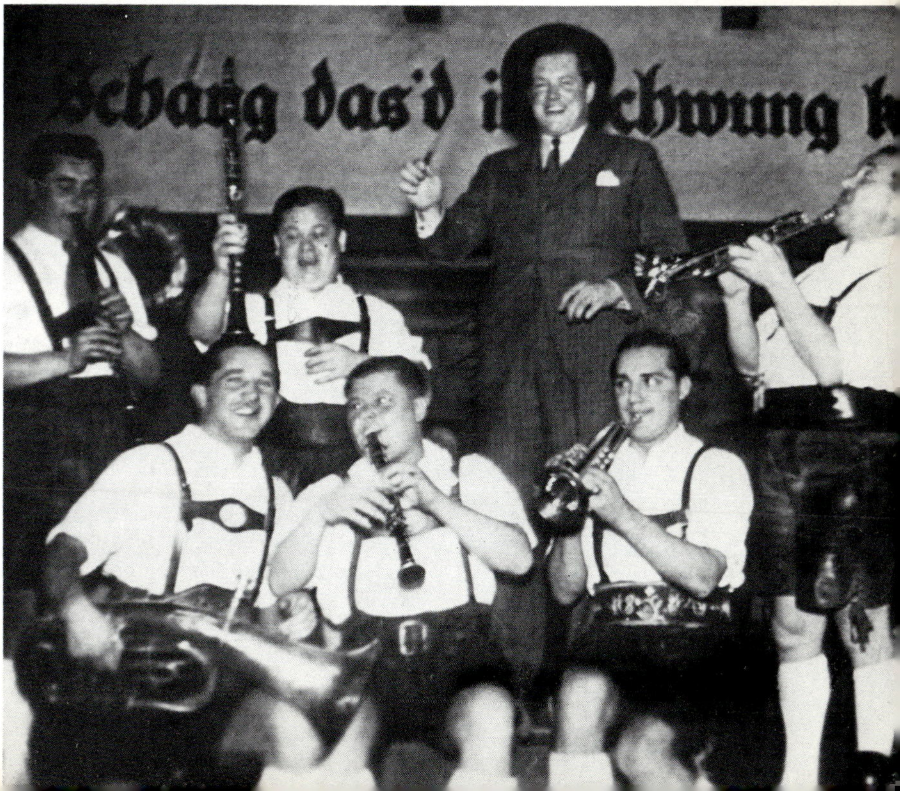
chang das'd i chwung

With Jan Baalsrud
in Lyngenfjord.

In north-east Greenland,
with miners waiting
for the plane.

each end and its roadway covered with rubble, thrown there to stop anyone suddenly driving across in the dark. You could plainly watch the Germans strolling about at the other end, some with rifles slung on their shoulders, some who seemed only to be admiring the view. The French soldiers and gunners begged us not to go on the bridge for fear of provoking a fight. The most sinister sign was that there was no permanent road-block on the French side, as if the officers expected the politicians to call off the silly ban any day and let them cross as usual; and events were to prove that many of them did.

It was all a scene to tax even Richard's powers of description. He wrote a careful and thoughtful piece, and we set up the gear in the main square to record it – here a church clock that had stopped, the empty fountains, the unmown grass and weedy municipal flower beds – and the recording car on the sidewalk in the doorway of a bank, which seemed a symbol of prosperity abandoned. I gave the usual cue to Sarney – We'll start in ten seconds from now – and on the ninth second a solitary French soldier came marching round the corner, whistling. He stopped and gave a mighty belch and then an even mightier fart which resounded across the silent square. Then he marched on, relieved, and started his tune again. It was all on that disc, the whistles, the belch, the fart and Richard's and my rude uncontrollable laughter, and we kept it in our growing collection of disastrous discs. I hope the Germans enjoyed it: they got all our souvenirs in the end.

Back in Arras, nothing had changed and nothing was happening. Brought up in the BBC, we still cherished the truth, but we found how little truth you can tell in a war. The best you can do is try to avoid the deliberate deceptions. People still spoke of our troops as being in the front line, and so they were. In the early days, that caused intense anxiety at home, where soldiers' families were left to imagine something like the front line trenches of the previous war – you could still see remnants of them here and there around Arras, among the enormous cemeteries. A single sentence from Richard could have relieved all that anxiety, but he could never say it: he could never explain that the people on the other side of this front line were not warlike Germans but friendly Belgians, or that the British army had not yet seen a German or heard a bang, except perhaps a few they had made themselves.

There is an extra hazard in broadcasting from a theatre of war which Richard was often to meet. It is all very well for a newspaper to report a thing which looks like news, but is really official propaganda. It takes days at least for the newspaper to get back to the army, and by the time it does the news is stale and nobody cares very much. But broadcasting is immediate. If by mistake we reported anything passed by the censor but misleading, it came back at us straight away. The whole army heard it, and were eager to ask us where we had got such a load of rubbish. For that reason, we seldom sent the official bulletins; they were too often propagandist, and if the BBC wanted them, we reckoned, they could always get them from the agencies. Between the BBC, the needs of the public at home, the censors, and the critics we lived among, whichever way we walked we were on tightropes.

The first way of escape we found was to make small feature programmes about obscure army units: not only the obvious glamorous ones, the infantry, artillery or cavalry, but people like the Catering Corps, the Pioneers, or the Ordnance Storekeepers. I don't suppose anyone remembers those programmes now – they were really rather dull – but our masters in the BBC liked them. Some were very short, ten minutes or so, and would fit into a news bulletin, some were longer, but the programme planners always found a 'slot' for them. Anything we sent from France was sure of an audience. For us, they were a prime exercise in public relations. Brigadiers began to come seeking for Richard, sometimes even for me. 'Heard that bit you did about the So-and-so's. Jolly good. Could you do one about us? The lads'd love it, and they really deserve it. They're doing a wonderful job.' The lads would love it? We knew the brigadiers would love it too. Everyone loved to hear themselves and their friends 'on the air', and to know their families were hearing it too, and not only their families but their lovers, and their old companions in the bar of the local, the members of their clubs, the people they had known at work. We had a sellers' market. And the programmes had the great advantage that the soldiers were speaking for themselves, and nobody could say what they said was anything but true.

Those mini-features were an immense amount of work; for some, we had to drive right back down the lines of supply to Normany or Brittany. But Richard and I were used to hard work, and Sarney fell in with it very readily. In the old days, we had done it to establish Richard's ideas of news reporting. Now we did it because we were selfish. We had a whole vast field of broadcasting all to ourselves, and we dreaded the BBC might want to send out a whole vast staff to do it. So we sent them not only whatever news there was, but every kind of programme we could think of, whatever difficulties we foresaw. The mini-features in particular brought Richard friends throughout the army. As we drove round the zone, it was everywhere 'Hi, Richard', or 'Good morning, Mr Dimbleby, sir.' Nobody who met him ever forgot him – his rather outlandish name, or his unsoldierly appearance, which he balanced by a strict observance of army etiquette. And he never forgot anyone he met. His memory for people's names and faces amazed me.

'Hullo, Mr Dimbleby. Remember me?'

'Of course, Private Jones. Did your wife hear the broadcast?'

'You bet, sir. And all the neighbours. Cheered her up no end.'

'And how's young Shirley's whooping cough?'

I never saw him hesitate. Once I was standing with a brigadier and watching him chatting up some rather dimwitted privates. I said something about his way of getting on with all kinds of people.

'Of course,' the brigadier said with a sudden surprising show of feeling. 'Of course he does. We all *adore* him.'

So they did, as an acquaintance, and it was one of the causes of his great success. And so did I, as a close friend and a constant companion. Thus I never had the slightest jealousy of the fame he was winning. He was so supremely good at his job I knew I could never do the same and did not even want to try. I was happy to play second fiddle.

A rather unwelcome chore - because it was so far from what we had come for – was to broadcast the concert parties arranged by ENSA. I forget what the initials stood for, but this was the organization that provided entertainments for troops. Some of their concerts were purely amateur, given by soldiers who had made themselves reputations as singers or comics. Some were purely professional, by parties sent out for the purpose. Those with most scope for disaster were a mixture of the two. Comparatively, broadcasting ENSA shows was easy for us. We could not record them, because with only a single disc channel we could not record continuously for more than 4½ minutes. They had to be live, and I think it was these that first persuaded the censors to trust us with live broadcasts. All we had to do, having once overcome the censors' jitters, was to ask the French radio to take on the technical work as Outside Broadcasts. So I found myself doing, after a fashion, the jobs of an OB executive and a Light Entertainments producer, and Sarney acting with the French as an OB engineer.

This was my only foray into the music hall world, and I knew I was out of place. I was in nobody's fan club. There were stars I had never heard of who were evidently famous, or thought they ought to be. Judging them only by the way they behaved, I grew to admire some and dislike some others. Gracie Fields was perhaps the most famous of all, and she was always modest and polite and wholly admirable. With her voice which could change from sweet tunefulness to something like a circular saw, she could hold an audience of soldiers enchanted, laughing their heads off one minute and shedding their manly tears the next, with plainly audible sniffs. She was indeed a genius of her kind.

I also remember with slightly shame-faced pleasure an unknown girl contortionist the licentious soldiery loved. From the wings of the theatre, Richard and I watched her tying her graceful body in knots with as much attention as anyone. 'David, let your imagination run riot,' he said in a piercing whisper. 'The possibilities are infinite!'

The great stars, of course, gave their services free, but some of them, I am sorry to say, seemed determined to squeeze the last drop of personal publicity from their generous deed. Consequently, they longed for their show to be broadcast. Gracie Fields was not one of these, but unless I am very much mistaken, Noël Coward and Maurice Chevalier were. I do not think either was the sort for an unsophisticated British audience, Coward too clever and supercilious and Chevalier too French. ENSA had unwisely put both these superstars in the same single evening's entertainment, with army amateurs to fill up the programme. We had orders for a live broadcast of the first half of the show but not the second, precisely forty-nine minutes of prime listening time.

That morning the ENSA man in Arras, a very young second lieutenant, rang me and asked me for God's sake to come and help. I was taken to Maurice Chevalier's bedroom. Chevalier was sitting up in bed, naked to the navel with a gold crucifix hanging among the fur. Coward was striding round the room looking like a caricature of himself: the blue silk dressing gown, elaborately casual, with his monogram on the breast pocket, the cigarette in a long holder.

'But my dear Maurice,' he was saying as I came in, and he took no notice whatever of my entrance, 'my dear Maurice, you are the greatest entertainer in the world today. They cannot be allowed to do this to you.'

'No, no, dear – Noël,' came from the bed, with a perfectly judged hesitation between the 'dear' and the 'Noël' which made it supremely viperish, 'you exaggerate. *You* are the greatest. It is you they cannot insult in this manner.'

'We must agree to differ,' Coward said. 'The point is clear. Neither you nor I will perform in the second part, which we are told is not to be broadcast.' He turned on me. 'I understand you represent the BBC. The solution is simple. You must broadcast both parts.'

'That's out of the question. The programme is scheduled and published. But your names are not in it yet.'

'You have authority to refuse?'

'Certainly I have.'

'And your name is –?'

Even in those days I hated feeling angry and always tried to avoid it, but that made me very angry indeed. I heard the ENSA man explaining, clearly not for the first time, that they were there to entertain a live audience of troops in the field, not a radio audience in England, and that the second half would be a fiasco for the troops if they both insisted on appearing in the first half. To no avail. I was so mad at their conceit that amnesia has released me: I have no recollection whatever of what happened in the end, whether both of them or neither of them appeared. Perhaps I robbed the BBC of a unique double billing, but I did not care. For once I was adamant, and I knew the BBC would support me. It did not like its employees to be bullied.

Having to parade for important visitors was often unwelcome – not the ENSA entertainers, most of whom came sincerely to do their best, but the official VIPs, the very senior generals and the politicians, who might take it into their heads to say something for a broadcast or for the press. The most senior of all, of course, was the King. Most people feel honoured to meet their King, and so did I. But – I ought to have known – the first and only time I met him turned into a farce. The whole press corps was lined up to be presented, and the King came along the line with a colonel who had been told to introduce us. It was not an easy job for the colonel. There must have been about twenty-five of us, including some foreigners with unpronounceable names, and he had to remember each name and the agency or the paper each represented.

He came to Richard first of us three. That was easy for the colonel, because the King already knew Richard who had been with him on a royal tour of Canada. They talked for quite a while. Next in the line was Sarney. I heard the colonel say confidently, 'And this is Mr Howarth, sir, also of the BBC.' Sarney said nothing.

Then the colonel saw me, and I saw him do a double-take. He knew me perfectly well, and knew he had flunked his job. I just had time to wonder what he would do. 'And next, sir, is Mr Sarney.'

'Ah, how do you do, Mr Sarney,' the King said, shaking my hand. 'So you three make a team. And a successful team, I must say. I've just been telling Mr Dimbleby I am among your regular listeners.'

I don't remember what I said, if I said anything at all. I couldn't let the colonel down. The King was left to believe – if he ever thought of us again – that I was Sarney and Sarney was me.

Nobody expected the King to be a strategist (though perhaps he was). We did expect it of the generals and politicians, but we got no word of wisdom whatever from them, no hint, even off the record, of hopes or fears or plans. The two I remember who most had an aura of ignorance were the French Commander-in-Chief, General Gamelin and the British Liberal Secretary of State for War, Mr Leslie Hore-Belisha. General Gamelin was a chief exponent of what came to be called the Maginot Mentality, the belief that France could shelter behind a fixed line of defence, and he was known for his dictum 'To attack is to lose'. Mr Hore-Belisha's recorded interest in the army was to make it more democratic, which may have been a praiseworthy aim but was irrelevant, to say the least, at that time and place.

Perhaps the interval between those two wars was just the wrong length, twenty-one years. Some of the generals of the previous war, especially the French, were still on their feet, if only just. General Gamelin was sixty-eight. His only senior, Marshal Pétain, was eighty-four, and already prepared to surrender to the Germans, though he had not yet openly said so, and the Chief of Staff General Weygand was seventy-three. The British generals were rather younger, but the Prime Minister Neville Chamberlain was seventy-one, and he had agreed that the British generals in France were entirely subordinate to the French, as they had been from 1914–18. It was not their business to criticize the French, who could reply with crushing force that they disposed ten times as many men.

It is certainly not my business, either, to be critical of those elderly gentlemen, only to report the indelible impression they made on us, and I am sure on many other people who met them on their visits. The impression was that they did not know what they were doing, or what they ought to do. I am not saying we knew any better; but it was their job to know, not ours. And I can report what we saw, and what we thought of it at the time. Churchill wrote long afterwards that the line the British had to defend was strong, but that winter he was still First Lord of the Admiralty, and he had not seen it. It was not strong. We had perhaps seen more of the French frontier than any other Englishmen, and it needed only two eyes and a little common sense to see that either the Maginot Line was absurdly over-elaborate and costly, or that the British line was absurdly weak. There, on the Belgian frontier, the French before the war had built a row of separate primitive blockhouses, and to avoid upsetting the Belgians had built them so that they could not fire to the front but could only defend one another by enfilading fire, a weak form of defence at the best. The backs of them had doors, unarmoured or very lightly armoured, approached across open fields. During the winter the British had done their best to patch up this line by building smaller gun emplacements between the French ones, hampered by the trouble of setting concrete when it was freezing, and they were laboriously digging a small anti-tank ditch in the ice-bound earth.

The worst weakness of this line was out of sight. To the north it ended at the sea, but to the south it ended in nothing. Between its end and the beginning of the Maginot Line was a gap of fifty miles which the French had not bothered to fortify. This was among the minor mountains of the Ardennes, and Marshall Pétain had declared there was no danger there because a mechanized army could not pass through the hills. He was wrong. It was precisely at that point that the German army passed through when they started their attack in the spring. The British line had been built in the hope of holding an attack from the east, but when the Germans reached it they came from the opposite side, the west and south, and as a line it never fired a shot.

Nor did the Maginot Line itself. The minds of the elderly generals had been fixed in 1918, and they had no conception of the new battle tactics the Germans had already used in Poland, and were planning to use with far greater strength against us: the blitzkrieg, a fast-moving war of self-contained tank units with dive bombers, in which fixed defences were no defence at all.

We often saw different bits of the British line, and we drove along it several times in the wake of visiting dignitaries. On one of those tours Harry Tufton, who had been everywhere with us and as I have said was a soldier of common sense, stood and looked at the line and asked us 'D'you think all this is the slightest use? Or are we in for the biggest bloody disaster in military history?' They were words to remember. This was the doubt that had haunted us all winter, ever since we went to the Maginot Line and Strasbourg, but of course not a hint of it could ever be mentioned in our broadcasts.

To that extent, we often felt we were guilty of deceit, or of conniving in deceit. But who were we to think we were right and so many experts were wrong? We never more than half believed our own opinion, and if we had sent an apocalyptic warning home, the BBC would rightly have told us to mind our own business. In war, if you see a weakness on your own side, it usually makes it worse to mention it.

Our business was broadcasting, not the nation's military fate. From that rather trivial point of view Christmas Day was a climax, although it was only halfway through the eight months we waited there. For this peak listening day of the year, the BBC wanted five broadcasts from 'the front'. They were prepared to send teams of staff to arrange them, but with our jealous policy of never saying No, we told them we could manage them all ourselves. It was crazy really. I doubt if three men have ever done five major outside broadcasts in a single day, let alone Christmas Day, and I do not think anyone but Richard, urged on by Sarney and me, would ever have claimed it could be done, and got away with it. The five were a general knowledge quiz at lunchtime, technically a rather complex kind of broadcast; then the biggest church service we could organize; then in the afternoon a piece in the Round-the-Empire programme which the BBC had made a tradition to lead up to the King's speech; and in the evening two Christmas concerts, one British and one French.

We had worked it all out assuming that we could drive the Humber pretty fast from each location to the next. We had not reckoned that the roads that day would be covered by black ice. We ought to have thought of it, because anyone who was in the Expeditionary Force will remember that the winter was exceptionally cold; but we always supposed we could cope with natural hazards, and of course we had the usual precautions, chains, ropes and shovels.

For the quiz and the service we had booked a very large hall in a town about twenty-five miles away. We got there by driving slow all the way with two wheels in the snow on the verge, hoping there was not a very large ditch underneath. Before we arrived, we quite thought our team for the quiz would not turn up; but they did, some more sober than others, and so did the faithful French radio technicians on whom we depended. So did the censor. He had missed his Christmas dinner, and was not in a festive mood at all. That was the memorable occasion I have already mentioned when the 'quiz master' at the London end asked us a question to which the answer was Calais, a name we were not allowed on any account to mention. Halfway through the forty-minute programme I became aware that I had assembled a team of ten, but now had only nine. The tenth had fallen under the table and was being sick.

The church service came very soon after, and so had to come from the same hall. We had expected Richard could introduce the service and then sneak out in time for the third broadcast, another twenty-five miles away; but on the ice we could not risk it. I had to be left to introduce the service – and first to eject our derelict team, mop up the sick, rearrange the furniture and microphones and admit a large sober and devout congregation and the Chaplain General to the Forces – if I have his title right. I don't know what the BBC thought of my introduction, but the Chaplain liked it so much that he said I was a loss to the Church. I didn't argue.

The piece in the Round-the-Empire programme was billed to come from a front-line dug-out. But that billing was written by somebody in the *Radio Times* with the usual vision of a 1916 line. It came from the front line right enough, but there were no dug-outs in that line, and Richard had to compromise and use a blockhouse. For once, he let the more picturesque illusion stand. This was not news, which had to be precise. It was a run-up to the King, and it had to be dramatic.

The British concert was from Arras. I got there with a lift from the French technicians. It seemed likely I would have to introduce the concert too, and not only the concert but each separate carol. I didn't know where Richard was, there was no possible way he could tell me, and I expected he was irrevocably stuck somewhere in a ditch, alive or dead; but I had never known him miss a cue, and he turned up at the last possible moment, shivering, after digging the car out of three ditches. I revived him with cups of coffee, to which the French had added a shot of brandy, and his microphone manner was as suave as ever.

None of us, though, could possibly get to the French concert, which was at least 150 miles away somewhere down the Maginot Line. I forget if we had ever expected to, but it did not matter. We had laid it all on in detail with the French, and one could always depend on them for an efficient Outside Broadcast and a passable army choir. They must have guessed we were not coming, or perhaps we sent them a message on the concert line from Arras. Anyhow, they found an English-speaking announcer who introduced each item.

All in all, it was a day of splendid confusion and delightfully near disasters, the sort of day that Richard throve on. Broadcasting House never knew the risks we had run: neither the risks of breaking our necks nor the risks, which would rightly have worried them more, of missing a broadcast. The art of broadcasting is often to hide the tenuous mechanism that holds it all together, and sometimes even to hide it from one's bosses. Someone back in our hotel had made an immensely powerful hot rum punch, and we went to bed well pleased with ourselves that Christmas night, and rather drunk.

As spring approached we began to get bored; so did the army, and probably everyone at home. Waiting for something to happen is always difficult, and waiting for a battle perhaps especially so. After a while anything else, even death and destruction, seem better. And for us, it grew harder and harder to think of any broadcast we had not already done. Richard began to wish he was in Finland, where the Finns were fighting a straightforward reportable winter war against the Russians. And when the Germans invaded Norway in early April, I longed to be there. I knew that country pretty well from many holidays, I loved Norwegians and the life they led, and I wished I was with them in their desperate fight. But I knew it was no good wishing. The BBC was not about to make me a reporter, or an observer as they still called it, and I had to admit to myself that Norway in April was no place for a recording car.

Perhaps the BBC noticed or guessed we were getting stale. Anyhow, in April they abruptly took Richard away and sent him to Egypt, where the shooting war had started in the desert. I didn't see him again until after the war, when he was rich and very famous. I don't think riches and fame had changed him, but I had no heart to pick up the bits of our friendship. So the day he left Arras was the end of something excellent in my life.

They sent out a replacement for him, of course, but it was

quite impossible for a novice to rebuild the network of friendship he had created in the army. Perhaps I ought to have stayed to try to ease things, but I was very tired and I could not face beginning all over again with somebody I had never met. So I asked for leave. They could hardly refuse it, because I had been there eight months with never a day off – hardly an hour off while I was awake.

Thus it happened that when the event came in France for which we had prepared so long, Sarney was the only one of the three of us still there. Richard was seeing action in the desert, and I was shamefully back climbing mountains in the Island of Skye, which was as far from London and France as I could get. I had come down alone from the top of the mountain called Sgurr Alasdair, and war seemed unthinkably remote, when I heard a rumour in the hotel that the Germans had invaded Belgium. I waited to hear it myself in the news – only an agency report, I noticed, nothing from Our Observer – and then I set off by the quickest way to London. There, it was obvious there was not a hope in the world of getting back to France: the war correspondents were among the first the army was hustling out of the country by way of Boulogne. Sarney drove the recording car back to Boulogne, and told me when I met him in London that he had been shot at from rooftops, not by the Germans but by the French. In Boulogne, the army had made him abandon the car and the gear and all our remaining property in the docks.

By missing the climax we had not missed much, except experience. With German tanks roaming freely round the countryside, the command of the huge French armies broke up at once into chaos. Since then, military historians with their maps and arrows have more or less analyzed the moves and counter-moves, but nobody on the ground at the time knew what was happening, where anybody else was or where they were going. All normal communications were cut; plans were made daily and abandoned; it was out of the question to write a coherent report, and doubly out of the question to send it to London. Above all, as we had suspected in Strasbourg and elsewhere, the French were divided; some were as determined as we were, but some were willing to be ruled by Nazism rather than fight it. The small British army, surrounded by much bigger French and Belgian armies, fought hard but in ignorance; they tried to march from Arras to the south, but then turned round and fought their way to the north, towards Dunkirk.

In both countries, generals and statesmen were sacked and others appointed. After two days M Reynaud, the French premier, telephoned Churchill, now abruptly made Prime Minister, to tell him France had lost the battle and was beaten. After about fourteen days the British were besieged within a small and shrinking perimeter round Dunkirk.

It was then that I met a general alone in a lift in Broadcasting House. I had known him in France, and he knew me. I think he was Director of Military Intelligence. Certainly, he had witnessed the débacle.

'What do you make of the situation, sir?' I asked him.

'We're finished,' he said decisively and without hesitation. 'We've lost the army, and we shall never have time or strength to build another.'

SEVEN

Extraordinary Seaman

That general of all people ought to have got it right, but he got it wrong. His black despair was not the mood of the country, or of the navy or the air force, or of Churchill, or right at the bottom of me. In the next nine days 338,224 of the army he thought was lost – including some French – were rescued by the navy and by hosts of amateur sailors in every kind of boat who picked them up from the beaches of Dunkirk and brought them home through air attacks; but all their major equipment was lost. It was just the disaster that Harry Tufton had foreseen, but we all – all the British, that is – in defiance of logic, came to think of it as a victory.

Nobody who lived in England in those days could avoid remembering Churchill's voice on the radio, punctuated by his growls and grunts: 'We shall defend our island, whatever the cost may be. We shall fight on the beaches, we shall fight on the landing-grounds, we shall fight in the fields and in the streets, we shall fight in the hills; we shall never surrender.'

He was not speaking to us, but for us, and to our friends and enemies. We did not need to be told; indeed, we could not have been told. Ever since 1066, the threat of invasion has united the British as nothing else could, and it happened again in 1940; and while such eloquence flowed far above our heads, each of us made his own humble decision and knew that this was what we were going to do. Old men and boys became Local Defence Volunteers, and were later called the Home Guard, and armed themselves, having nothing better, with ancient pikes, pitchforks, great grandfather's cavalry sabre from the kitchen wall, a few shotguns and sporting rifles, home-made petrol bombs to throw suicidally at tanks, and anything else that came to hand, even clubs; housewives sharpened their carving knives, and were determined to defy the German army and its fearsome equipment. 'You can always take one with you' was the phrase.

Among all that genuine gallantry, my own decision was made, like most of my decisions, for foolish reasons. In the main, they were negative. I was sick of the army. I didn't know anything about flying, and it was too late to learn; invasion was said to be coming any day, and whatever one did would have to be done at once. But the navy: I did know how to handle a boat, and the navy had shown at Dunkirk it was not too proud to use amateurs. There was some shame in my decision, too. When Norway was invaded, I had hoped to be there but was stuck in France. When France was invaded, I was ignominiously on leave. At the time of Dunkirk I had tried to find out how to volunteer, but had left it too late. I did not know whether I was a coward or not, and suspected I was. In fact, I never did find that out, and still suspect I am, but in the hope of putting it to a test I ran away from the shelter of the BBC to a naval recruiting office in London and offered to help them. 'Fine,' they said, 'report to the naval base at Lowestoft tomorrow morning' – and to my surprise they gave me a free railway ticket. So I received a grandstand worm's-eye view of that famous summer, and, like so much of war when seen from below, it had an agreeably lunatic air.

Lowestoft is on the east coast, close to Yarmouth where the Paget story started, and in 1940 just north of the middle of that part of the coast considered most likely for Hitler's invasion, which extended from the Wash down to Kent.

Waiting for the train, I went to the station bookstall for something to read, and saw a small book called *Brown's Rules of the Road at Sea*. Just what I need, I thought: I had sailed boats, but never at sea. The rules I remember from that journey are in verse.

> Outward Bound,
> Don't run aground

is a philosophical injunction I have found useful in all sorts of circumstances.

> Green to green or red to red,
> Perfect safety, go ahead

is more limited in scope, but comforting. At Lowestoft, armed with what seemed to be wisdom, I joined the day's catch of recruits. We lined up, and somebody came along the rank asking each of us 'Stoker or second hand?'

I don't know if anyone knew what he meant. I didn't. Second hand seemed derogatory, but stoker? I saw myself shovelling coal in the guts of a battleship, so I said second hand.

They made us into two groups, stokers and second hands, and another somebody asked our group, 'Any of you lot navigate?' Nobody answered.

'What, none of you?' he said, and seemed disappointed.

'Perfect safety, go ahead,' I thought, and I heard a voice saying 'Yes, sir, I think I can, sir,' and realized it was me.

Encouraged, two others said they could. One turned out to be a Thames tug skipper, and the other a young man who claimed to have crewed in the Fastnet race. We were marched off to get our kit, huge armfuls of clothing.

'Here, what's going on?' the tug skipper said, picking over his bundle. 'I've got a collar and tie. They said navigate, didn't they? You don't need a collar and tie to do that in.'

'And where are my bell-bottom trousers?' the Fastnet man said, petulant. 'I only joined for the bell-bottoms, and a nice little jumper with a lanyard.'

They both turned on me. 'Hey, you got us into this pickle. Why didn't you keep your trap shut?'

'The man seemed to want us to navigate,' I said, defensive. 'So I said I'd have a go. It's not all that difficult. I read it on the way here in the train.'

'Cor stone the crows up a tree,' the tug skipper said.

'They'll probably give us lessons,' I said, to cheer myself up.

'Whasser matter, boys?' the store-keeper said, still handing out his bounty. 'You're petty officers, you are. Didn't they tell you? Lucky lads, if you ask me. You don't get no lessons, you give 'em.' And like it or not, that is what we were.

Early next morning, seven of us new-fangled petty officers, precariously dressed and ready to run for it if we saw anyone who looked as if he wanted to be saluted, were sent by train to Brightlingsea, sixty miles or so down the coast towards London. With us were seven stokers and seven seamen who seemed to be second hands, who had kept quiet about navigation. All were safely in bell-bottoms except us. At Brightlingsea there was a blackboard with seven names chalked on it, apparently of ships, and we chose one each. I picked the name *Lamouette*. I thought *Lamouette* was French for The Kiss, and I liked the idea of a ship called HMS *The Kiss*. I was disillusioned later to learn it meant only Seagull. We went on board, I with a stoker who had been a garage mechanic in Cornwall and had brought his electric guitar with him, and a very young seaman from Lancaster who said he had never seen the sea till the day before, not even from Blackpool beach. No destroyer, no frigate even, not much of a seagull. *Lamouette* was a cabin cruiser, clumsily converted from a naval picket boat of the war before. But I was captain of her, and the other two were my crew.

The proud captains were summoned ashore again, and met a sub-lieutenant, the first officer I had seen. 'Seven boats here,' he said, 'and they want them in Lowestoft in a hurry, God knows why. But only one chart. Which of you is the best navigator?'

'That bloke,' the tug skipper said, and pointed at me. 'He learned it in a train.'

'OK,' the sub-lieutenant said, and gave me the chart. 'You're flotilla leader. Better keep well off Harwich, there's a minefield there. Can you start at High Water a.m. tomorrow? That's about seven.'

It was a beautiful chart. It showed Denmark on the right hand side, and Bergen in Norway near the top. It showed London and Harwich, but not Brightlingsea, which is not a significant place, nor any minefields, nor any buoys or sandbanks. But the sixty miles to Lowestoft did not look very far; about two inches.

So I had been all of thirty-six hours in the navy, entirely bewildered, before I was sent to sea in charge of not one of His Majesty's ships but seven of them; not his best or biggest ships, it was true, but HM ships they undeniably were, and a few weeks later they gave us white ensigns, which proved it. They were a funny fleet. The tug skipper had a magnificent seventy-foot diesel yacht, complete with bottles of whiskey, nine-tenths empty. There was a small American cabin cruiser, obviously fast, and a river cruiser which could hardly move at all and went round in circles if a breeze caught its upper works. Most of them broke down from time to time and had to be taken in tow. They all had compasses, but all of them pointed in different directions. I hopefully set a course on *Lamouette*'s compass to take us clear of Harwich. It was easy, because I could see Harwich as soon as we cleared the harbour.

Off Harwich, and all that day, we were miles out of sight of land. It did not strike us as odd to be out in the North Sea on a cloudless day, in the middle of the invasion area, with no guns, no national flags, and no way of explaining who or what we were. The navy had sent us there, and the navy, we all believed, knew what it was doing. The only suspicious thing was that we never saw a ship. Everyone else had gone. We had an uneasy feeling they all knew something we had not been told, or had not understood. In fact, it was a thousand years since that bit of sea had been so empty before.

In the afternoon we stopped and had a committee meeting. My stoker entertained the fleet with the only tune he knew on his electric guitar: it was called 'Begin the Beguine'. We did not know how far we had come, but it was not very far because of the breakdowns. It was obvious we would not see Lowestoft that night, and obvious too we could not stay together in the dark without any lights. We agreed to take a turn to the left and go on until we saw the coast again, and then have another meeting.

As dusk was falling we saw it, low, straight and featureless, not a town or a house anywhere. I was sure we had come beyond Harwich but not as far as Aldeburgh, a small but recognizable town. Between those two, there was only one dent in the coastline on the chart, and we decided to look for that. It proved to be the mouth of the River Ore.

I have sailed into that tricky entrance several times since then, but always with the proper chart and knowing the leading marks and wondering by how many strokes of luck all seven of us got in that night – as we did, and made fast to the river bank. I walked up the bank and across some marshes and found a telephone box, and dared to ring up the duty officer in Lowestoft to confess what we had done. He said he had never heard of us, but we seemed to be doing all right, and to carry on in the morning. It was beautiful, eerie and dreamlike. When the last of us switched off his engine, it was perfectly peaceful and quiet, no sound but the faraway calls of curlews. Some of us started to whisper, then thought it was better to talk loudly in English. In the heart of England's alleged defences we might just as well have been Germans, yet nobody had seen us or heard the row we had made. Not even a dog had barked. We made our supper and settled down for the night. It seemed a good life, at least a change from the BBC and Arras.

Going out at dawn, the river cruiser tried to do one of its circles and ran aground on the bar. We left him there to float off with the tide, and told him he only had to follow the coast and he was sure to see Lowestoft in the end. It was true there were no more nagivational hazards, or none that we knew of. In fact, there is a row of sandbanks off shore where at low water you can almost see the seagulls standing, but we did not know they were there, so we did not worry. The only hazard that day was the breakdowns, which were more and more frequent. Sometimes, with the tide behind us, we made good progress; with it against us, we often went backwards.

Then Lowestoft. That was a hazard, though of a different kind; a defended port, we supposed, and we were much more scared of our own side than we were of the Germans. I got there first; the faster boats had been towing ones that stopped. I had not seen the port when I was there before, and now there was some flurry going on inside. There were guns on the quay, which trained on us when we moved, a mass of trawlers, lights which flashed morse that we could not read, soldiers and sailors running here and there. I hovered around outside, in the hope of persuading them we meant no harm. In the end, I had to take the plunge and motor in through the entrance. A harbour-master or somebody bellowed through a megaphone, but I could not hear what he said. Once in, I came quite gracefully alongside a very high quay, and heard from up above me a loud voice like Jove in a cloud.

'And who the hell are you?' it said. I looked up and saw a man with more gold braid than I have ever seen or imagined: a lieutenant-commander RN, it turned out. Of course I didn't know who the hell we were.

'Well, we've come from Brightlingsea,' I said. 'They told us to bring these boats to Lowestoft. This – is Lowestoft, isn't it?'

He didn't answer my question.

'From Brightlingsea?' he said. 'Good God! Good God! And d'you mean to say nobody shot you up on the way?'

'No, sir,' I said. That was the only misfortune we had not seriously thought of.

'Hm,' he said. 'Better throw me a rope, then.'

Ever since then I have had the greatest affection and respect for the Royal Navy. I came to know that if you tell it you can do something, it believes you and tells you to go ahead and do it. I came to know that lieutenant-commander too, as well as a petty officer is likely to know a lieutenant-commander. He was a very kind man.

'You gave us the fright of our lives that day you came in,' he told me later.

'You gave me a fright too, sir. I thought you were God, or St Peter.'

'You were never more mistaken,' he said. 'We couldn't guess who you were. No ensign, no weapons that we could see, didn't read our signals. We couldn't tell what to do, sink our blockships to seal the harbour or blow you out of the water, or what?'

'Thanks for not blowing me out of the water,' I said.

'No thanks to me. We phoned the Admiralty. They thought you might be Dutch refugees or German deserters, and told us to get you alive.'

'I'm sorry we gave you all that trouble, sir.'

'No trouble. Nothing much ever happens here.'

I had just begun to learn by the time we got there – less about the sea than about myself and other men. After our stormy start, the tug skipper and I became friends. I had been shamefully boastful and clumsy. All I had really discovered in the train was that coastal pilotage (not real navigation, which is much more difficult) was mostly an application of simple maths which I had been taught long before and still dimly remembered. I was sure I could figure it out, and so I could. But the tug skipper was an expert. He was not much older than I was. He had had to leave school at fourteen, and for years and years he had worked all day as a ship's boy or a deckhand and studied navigation in night classes, and at last, quite recently, had won through to his skipper's ticket. All the time, as I blundered along, he had known exactly what he was doing – had known that with luck we would get there, and without luck we would not. But he had never said a word. He was supremely patient and self-controlled. Like many wartime friendships, ours was cut short, because he was posted somewhere else. That is why I do not even remember his name, but I remember him with affection and respect. He gave me a second lesson in the humility Sir J. J. Thomson, unknowing, had begun to teach me; but he had gone before it had really sunk in, and I was never able to tell him I had learned it.

The lieutenant-commander was right; nothing much happened in Lowestoft, except to us. It was full of trawlers, each with a gun, but they very seldom went to sea. We went to sea every night – or every night our engine would start. Our job was to patrol from dusk to dawn, each boat from one off-shore buoy to the next; in theory, it made a line of boats which covered the whole of that coast. Churchill wrote long afterwards: 'Far out on the grey waters of the North Sea and the Channel coursed and patrolled the faithful, eager flotillas peering through the night.' Did he mean us? We certainly peered through the night, but we were hardly the ocean greyhounds his rhetoric implied. The ocean greyhounds simply were not there, and never had been. The front line of England was on the beach, and we were three miles in front of that, and outside us, as we knew very well, there was nothing and nobody between us and Germany.

Soon, when they gave us white ensigns and more appropriate charts, they armed each boat with a rifle, a revolver and a rocket. Our orders were, when we saw the German fleet coming, to fire our rocket which would alert the defences ashore and indeed the whole of Britain, and then of course, in the words of Nelson's last signal at Trafalgar, to 'Engage the Enemy more Closely', with our rifle and our revolver. It seemed fair enough: the Home Guard, we knew, were less heavily armed.

The buoys were about three miles apart, and it was a constant but soluble problem in the strong tide to pick up your second buoy. If you missed it, you were very lost indeed, and were also on the beat of another boat, and each of you would think the other was German. The first lost boat I met was a big one I did not know, with a sub-lieutenant in charge: I know that because

I shone a torch on him. He had no business to be there and we almost tried to fire our rocket, but he shouted to ask me where he was.

'I know but I can't tell you,' I said triumphantly. 'I'll escort you to harbour if you like.'

'Well, f—— you,' he shouted, which sounded English enough, and he disappeared and I never saw him again.

That amateurish patrol went on all summer until September. At sea we watched the season passing, and also watched the progress of the war. At first the nights were quiet and the shore appeared deserted. Then we began to hear the German bombers coming in from the sea late at night, and going back early in the morning, and the sky to the west was lit by flashes, and the air shook with the distant thunder of bombs; and later still in the summer our own bombers outward bound in the evening, and homeward just before the dawn came over the sea and lit the sad steeples of Lowestoft. We sat through it all, motoring to and fro between our buoys, happy to think we were invisible.

For the first time, I was living in equality with fellow-countrymen of every class and every education. At my age it should not have been a revelation, but it was. Most were innately kind; I liked them all in varying degrees, and they happily put up with me if I did not pretend to be anything I wasn't. I began to think those were the qualities I valued most – kindness and freedom from pretence; a conviction that has grown in me ever since. It was the only time in my life that I was known as Dave.

Perhaps in remorse for the tug skipper, I set myself to learn navigation in earnest. It fascinated me. I bought the first two volumes of *The Admiralty Manual of Navigation* – the second, on nautical astronomy, taxed what wits I had – and the nautical tables to go with them. I also bought a very old sextant, just to see if I could observe the latitude of Lowestoft and get it anywhere near right. Most people who saw me taking sun sights on the pier laughed, just as ancient mariners laughed when sextants were first being used in the eighteenth century.

One who didn't laugh was a very young man, not long out of school I think, called Peter Mansfield. He was the lucky second hand who had picked the fast American cruiser in Brightlingsea.

Trundling around in *Lamouette* I envied him, and he knew I did. He also had an exceptional stoker called Fred, and between them they had made their boat the most efficient of all; they were both people who liked to do things as well as they possibly could. The boat was called *Quicksilver*, like my brother's childhood tricycle, but with better reason: she was smaller than most, but flat out she did 18 knots.

Peter shared my new-found passion for navigation. We learned it together and set each other exam questions. Indeed, he shared all my thoughts and aspirations, within our environment.

When we had nothing better to do we went for peaceful country walks together – but not very far because we were told that if the invasion began, wherever it was, an extra large green rocket would be fired from the naval base, and we did not want to miss that.

The carefree life seemed to come to an end for me when *Lamouette*'s engine died peacefully of old age. My stoker gave it something like the kiss of life, but failed and went back to his electric guitar. I tried too, so did the naval base, but it was pronounced irrevocably dead. The poor old boat was towed up the river and put on a growing heap of derelicts. I was sent to a much larger boat, or ship, commanded by a sub-lieutenant with two second hands and a crew of ten.

I hated that ship – partly perhaps because I had lost my independence, but mainly because of the other second hand. He was a real second hand, which I had learned was a fisherman's term for a mate: a foul-mouthed, sanctimonious, smelly, grizzled little Scotsman from a fishing port on the Moray Firth. I did try hard to like him, but I couldn't. He quarrelled with everyone all the time, and most of all with me. Rightly, I suppose, he looked on me (and the sub-lieutenant) as upstart ignorant amateurs, and he never stopped telling me so: man and boy, he said again and again, he had been at sea since long before I had 'sooked at my mither's tits' – a phrase which offended me. If the sub-lieutenant asked me to take the wheel, the old wretch would shove me out of the way shouting 'Man, he'll have us all agroond. He dinna ken naethin.' What was more, he had infected the crew. They seemed to be happy enough to tolerate me but they quarrelled and argued among themselves non-stop. His ignorance was so profound, his thoughts so tangled and his language so incomprehensible and obscene that I could make nothing of him, and was miserable.

He got rid of me pretty quickly, and in a rather peculiar way. On the deck above the crew's quarters we had a Hotchkiss machine-gun. The Hotchkiss had already been obsolete in 1918 and had been kept somewhere, covered with grease, for twenty-three years. You had to know its tricks. If you cocked it, the action pushed a round into the breech, and you could not uncock it unless you could get the round out; the only way to do that, so far as I know, was to fire it. Moreover, if you let go of it on its mounting, it hung there with its muzzle down instead of up.

With that introduction, you can see the point of this story a mile away. One evening, we were all sitting round the table having our tea, except the gunner who was dutifully manning the Hotchkiss above us because the air-raid warning had sounded. He let go of it, it fell muzzle-down and he absent-mindedly pulled the trigger (he said it pulled itself). The bullet came through the deck above, through a loaf of bread, neatly through the middle of the table between all our toes, through the floor and out through the bottom of the ship.

The outburst of rage was terrible. Everyone but me was shouting awful vengeance on the gunner, and the Scotsman seemed about to do himself an internal injury in his fury and indignation. I was laughing. It struck me as funny, and funnier still when I heard between the oaths the sound of running water under our feet. I pulled up a hatch, and found an elegant little fountain in the bilge. I climbed down and put my finger in the hole – not that it mattered, we were not going to sink for a long time, but it seemed that somebody ought to do something.

I was still down there, still laughing and still with my finger in the hole, when somebody shouted above the din that a bloody great green rocket had gone up. I scrambled up, took my kitbag and deserted. Nobody took any notice of me, they were still arguing. I could hear them far down the quay.

I do not know exactly what I meant to do, but after Norway, France and Dunkirk I was quite determined not to be ignominiously absent from another invasion, this time in a ship with a hole in the bottom. I hastened down to the naval base but it seemed to be teeming with officers and I supposed they were all too busy to want to hear my petty troubles. I went on round the harbour, until I saw the *Quicksilver*. She looked homely and friendly.

'Peter,' I shouted, and he stuck his head up through the hatch. 'Peter, I can't stand that ship I'm on. Can I join up with you?'

'Of course,' he said. 'I was hoping you would.'

We sat up most of that quiet night, perfecting a plan we had thought about before, and the first thing we heard in the morning was that the invasion alert was off. It was not just a local mistake. I know now from histories of the war that this was 7 September, and army GHQ had issued the code-word Cromwell, which meant 'invasion imminent'. They had done it for two bad reasons. They thought the next few days were the likeliest for invasion, largely because the moon and tides were right, and they had no code signal for anything between eight hours' readiness and action stations. To any normal person the word imminent meant that the invasion fleet had been sighted and was about to land, and that fleets of troop-carrying aircraft were actually on the way. Here and there all over the south-east of England, Home Guards rang the church bells to call out their colleagues. Immense numbers of people listened and watched the sea or sky at a new peak of tension; wives left at home with the children switched on the radio, hoping to hear what was happening, and heard nothing.

In his own history, Churchill explained that he had not been told, and added, 'It served as a useful tonic and rehearsal for all concerned.' It was just as well he did not say that at the time: it was patronizing, complacent and untrue. The hundreds of thousands of citizens who for three months had shown every night that they were ready to die might almost have rebelled if they had been told they needed a useful rehearsal. Churchill, seeing it from on high, might have felt he had to protect his generals. Everyone who saw it from below understood exactly what it was, and said so: a supreme cock-up.

Such a mistake turns the chain of command on its head, which may be good for it. Every officer, whatever his rank, had to face his juniors after a uselessly anxious night and say 'Sorry, boys, some high-up made a cock-up. It wasn't me.' And every Home Guard, air raid warden, fireman and roof spotter had to give the same sort of explanation to his wife. In my experience, it makes soldiers and sailors happy, once in a while, to know that somebody right at the top has been caught, as the saying goes, with his trousers down. It confirms a lurking suspicion that war is a dangerous, inconvenient and silly charade which nobody can escape from once he is involved. But it must not happen too often.

That abortive 'Cromwell' helped me out of trouble. I crept round to the base next morning, and Peter came with me and waited outside. Luckily the lieutenant-commander was on duty. He listened to my halting explanation of what I had done and why, and I had never seen him less pleased. But he also looked wan and tired, like everyone else; his mind was not on punishment.

'What ought I to do with you?' he said, giving me the chance to say I wanted to join Peter in the *Quicksilver*.

'We've had an idea, sir,' I said. 'He's outside. Can I bring him in?'

He came in, and we both stood at attention with our caps under our arms.

'Sit down,' the lieutenant-commander said, and we knew we were winning. 'Now, what's the idea?' he asked. 'It had better be good.'

'We want to be the Lowestoft rescue boat,' we said together. 'Mainly for the bombers that ditch offshore before dawn. I suppose it looks better to them than crashing on land, but there's nobody here who can go off quickly to pick them up. We could. With two of us, the *Quicksilver* could be on two minutes' notice night and day. We could take the doctor off to the ships that call him, too.'

'What would you need?'

'Nothing, sir, except stores. We've made a list, but we ought to ask the doctor.'

'And when would you propose to start?'

'Tonight, if you can let me go.'

We talked around it, and in the end he said, 'It seems possible, and possibly useful. I can only give you a qualified yes. We'll have to ask the air force. But I can't see any reason why they should object. Meanwhile, Howarth, what's to be done about you? You ought to be on defaulters, but frankly, I can't be bothered this morning. Suppose I post you to the *Quicksilver* with effect from yesterday? That would get you off the hook. Is that what you both want?'

It was; or more than enough to start with. We had got a new job.

It was none too soon. Whenever in the past the English have expected invasion, they have relaxed about the middle of September and relied on gales and fog to defend them. In 1066 the invasion succeeded because King Harold's army and ships relaxed a few days too soon. They began to go home on 14 September (by the Gregorian calendar). On the 19th King Harald Hardrada of Norway invaded Yorkshire, and on the 28th Duke William of Normandy, delayed by an early gale, made his landing at Pevensey and marched to Hastings.

In September 1588 the English held a service of thanksgiving for the defeat of the Spanish Armada, and in September 1940 they relaxed again; but, unlike 1066, the timing was right. By about 20 September people believed unofficially that Hitler had missed his chance. If he had been ready in June or July his army could have landed without getting its feet wet, as we had landed in the mouth of the River Ore on our way to Lowestoft. Whether he could have maintained an army once it was ashore was always more doubtful. But he was not ready then: his three commanders-in-chief were arguing and passing the buck to one another. By September, he was as hopeless as Napoleon: Napoleon could not launch his invasion without naval command of the Channel, and he finally lost it at Trafalgar. Hitler could not do it without command of the air above the Channel, and he lost it in the Battle of Britain. The crux, as we learned much later, was the great daylight raid on London on Sunday 15 September (which I happened to witness because I was on weekend leave). On the 17th, when Hitler had counted the losses of that raid, he postponed the seaborne invasion until the spring – which meant for ever.

So in our microcosm of Lowestoft, soon after that abortive

'Cromwell', the nightly offshore patrol was cancelled, the boats were laid up and the second hands and crews dispersed to other and probably duller jobs. *Quicksilver* was the only boat left in the harbour, and Peter and I the only privileged second hands. We painted H.M.M.L.I. on her bows. No doubt His Majesty had other motor launches in other places, but *Quicksilver* was the only one he had in Lowestoft. That autumn our mild adventures continued. But our primary hope, of finding the crews of wrecked bombers, was a failure. We were ahead of our time: it needed equipment that did not yet exist. Farther south in the Channel, where crashed aircraft were even more numerous, the Germans tried seaplanes marked with the Red Cross and our fighters (since Red Cross aircraft were not foreseen by the Geneva Convention) shot them down; and the RAF used motor launches of their own, and the Germans shot them up. To have any hope of finding a rubber dinghy from another small boat in the sea at night, you had to have some kind of radio homing device, or some kind of very plain visual signal, and as far as I knew the dinghies we were looking for had neither.

Above all, you had to have an accurate idea of where to search, and it was too much to expect a bomber navigator, coming back from a distant raid and on the verge of a crash that would probably be fatal, to signal exactly where he was, or where he would be when he hit the water. Sometimes the positions the air force gave us were thirty miles offshore. That was pretty hopeless, but we always went out there and tried. Even at ten miles off we never found anything. Perhaps there were never any survivors to find. Nobody could know.

But it was always invigorating, to say the least, when we roared out of harbour at three or four o'clock in the morning, hoping at last to be lucky; Peter or me steering and the other one working out the course to the position we had been given and keeping the dead reckoning, and Fred purring over his engines, which never faltered. At that time of year our bit of sea was always rough for a fast 28-foot boat, but it is marvellously relaxing in a small boat to be entirely freed from worry about your own safety. With somebody to search for, risks really did not cross our minds — except the risk of hitting floating wreckage, of which there was plenty, and there was nothing we could do about that. Nowadays,

I confess, I sometimes secretly smile at yachts festooned with expensive safety devices and electronic aids to navigation. I do not think we even had a lifebelt. We had no intention of falling overboard, and if we drove the boat too hard and sank it, nobody was going to come and look for us, so it was clearly better to sink with it as quickly as possible and get it over. For navigation we had the right charts, parallel rulers, tide tables, a pencil if we could find it, a wristwatch, a lead line and a compass, and that is all you need to go anywhere. Ever since those nights I have known that if you go to sea in boats you ought to expect to look after yourself whatever happens, and not expect to be rescued by anyone else.

When we had reached the position where the crash was supposed to have happened, we slowed down and began a square search, as scientifically as we could, allowing for the distance a dinghy might have drifted in the tide and wind, and hoping the men we were looking for would see us or hear us and at least have a torch they could flash.

Going slow, we were more aware of the isolation. I have seldom felt lonely at sea, or anywhere else, but normally in a boat one is going somewhere, not merely to and fro on a set of compass courses, and that sea was so utterly empty – excepting just possibly an even lonelier dinghy. But when the dawn came up we often sighted trawlers approaching, which had come out of port well behind us on the same mission, and we handed over the job to them. With their much greater height of eye they could see better than we could in daylight. They were also at greater risk because they were more visible from the air. They never succeeded either.

We had some success with odd jobs like taking out the mine disposal experts. Floating mines were often reported by the army, and by the time we reached them they were bobbing about most lethally in the surf. The admirable experts grappled with them from our rubber dinghy and usually lassoed them with a rope, so that we could tow them out to sea in the hope of detonating them in safety. Towing a mine, we found, you have to keep moving, or the mine has a distressing way of catching you up. It is quite difficult to detonate them without blowing yourself up too. The only way we knew was to shoot at them with a machine gun, and it was a matter of luck to hit them at all when you glimpsed them in the waves, let alone to hit them on one of their horns, which would set them off. In rough weather we always missed, and then the only thing was to shorten the tow-rope and take them into harbour, where the experts could de-fuse them in calm water. When we approached the harbour flying a red flag with a mine swirling around in our wake, it was fascinating to see people vanish as if we had some very evil smell. Inside, we cast the experts off in the dinghy, and left them most thankfully to beach the things and make them safe.

Also successful, and rather more exciting, was the job of taking the doctor off to ships that had sick or injured men. Most of them were in minor coastal convoys, and they were nearly always off Lowestoft in the night. It was easy to find them, and to put the doctor on board and wait to take him off again, with or without his patient. The exciting part was finding the harbour again. Peter and I both had very good night vision, and I think we might justly have claimed to be experts at finding that harbour in the dark. We had studied the problem like nobody else. The town formed a hump that you could always discern against the night sky, however dark it was. Directly below the top of the hump the shore was steep-to, and you could approach it in safety until you could see the breakers. If there were no breakers, which was rare, you crept in on the lead-line (we had no echo sounder) to the three-fathom mark. From there we knew the compass course that would take us close but not too close to the two moles that enclosed the harbour entrance, half a mile or so to the south. Off the entrance there was an eddy where the river current met the tide, and if you could not see the eddy, you could feel it. Then a cautious course westward until one of the moles was in sight, and a moment's hesitation while you decided which mole it was, the north one or the south one. Finally, when you had made up your mind, you opened both throttles wide before the boat's head could swing off, and if you had played your hand right you roared through the entrance at a very impressive speed. It was just one of those tricks that are really much easier than they look, a very early paragraph in any manual of pilotage, but the doctor, who had seen nothing but blackness, always kindly pretended he thought it was witchcraft. One night after a rough ride, when he was nearly as wet as we were, he put his patient into the ambulance that was waiting and said to the lieutenant-commander, who usually turned out to see what was happening, 'Remarkable! These two fellows *smell* their way in.'

It was getting wet that made us ask for something we had not foreseen. After a few hours at sea in the late autumn everything on board was soaked, and it was really impractical to live on the boat. We needed some sort of building on the quay with a stove in it. They gave us a fish salesman's office, which had a kitchen range and the kind of high desk where nineteenth-century clerks used to sit on stools, writing up their ledgers with quills.

Our cookery on that stove was simple. We drew our rations on Monday, mainly a huge lump of beef, ten times the civilian ration, and a sack of coal. We hacked the beef into bits and made a stew. It was stew again on Tuesdays, and then as the week went by we topped it up with potatoes and a daily dose of curry powder.

It was an odd-shaped building they had given us, with a roof of single pitch so that the front wall was low but the back wall was very high and was made entirely of small panes of glass, like a greenhouse. We therefore had to contrive a very large black-out curtain. The only material we had was army blankets, which were plentiful. The curtain took fourteen of them.

On our first night in this novel home we borrowed a step-ladder, and by putting two of its legs on the desk and two on the stove I could just reach the top of the glass; but to make room on the stove we had to take off the simmering pot of curry and put it on the floor. To climb the ladder I took off my leather fisherman's seaboots, like an old-time sailor climbing the rigging, and I stuck up the blankets with drawing pins. I had just finished and was climbing down, admiring my handiwork, when a lot of things happened at once. The air-raid warning went off, which made all the trawlers in harbour fire their machine guns uselessly into the sky, and I saw the blankets begin to peel off from the top. Peter saw them too, and for fear of the air raid warden he turned the light off. I jumped down in a hurry.

I don't know, but I think it may be a unique experience to be in the pitch dark in an air raid, trying to fight your way out from under fourteen army blankets full of drawing pins, with one bare foot wedged in a pot of curry.

In the end, the winter caught up with us. There were days or even weeks when the seas came over the harbour walls, and no trawler skipper would have risked the entrance unless he was desperate, or dreamed of going out if he was in. We fretted inside, with nothing to do except crouch over our stove and try to protect our boat from bashing itself to pieces against the quay. It had all been an excellent experience but it was coming to an end, as everything does in wartime. I had never been taught anything to fit me for it, and was given no training whatever; nor was Peter, as far as I know. We had taught ourselves, which is the best way to learn anything. In a big warship, we could never in years have come to know the sea so intimately.

But we did not know anything at all about the navy, the real navy, except that it had been wonderfully tolerant. We were still in no way qualified to be petty officers. Petty officers, especially chief petty officers, are the backbone of a navy, the men who know all the answers and all the rules and precedents. If we moved somewhere else as petty officers we would have to go right down to the bottom and start again, and give up the strangely independent life we had won. There was nothing attractive in that. So, if we moved, the only way we could move was up. We went to see the lieutenant-commander again, and he sent us to see the naval officer in charge, who was a captain. I had not met him before, but he seemed to know us.

'Ah, you two again?' he said. 'What can we do for you this time?'

'Sir, we wondered if we ought to apply for commissions.'

'I've been expecting that,' he said. 'Why didn't you do it months ago?'

'We enjoyed being here, sir. But there won't be much to do in the winter.'

'No,' he said, 'not much for you, and damn-all for me. But I'm too old. At your age, you ought to try for something more important.'

'That's what we were beginning to think, sir.'

'Very well. Sorry to lose you, but we've no right to keep you here. We'll fill up all the forms, and I'll wish you luck.'

And that was that. As we turned deferentially to go, he said to a younger officer, 'You know, it's a scandal the way we waste our man-power.'

We took it as a compliment.

EIGHT

Sunday in September

Usually, it is not in the nature of a battle to have a passive audience; but the great daylight air raid of September, 1940 was watched by tens of thousands of people all over Kent and East Sussex and in parts of Surrey. I happened to be watching, because I was at home on weekend leave. It is not really part of my story but it does illustrate the anomaly of that war, which put the old and the young of both sexes in the greatest danger while a large proportion of the able-bodied men like me lived in safety.

Home by then was Charles Darwin's house at Downe in Kent. Downe was a country village, and it still is, but it is only twenty miles or so south-east of central London, a few minutes as the bomber flies, and the house was half a mile from the runways of Biggin Hill, which was one of the principal fighter airfields. In that month of September, Fighter Command of the RAF regarded Biggin Hill as the centre of the hottest hundred square miles in the world. The house, so near the centre, was large but fragile; my mother told me in a letter that nearly sixty people were sleeping in it. It was a major disaster just waiting to happen: by what seemed a miraculous chance, it never did.

Our father was sixty-three, and in uniform for the first time in his life, a private, later a lance-corporal, in the Home Guard. Nowadays, of course, the Home Guard has become a national television joke, and a very good joke too: Dad's Army with its shambling drill and absurdly inadequate weapons. He was very proud of the uniform, and of the stripe when he got it, but he always saw it as a joke at the time, and said he would be worse than useless. In fact, it needed immense courage to be determined to attack the German army, as the Home Guard was, knowing that they would be messily killed at the first encounter. Besides his uniform, he was given a tin hat and a rifle, he said, of the Iron Age; it weighed a ton and jammed if you put more than three rounds in the magazine, and he never fired it.

Useless or not, the Home Guard gave him a new lease of life. For the first time, he began to make friends outside his narrow circle of academics, and outside his own class, among the artisans who lived in the village and like him were too old for the Army, and especially among the boys who were too young for it. He showed those boys a fatherly affection I didn't know he had in him, and I liked him better for it. There was only one chink in his courage: he was what he called a mild case of claustrophobia. In the early part of that September, when Biggin Hill had heavy raids every night, he found he did not like to be in the house. If he was not out on duty when things were at their hottest, he put his tin hat on and took his archaic rifle and went out alone to see what was going on. On one or two nights, I went with him. If the house was hit, he said, we would be much more use outside it than inside. I had never seen bombing on such a scale, and I was healthily apprehensive; but when he was out in the garden or the surrounding woods and fields he seemed perfectly calm and even amused, especially when it seemed advisable to lie flat on our fronts. 'Illogical posture! You get your head down but you leave your backside sticking up in the air.' And again – 'Damn noisy, but in the open I doubt if it is mathematically more dangerous than a thunder storm.'

That weekend my brother was also at home; he too was in the Home Guard, because he had a 'reserved occupation' which he strongly felt was ignominious. Our cousin Paul Mayhew was also there; he was twenty, an Oxford undergraduate and a fighter pilot on leave from Biggin Hill (he was killed soon after, the most awful tragedy in our family). On that relaxed and leisurely Sunday afternoon, we heard the fighters from Biggin Hill go up, which was not at all unusual, and then a most unusual noise, the roar of huge numbers of aircraft overhead – but no bombs.

Downe House had a small flat roof among its complex gables, and there was a rickety ladder in the loft which the fire-watch used. Led by Paul, we clambered up there to have the best possible view. Coming high over the trees to the south were wave after wave of German bombers, hundreds of them, we soon lost count.

I don't suppose anyone anywhere had ever before seen so many aircraft in the sky at once as everyone saw that day. They were not pretty, like the silvery bi-planes we had seen from the Dolls' Hospital in the first daylight air raid of all; these were black against the sky, and they came on in tight formations, hideously determined. But round and among them were the fighters, much smaller and fewer. Paul gave us an expert commentary, hopping with excitement at the great dog fights above his head, half wishing his squadron was on duty and half thankful it was not, and often interrupting himself to ask if we thought our mother was making cucumber sandwiches for tea. She was, but no butter.

For the first time, the bombers were taking no notice of our local target, the airfield. They were going beyond us, to London. Around us, nothing was falling out of the sky except the wreckage of battle. Sometimes a bomber disintegrated in a cloud of smoke, leaving nothing but fluttering pieces. Sometimes they fell intact, turning over and over like the autumn leaves which were also beginning to fall. Sometimes a Hurricane or a Spitfire was instantly destroyed, or came straight down with its engine screaming to bury itself in the woods. Always, British or German, one longed to see parachutes detach themselves and open. To shoot a bomber down was a triumph, but one could not wish the men in it to die. Before dusk, the whole northern horizon was an evil cloud of smoke. London was burning.

We walked down to the village pub as evening fell. Everyone in the bar was saying old Goering had changed his tactics, as indeed he obviously had, for better or worse. When we came back it was dark, and we climbed up to the roof again. From north-west to north-east was a wall of flame, a fire we reckoned was twenty miles in length. It seemed impossible that there were many people alive at the roots of those flames, and we went to bed sadly expecting a flood of refugees by dawn, looking for sanctuary in the countryside. But London and Londoners, of course, were tougher than anyone had thought they possibly could be. At dawn, the fires were still burning. Bombs had been falling into them all night, each one casting up flames to new heights. But there was not a single refugee; not a soul came trekking through the village.

I had to go through London next morning to get back to

Lowestoft. My brother was still commuting to his work in the City every day, and said the trains would probably still be running, not as usual but in the general direction of London. I caught one which passed through the slums to the south of the docks, where hundreds or thousands of the poor little nineteenth-century houses had fallen down in smoking ruin; but the train was packed with regular commuters, who observed their strict convention of never speaking, and nobody made any comment on the tragedy we saw from the windows. The train came to a final stop at London Bridge station, and everyone got out and walked across the bridge. Even in the commercial heart of the city, a great many buildings were still on fire, the nearest a house in Black Raven Alley at the northern end of the bridge, where I had lived in a top-floor flat before I moved to Carnaby Street. The firemen were still at work on it, obviously tired out, scorched and black with smoke. They had already been hard at it for eighteen hours. Admirable men, but it was not done to stand and watch.

On the other side of the road, still intact, was the monument where the other fire of London started in 1666 – also on a Sunday in September. That reminded me that I had been within a few yards of where Samuel Pepys rowed out to midstream to escape the heat, before he thought of rowing up to Westminster to tell the King what was happening and advise him to order fire-breaks to be made by blowing up houses in the path of the flames. I had also been close to the ale-house in Bankside on the other shore of the river where he sat the same evening and began no doubt to compose the most famous descriptive passage in his diary:

Poor people staying in their houses as long as till the very fire touched them, and then running into boats or clambering from one pair of stairs by the waterside to another. And among other things, the poor pigeons I perceive were loath to leave their houses, but hovered about the windows and balconies till they were some of them burned their wings, and fell down . . . At last met my Lord Mayor in Canning Streete, like a man spent, with a handkercher about his neck. To the King's message, he cried like a fainting woman, 'Lord, what can I do? I am spent. People will not obey me. I have been pulling down houses. But the fire overtakes us faster than we can do it' . . .

And as it grew darker, [the fire] appeared more and more, and in corners and upon steeples and between churches and houses, as far as we could see up the hill of the City, in a most horrid malicious bloody flame, not like the fine flame of an ordinary fire . . . We stayed till, it being darkish, we saw the fire as only one entire arch of fire from this to the other side the bridge, and in a bow up the hill, for an arch of above a mile long. It made me weep to see it. The churches, houses, and all on fire and flaming at once, and a horrid noise the flames made, and the cracking of houses at their ruine . . .

After that weekend my dark damp nights in the North Sea were never the positive pleasure they had been before. Like thousands and thousands of other young men, I worried about what my family were going through at home: my father under his tin hat in the garden, my mother inside that tottering overcrowded house, my brother in those evil commuter trains. It was wrong to be doing anything one enjoyed when so many more worthy people were doing things they hated.

NINE

Flags at Scapa

Peter and I knew a move would separate us. I regretted it, and so did he I think; but things like that in wartime are out of your own control. It happened more quickly than we expected. There was a medical and in spite of his excellent vision he found he was colour-blind. That is one thing the navy is adamant about; if you are colour-blind you cannot be a naval officer, except perhaps in a clerical job; and that is that. So he joined the Royal Marine Commandos, the most belligerent of all fighting units, which was generally regarded as a one-way ticket. He was a very kindly and gentle person, and I often wonder sadly if he survived. I doubt it.

A week after shedding my lower-deck uniform, I dined in a stone-built mansion at Scapa Flow in the Orkney Islands off the north coast of Scotland, attended by petty officer stewards. I was a member of a mess which had only four men in it: the Admiral commanding the famous naval base, his chief of staff, who was a captain RN, his paymaster-commander, and me – the Admiral's flag-lieutenant. I was reduced again to the total confusion of my first few days at Lowestoft, and I was dumb with shyness and awe. But the others were very kind; in my experience, most senior naval officers are. The Admiral, Sir Hugh Binney, was endlessly patient with my ignorance, and his COS remarked, soon after I arrived, how much good it would do them to have somebody 'from the outside world' to talk to. Among themselves, he said, they had nothing to talk about except bars in Alex. But it was a drastic change from Lowestoft. There, I had wandered around in a sweater and seaboots, and nobody cared. Here, it was a clean shirt twice a day. Life seemed to be getting serious.

The navy must have chosen me for the appointment by wartime logic, which by normal logic is well known to be back to front and upside down. I had done the usual two months' training of a sub-lieutenant RNVR. I think I passed top of my division, or nearly top, in navigation and seamanship, and I know I was bottom in OLQs, or Officer-Like Qualities, which was a healthy shock to me. Perhaps one reason was that I have never been able to shout, and have always been reluctant to try. As one of our tests, each of us had to drill a small squad of our fellow candidates. My squad knew me and my weakness very well, so when I gave them 'Form fours', 'Right turn' and 'Quick march' they obeyed smartly enough. But as soon as they were marching, they played an age-old trick on me. They pretended they could not hear my pathetic pleas to halt, and they marched on resolutely into the distance, round a corner and out of sight, dismissed themselves in the canteen and ordered coffee, leaving me alone in the middle of the parade ground with the chief petty officer, who was the examiner.

'Well, that was a right old cock-up, that was,' he said, and wrote zero on his mark-sheet. He marched me to the canteen to order them out again, but we found they had also bought coffee for him and me, and as it was a cold morning we used common sense and stayed there.

On the basis of that débacle, the navy gave me an appointment which needed no navigation or seamanship whatever, but all the OLQs in the world. On my journey to the north of Scotland by train – first class now in my proud new uniform with its single wavy ring of gold – I was carrying in a cardboard box a set of aiguilettes, the gorgeous drapery of gilded cords and tassles which adorns a flag officer's staff.

In olden days, of course, a flag-lieutenant was in charge of the Admiral's signal flags: it was Nelson's flag-lieutenant, John Pasco, who ordered 'England expects' to be hoisted, and even proposed those two words instead of 'Nelson confides', because they needed fewer flags. But by 1941 signalling was a highly technical speciality of cyphering and electronics, and a reserve sub-lieutenant was not expected to understand it. The flag-lieutenant's job had shrunk: all I had to do was take care of the Admiral himself. I did my best at it, not because he was an admiral but because he was a much older man and I came to like him very much, and did not think he took enough care of himself. In the back of my mind I was always misquoting,

'You are old, Father William, the young man said,
The few locks that are left you are white.
And yet you continually stand on your head.
Do you think at your age it is right?'

He did not stand on his head, but in his inspections of the defences of Scapa he was always getting wet through with rain, salt spray or sodden snow, or all three together. He seemed to think nothing of it, but I was sure it was not good for him, so I naturally carried dry socks for him in my pocket, and if I produced them at a tactful moment he thanked me and put them on. I would have done the same for any favourite uncle, and indeed he behaved to me more like an uncle than an admiral. From him I began to learn how the navy works and thinks, and he patiently explained the trivia of naval etiquette: when and when not, for example, to wear the ostentatious aiguilettes, when and when not the loyal toast could be drunk sitting down, and the formalities of getting into and out of a boat: embarking from shore or ship, the most junior officer goes first; disembarking, the most senior does so.

Even within the narrow scope of the job, there was very little I could do for him. Nominally, I was in charge of his domestic staff and the requisitioned mansion, which is called Melsetter, and his drivers and cars, and the coxswain and crew of his barge, which of course was a high-speed power boat. But each of these departments was run by a chief petty officer who had made it his life's career and was as efficient as only a naval chief can be – a sort of maritime Jeeves. I was an amateur, they knew it and so did I, and I had to use far more tact in not annoying the chiefs than in not annoying the Admiral. But when they found I was not going to throw my weight about they became my allies and tutors and told me in whispers what I ought to be doing, like prompters in a play. They taught me the esoteric niceties of naval language, polite and impolite. But I did not always use it. When the Admiral's car was at the door of the house, it seemed natural for the chief to report to me, 'Car's alongside, sir', and if the

Admiral was in it, 'Admiral's coming aboard, sir'; but it would have seemed affected if I had done the same.

Nothing, I am afraid, could have made me a competent flag-lieutenant; I was always gauche, and still am, on social occasions. Only two things made the experience bearable. One was the Admiral's kindness, and the other was the place. Most people posted to Scapa loathed it, because it is bleak and wet and windy, and by ferry and train at least thirty-six hours from anywhere. But most of them had to live in ships, or in sordid and formal camps of huts ashore. I lived in luxury. Melsetter is near the south end of the island of Hoy, and Hoy is quite different from the other Orkney islands. The others are low-lying and green, but Hoy is mountainous and barren, the sort of place I love.

So whenever I had a half-day's leave – which was often because there was so little for me to do – I put on something like my Lowestoft rig again and climbed to the top of the hills and walked along the superb sea cliffs on the westward side of the island. There were tens of thousands of people stationed in Scapa but up there I never saw anyone at all, and the ships of the fleet were out of sight. The clifftops, and the swell of the open Atlantic bursting a thousand feet below, and the heather and inquisitive northern sea birds, gannets, petrels, skuas, puffins, gulls and sometimes a great northern diver, returned human life to its proper proportions again; one could tritely reflect (before the atomic age) that whatever happened in the war, whatever wounds humanity inflicted on itself, those cliffs would still be there with the same seas bursting at their feet.

At about that time I had a letter from the BBC. They told me I was on a list of 'indispensible' staff whom they could claim back from the forces; but they added, 'We are quite willing not to embarrass you by taking any action if you are happier where you are. Are you?' I hesitated a long time: it was good of them to think my happiness counted. Was I happier, come what might, in the navy? Up on the cliffs, leaning against the wind and rain, I concluded I was.

My Admiral's title was ACOS, Admiral Commanding Orkney and Shetland, but his command extended to the Faeroe Islands and Iceland, so we had to travel. Our first journey was short but uncomfortable: across to an air force station on the mainland of Scotland in a single-engine four-seater biplane in a gale of wind. The Admiral stood and looked at the archaic plane and the shredded clouds whirling in from the west. 'Well, Flags,' he said, 'I suppose we mustn't let the air force see we're frightened.' And treating it like a boat, I climbed reluctantly in and he followed.

I soon knew I was going to be sick, and there was nothing to be sick in, so I took my aiguillettes out of their cardboard box and put them on, and was sick in the box and hid it under the seat.

When at last we reeled into the airfield he turned round to me from his seat in front with the pilot, and no doubt saw I was green.

'Didn't you enjoy that, Flags?'

'No, sir. I thought it was hellish.'

'Really? So did I, to tell the truth. And now of all things, look, a guard of honour. Can we make it?'

'I'm ready to try, sir.'

He clambered out of the detestable machine, shook himself like a dog, saluted and marched erect in the howling wind along the ranks of airmen presenting arms. I tottered in his wake, unsure if my knees were about to buckle under me, and hoping not to disgrace him or the navy.

Poor man, he had to give two lectures that afternoon and inspect four more guards of honour, getting wetter every time ('Do you think at your age it is right?'). When we went home it was calmer, but as we approached Scapa Flow across the Pentland Firth there was an air-raid alarm and the whole of the Scapa barrage went up. That barrage was impressive from the ground, but more than impressive from on top in that giddy aircraft. It is unlikely they were shooting at us, but I was far from sure at the time, and so was the pilot. He made an abrupt turn to port, slid over the top of Hoy, ducked down to wave height behind the cliffs and took a long detour round the shell-bursts to approach from the north. I was so glad to be on the runway again that I forgot the disgusting cardboard box I had hidden under the seat. I wonder who found it.

Our next journey was longer and much more eventful. In May 1941 the Admiral decided to visit the Faeroes and Iceland, and the six-inch cruiser *Arethusa* was appointed to take him there – and me. The Faeroes are delightful, a group of islands as sharp as a set of carnivorous teeth, with a scattering of white-painted wooden houses which reminded me of the outer islands of Norway; they were in fact a Danish colony which had joined our side when Denmark was invaded by the Germans. I doubt if any cruiser had ever been among them before, and our principal purpose, I think, was simply to 'show the flag' – which after centuries of practice the Royal Navy does very well. Everyone on shore (there were not very many) stopped what they were doing to watch and wave as we steamed through the narrow sound, and it was a gala day when we anchored off the capital, Thorshavn. Fishing boats came out loaded with people to have a closer look while others, I must add, on their way out to fish, ostentatiously motored past us without a glance. A proportion of islanders everywhere refuses to be impressed by visitors, and wishes they would go away. We invited the leading citizens and their wives on board for drinks: they stepped on to the quarter deck with flattering expressions of awe and went away again cheerful and reeling, and they gave a reception for us ashore.

Then Iceland, which was well accustomed to naval ships. On 19 May we were at anchor off Reykjavik, and on that day something happened in Norway – the sort of thing I was to learn much more about in the next few years. On the south coast of Norway people saw two very large German warships escorting a convoy to the north. One man who saw them had a friend called Odd Starheim, who he knew had an illicit radio transmitter hidden on a farm. He also knew, and so did Starheim, that the Germans were already homing in on the farm with radio direction finders, and if one more signal were transmitted they would get bearings of it and find out where it had come from. One party of them was camped on the only approach road to the farm, and Starheim had already dug a hole to bury the transmitter.

It was a problem to get a message through to him. That was solved by his girl-friend; she often went to the farm, and the Germans knew her by sight. She volunteered to take the written message, tucked it in the top of her stocking and walked through the German party, politely saying good evening. When Starheim saw it he knew it was important enough to risk his life on, and hers. He sent the signal to England, buried the transmitter and began a long and successful escape to neutral Sweden. That intrepid girl with the note in her stocking started a naval battle which ranged three thousand miles over the Atlantic, the first that was ever controlled entirely by radio.

Starheim's signal reached the Commander-in-Chief, Home Fleet in Scapa: I don't think he ever knew or asked where the information had come from. Reconnaissance Spitfires were sent to hunt for the big warships and spotted them in a fjord near Bergen. One was identified from photographs as Germany's newest battleship, the *Bismarck*, and the other as the heavy cruiser, *Prinz Eugen*. Then the weather closed in, and when it cleared they had gone.

It was a problem for the C. in C. to guess what the Germans were developing: perhaps an invasion of Iceland, perhaps only a reinforcement of north Norway, perhaps a break-out of the two big ships for commerce raiding in the Atlantic – in which case they might come north or south of Iceland, possibly south of the Faeroes or even close to Shetland. The Home Fleet had two battleships in Scapa Flow, the *King George V* and the *Prince of Wales* – the latter so new that she still had the builders' men working in the gun turrets – the old battle cruisers *Hood* and *Repulse*, and the new aircraft-carrier *Victorious*, which had flown on her aircraft for the first time the day before. The *Bismarck* was known to be bigger, more heavily armoured and probably faster than the British battleships, and the British had a great respect, dating back to the Battle of Jutland, for the strength and quality the Germans put into their major ships.

The C. in C. waited two days (so that he would not run out of fuel before the Germans) and then sent the *Prince of Wales* and *Hood* to watch the Denmark Strait between Iceland and Greenland. He followed with the *King George V* and *Victorious* for the channel south of Iceland. Between them, the two parts of the fleet had ten cruisers and twelve destroyers; and in Reykjavik, detached and somewhat forlorn, were we in the *Arethusa*.

The *Bismarck* and her consort were next sighted, steaming very fast westward in the narrow channel north of Iceland, by the eight-inch cruisers *Norfolk* and *Suffolk*. Neither of them was anything like a match for her; they were ordered to shadow her and report her position, course and speed. We were sent out of Reykjavik and anti-clockwise round Iceland in case she went back the way she had come.

In the spring the channel north of Iceland was eerie. To port was an almost permanent bank of fog concealing the Iceland rocks and a minefield, to starboard the uncharted edge of the sea-ice, uncomfortably close. Between the two, the lane of clear water was only three or four miles wide. I would have like to be up on the bridge with the Admiral and Captain to watch how such a problem of navigation was solved at 32 knots, but there was nothing for me to do up there and I would only have been in the way. So I attached myself to the deciphering staff, who were more than busy with the stream of signals coming in night and day from the Admiralty and other scattered ships. Through them we watched the evolution of a monstrous hunt, and there is no denying it was exciting. It was made more exciting, and the channel more eerie, by not knowing whether the *Bismarck* was coming through it in the opposite direction and closing with us at 64 miles an hour.

It was obvious to me that all the regular officers, which was nearly all the others, were saying they hoped she would, while I was secretly hoping she would not. Perhaps I was cowardly, but I think I was realistic. Of course we were not officially expected to fight her, but it was impossible to imagine we could avoid it; and we would not have tried to avoid it. Our six-inch guns fired a shell of 105 pounds with a range of fourteen miles, the Bismarck's thirteen-inch guns fired a shell of 1750 pounds with a range of twenty-two miles – and their gunnery was radar-controlled while ours was not. We would all have been swimming before we knew she was there. Possibly, though it is doubtful, we could have got off a signal before we sank. But there was nothing behind us to stop her escaping back to Norway if she tried, so the only significance of the signal could be that the hunt was over and everyone else could go home. It hardly seemed to me worth so many men being drowned in that steel-grey icy water, but I was careful not to say so.

We were still passing through that sound to the westward at 5.49 in the morning of 24 May, when the *Bismarck* and *Prinz Eugen* met the *Prince of Wales* and *Hood* ahead of us in the

Denmark Strait, and there, in sight of the ice, among all the routine signals, we deciphered the words from the rear-admiral commanding the *Norfolk* and *Suffolk*: 'Hood has blown up.'

Was it I who woke my Admiral with it? Or had he been up all night? I don't remember, but nobody in the navy will forget the shock of it. *Hood* was an old ship, laid down in the First World War, and for twenty-two years she had been the biggest and best-known warship in the world; many people, and I was one, also thought her the most graceful. In all those years this was her first battle, and she had lasted six minutes. The *Bismarck* sank her with her second salvo at fourteen miles.

I have often remarked on one fundamental difference between a navy and an army: soldiers fight against other men, but sailors see themselves fighting against ships. In a naval battle your aim is to sink the enemy's ship, and if you succeed your next immediate duty is to rescue the survivors of her crew; a man in the water is everyone's ally, whichever side he was on. This duty has been acknowledged ever since sailors took over from soldiers in battles at sea at the time of Drake. So in the back of a sailor's mind there is a trace of chivalry which has almost vanished from armies.

But that signal brought a new purpose into the fleet. After it, to get the *Bismarck* was more than a matter of strategy, it was a matter of pride and naked revenge, and I do not think any of us spared a thought for the ordeal of her crew. Only two men were saved, I think, of the *Hood*'s huge complement, and most of the regular navy lost friends in her. But at least their death was instant. The *Bismarck*'s crew saw death coming for three more days and nights.

In the signals cabin of the humble *Arethusa*, we marvelled as the navy deployed its strength to catch that single ship. The signals were fragmentary, because ships were concealing their position, but before it was over we had plotted on the Atlantic chart (of which I got glimpses from time to time) five battleships, two modern carriers and two battle cruisers converging from ports as far apart as Scapa, Nova Scotia and Gibraltar. Also out in the hunt were about ten cruisers, twenty destroyers and probably fifty aircraft.

The hopes of the regular officers of *Arethusa* went up and

down, and so did my shameful fears. After she sank the *Hood* the *Bismarck* continued to the south away from us, leaving a wake of oil but still moving at high speed, which showed she had been damaged but not badly. In the night that followed the shadowers lost her and the *Prinz Eugen*, and for thirty-six hours the Commander-in-Chief believed they were coming back either his way, south of Iceland, or our way, north of it, and he told us so. Then she was sighted again by an aircraft, steaming south-west on a course for Brest in France. We knew with mixed feelings that whatever happened we were out of it, and we put back to Reykjavik where, next morning, the hills around us were as peaceful as ever.

The signals gave us the bare bones of what was happening that night, but left most of it to the imagination. Off Iceland it was tolerably calm, but down there off France there was a gale. Aircraft from the *Ark Royal*, coming up from Gibraltar, took off while the ends of the flight deck were rising and falling fifty-five feet. On their first strike they saw the cruiser *Sheffield*, mistook her for the *Bismarck* and attacked. Luckily, their torpedoes had a new kind of magnetic pistol which did not work. Five exploded when they hit the water, and the *Sheffield* managed to dodge the rest. On a second attempt in the dark they found the *Bismarck* and hit her with two torpedoes on her only vulnerable spot, the propellers or rudders or both. She was not far from safety in Brest, but she was out of control, steering erratic courses very slowly. All the rest of that night, her crew must have known the end was coming with the dawn.

After dawn, she was pounded at point-blank range by torpedoes and the heaviest guns. Her crew fought back until they had nothing left to fight with. She was so superbly built that for two hours she would not surrender and did not sink. At the end, she was a silent wreck, burning from end to end; her inside was a furnace which could be seen through the shell-holes. She was still flying her flag when she heeled to port, turned bottom up and vanished. In the last minutes, men could be seen running about on her upper decks, with a choice of burning or drowning. The impersonal fight against the ship became human.

A cruiser and a destroyer stopped for survivors. It was too rough to launch a boat, but they threw ropes and let down scrambling nets. Many men were too injured or exhausted to climb them and fell back into the sea, but 110 were saved, perhaps one-tenth of those who had sailed in her.

The British had made many mistakes in the hunt: it ought not to have taken so many ships to find and destroy only one, even the *Bismarck*; and the *Prinz Eugen*, which had vanished in the Atlantic, ultimately came into Brest with engine trouble. The feeling in the fleet was of relief, but not at all, I think, of victory. My Admiral had been away from Scapa much longer than he intended, and we left the *Arethusa* in Reykjavik and flew back to Scotland in a Catalina flying boat of the RAF, hiding under the clouds from what I was told were German Dorniers, a very long and tedious and anti-climactic flight.

Back in Scapa Flow we and the fleet had distinguished visitors, as usual; among them the Duke of Kent, a younger brother of the King. Strictly speaking, he was the guest of the Commander-in-Chief, not of my admiral, and on his first day he was bidden to lunch on board the flagship named after his father. The Commander-in-Chief wanted to keep his own flag-lieutenant with him, so I was told to take his barge, with his coxswain and crew, to fetch the royal guest from the airfield. With him on board we roared back across the Flow, saluted by all the scores of ships at their moorings, and as we approached the flagship I observed that her enormous crew was lining the rail, ready I suppose for the orders 'Off caps' and 'Three cheers', while every available admiral and captain of the fleet was assembled on the quarterdeck, the Royal Marine band was at attention, the signallers were standing by to hoist a royal standard and a posse of boatswains was lined up to pipe the visitor aboard.

The navy does that sort of thing in style. A barge approaches at full speed; at exactly the right moment her coxswain goes full astern and lays her precisely alongside the companion ladder, while his bowman and sternman perform a drill with their boathooks.

That was what we did – or began to do. At the crucial moment, the barge would not go astern. We hit the flagship with a gruesome crunch. The bowman lost his boathook overboard, but grabbed the rail and did not go in himself. The sternman fell into the cockpit, his boathook flailing, and the Duke, his pilot and I, who were in the cockpit, fell in a mingled heap. I could not see what happened on the quarterdeck far above. I was only aware, as I crammed on my cap again, helped the Duke up and tried to dust him off, of hundreds of heads peering down at us, a good many with gold-braided caps, wondering I suppose if rescue or first aid were called for.

They were not. The coxswain motored round in a circle very gently, and came alongside again dead slow. The Duke went up the ladder with his pilot and me behind, and the whole thing began again from the beginning: the crew doffed caps, the boatswains blew their pipes, the standard was hoisted, the band struck up 'God save the King', which seemed unusually apt, and everyone in sight was saluting. The episode had been so unspeakable that I don't think anyone ever mentioned it. It wasn't my fault, of course – it wasn't even 'my' barge or 'my' coxswain – but probably most of the hundreds of people who saw it thought it was.

The next day I redeemed myself, or so I thought, by a display of OLQs, but nobody saw it at all. The Duke was coming to lunch with us at Melsetter, which meant he had to be driven the four or five miles from the landing stage, with other exalted guests, in a procession of cars. At the last minute I thought I would drive on ahead, all alone, to make sure the road was clear. Any good flag-lieutenant would have thought of it long before.

The house at Melsetter had two drives, and we normally used the back one because it was the first that one came to. For the state occasion, however, the Admiral had decreed we should use the front one, which had a display of daffodils that was worth seeing in Hoy. So I drove past the back entrance and on to the front one where I found the army, who had been mending the road, had parked a steamroller inside our gate and had all disappeared for their lunch. It was hissing in a menacing way, and stopped us getting in as fiercely as Cerberus stopped people getting out.

I had wanted to drive a steamroller ever since I had a wooden one as a child, but nobody had let me. I took the opportunity and climbed up. It looked perfectly simple. I think there were only two controls. One was obviously the steering, so the other must be the steam. I tried it and the machine gave a promising gasp and moved perceptibly backwards, so I turned the wheel the other way. It chuffed triumphantly ahead, but dreadfully slowly: probably it had hardly any steam up. I peered anxiously over the aiguilettes on my shoulder in case the VIPs were coming. But we beat them to the gate and turned right, leaving the driveway clear; and I still had time – but only just – to drive my car to the house and wash the incongruous coal-dust off my face.

You do not often see a naval officer wearing *aiguilettes* and driving a steamroller, and it was a pity there was nobody there to watch, except some sheep.

A less important visitor, but more important for me, was an army captain called Mitchell. I did not know at the time, but he had not come to Scapa to see the Admiral or the fleet; he had come to have a look at me. I learned by degrees that he was mixed up with the Secret Intelligence Service which had established Odd Starheim in occupied Norway with his transmitter; that he had sent a couple of Norwegian refugee fishing boats back to Norway from the Shetland Islands to put agents ashore there; that there was a need to send many more in the future; and finally that Mitchell did not know much about boats and was looking for someone who did.

Of all the jobs I ever heard of in war, that would have been my first choice: boats, Norway, individuality and independence, yet with the status of a naval officer – a job that was unique and had no precedent, either in peace or war, yet was certainly useful, if anything whatever in war can be said to be useful.

I was very sorry to leave my fatherly Admiral, and he, kind and forgiving as ever, reported he was sorry to lose me. I could not believe it. And in late May or early June of 1941 I flew to Shetland in a Blenheim bomber which happened to be going that way. I could not see out of it, except through a round hole in the floor, so my first glimpse of the islands where I lived for eleven years was vertically downwards: first the sea breaking on rocks, then sheep and a peat bog distressingly close underneath, and then thankfully a tattered sandy runway, where Bob Mitchell was waiting to make me feel welcome. Typically, it was blowing hard and raining.

TEN

The Shetland Bus

This brings me to the awkward moment in any author's autobiography, the moment when he starts to write books. Should he assume the people who read his own story have read his earlier books or not? If they have, they will know all they want to know of their subjects, and probably all he can tell them. If they have not, then why have they chosen this one from the library shelf – or even bought it? I have written over twenty books, and the first was published thirty-two years ago. I think the safest assumption is that anyone who reads this has at least heard of some of the others, but has probably forgotten what they were about.

An author meets this dilemma in its acutest form when he is asked to lecture about his latest book, or about his books in general. I learned long ago to avoid these invitations when I politely could. They are doomed to fail: if you interest one half of your audience, you bore the other half. But the first time I did it, I could not escape. My first book was about what I did and what other people did in the four years after I landed in Shetland. In America, it was called *Across to Norway*, in Britain *The Shetland Bus*, and in Norway *Nordsjobussen*, which means 'The North Sea Bus' – the latter titles being the secret nicknames the Norwegians in Norway gave to the work we did. I read the book again the other day, and I was ashamed of it; it seemed unbearably pompous. But it sold enormously well because I had a very good ready-made story to tell. When it was published in Norway I was invited to go there. The publisher and several wartime colleagues met me in the snow at Oslo airport. 'Ovart,' they said (no foreigner tries to pronounce Howarth, however fluent he is), 'Ovart, you have to give a lecture on Friday, and it has to be fifty-five minutes exactly, because the King's coming and he will never sit still for an hour.' They told me they had reserved the Aula, the great hall of Oslo University, and invited the diplomatic corps. There was no way out, short of falling down dead.

So I had the chance (and once in a lifetime is enough) to begin a speech with one of those resounding introductions: 'Your Majesty, Your Royal Highnesses, Your Excellencies, Mr President, Ladies and Gentlemen'. The Majesty was King Haakon, the Royal Highnesses were the Crown Prince, now King Olaf, and several of the younger princes and princesses, the Excellencies were quite a crowd of ambassadors, and Mr President, though he sounded well, was not the head of a republic but only of the club of ex-saboteurs and spies who had largely run Norway during the German occupation and were running this affair. It was a pity there are no lords in Norway. I would have liked to put in 'My Lords'.

I remember that introduction very well, but I do not remember a single word of what I said after it. However, after fifty-five minutes the King was still sitting there and not looking restless. When I had finished I was called down from the platform to meet him. 'Thank you, thank you,' he said. 'You spoke to our hearts. Can you come to luncheon with me tomorrow?'

That glittering evening evolved directly from the wet and windy morning when Bob Mitchell met me at the Shetland airfield. But a long dramatic chain of events connected them, and neither Bob nor I foresaw it. I do not intend now to write about each link in the chain; it is all in naked print in the book I wrote in the early 1950s, if anyone still wants to read it. Now I shall only write of the effect it had on me, the ways it changed me, the things that have stuck in my mind ever since.

It is not only I who have changed; Shetland has changed now, since North Sea oil made it prosperous. In 1941, my first impression through the hole in the floor of the bomber was not far wrong: the barren off-shore rocks, round which the sea is never still, the thousand-foot cliffs (though I could not see them through the hole), the sandy or rocky bays in between, the sheep and peat bogs, and the wind and rain. You had a feeling then that humanity was only just succeeding in clinging to that wild, remote and sodden bit of earth. The Shetland men were fishermen and very small-time farmers, the wives and daughters knitted day and night for a pittance. You found out only slowly that most of the men, who looked as if they had struggled there in poverty all their lives, had been in the merchant navy when they were young and had travelled the world before they came back to the same few acres of bog and rock, for no reason except that it was home. They were very kind and friendly, but they were like a large family; they had a language of their own, a broad Scottish dialect with nearly a thousand old Norse words which had been in general use since Viking times, so it was impossible for an outlander to become one of them. I married one, and lived there eleven years, and learned to understand the language (I did not speak it because that only made them laugh), but as they had known me first as a naval officer I always remained Mr Howarth. After the war, had I been born a Shetlander I would have been Davey, with a nickname to distinguish me from other Daveys. I wished I could be. But during the war I was more concerned with Norwegians, who were much less respectful in their speech. To them, I was always Ovart or the familiar *du* – no Mr, and they had no word corresponding to Sir. When their own Crown Prince came to visit us, I noticed that even he was also *du*. '*Du*, Olaf,' they shouted to him, and '*Du*, Ovart' to me. They were only formal with people they did not like, and rank in itself meant less than nothing to them.

In Scapa there had always been a precedent for everything, and everyone had been told what he ought to do, even if he could not always do it. But our job in Shetland had no precedent at all. It looked straightforward on paper – to keep open some sort of sea route to occupied Norway. But in practice it was far from straightforward, and nobody had tried to tell Mitchell how to do it. Nor did he try to tell me.

He and I were appointed not by the navy or army but by SIS, the Secret Intelligence Service, and the new outfit called SOE, which was just beginning to organize resistance movements in the countries the Germans had overrun. Both these offices, our only bosses, were in London. We were very much on our own.

Luckily, we always agreed. He was no more a copy-book officer than I was; even less perhaps, for although he was dressed as an army captain – soon a major – and had seen some hair-raising fighting in Norway when it was invaded, he had never been in the army and was more a musician than a soldier. He was only about my own age, still under thirty, but he was an old hand in the all-absorbing world of espionage, while I was pitched into it headfirst.

A very few things were obvious from the beginning. Everyone knew, or ought to have known, that it would be very dangerous – not for Bob or me, but for the crews who sailed to Norway and landed agents and weapons and radio transmitters – not to mention the danger for the agents. Being an intelligence operation, the whole thing had to be under British command, but we would have to use Norwegian boats, because there were no other small sea-worthy boats we could get, and because a Norwegian boat, we believed, could pass with luck under German eyes as a peaceful fishing boat. For much the same reasons, we would have to use Norwegian crews. Another fact was that the crossings could only be made in winter, because so far north it is daylight all night in summer, and you cannot make secret landings on a hostile coast in daylight. The shortest crossing there and back was 360 miles, and some were likely to be a thousand or even two. The winter seas north of Shetland are some of the roughest in the world. This made the enterprise unique: nobody in history had ever deliberately made such long voyages in such small boats and on such stormy seas. Even the Vikings sailed in summer. So did the Biblical sailors of the Mediterranean and most of the explorers in later centuries. The Germans were going to do all they could to stop us, but the greatest danger was going to be the weather.

Before I arrived, Bob had already acquired an office in Lerwick (which was the only town in Shetland and the only operating harbour) with two British sergeants and a civilian cipher clerk. He was living in a large house about ten miles away with the old Norse name of Kergord or the modern English name of Flemington, and at first I lived with him there. The plan was to use Flemington as a house where agents could live incommunicado while they were waiting to cross to Norway. We urgently needed somewhere else as well: a very well-sheltered harbour for six or eight boats, with a building for fifty or sixty crewmen (and me) to live ashore – preferably a place where the boats could come and go without being seen by anyone, not even the navy, the army or the coastguards.

We spent most of the long light evenings that summer looking for it. It was a perfectly delightful occupation with a congenial companion. We drove or walked to deserted bays and coves (called *voes* and *geos* in Shetland). Some had a cottage or two at the head of them, where kind ladies gave us tea and bannocks, some had nothing at all except the birds which dive-bombed us, and the seals which flopped off the rocks when we came very near and watched us, mildly surprised, from the water. For weeks we could not find anything that would do. All the bays were open to gales from one direction or another. Some were shallow, or full of rocks. Most were inaccessible from the land, and would have needed miles and miles of new road. None had anywhere so many men could live ashore. We thought of building a camp, but time was getting short, or of chartering an old passenger steamer and using it as a base ship, but that would have been conspicuous from the air and asking for trouble.

It was August before we visited a place called Lunna. We had often seen it on the maps and charts, but always turned it down because it was twenty-five miles from Lerwick or anywhere else. I fell for it as soon as I went there. It had a small land-locked harbour, invisible from the sea, with a stone pier, only half-ruined, where the boats could lie alongside at half tide. Above on the hillside was a large, gaunt, grey house, empty but furnished, with outbuildings that would do as stores, and there were no other buildings in sight except two cottages, a small, very old church and a lot of even older ruins which might have been a monastery in the time of St Columba. It was just the sort of place the Celtic monks would have chosen; beautiful, austere and so remote that it seemed not to be part of the world of men. It even had a road. It was not a very good road: the last four or five miles were only a farm track, partly founded on peat and partly on rock, and when we brought loaded trucks along it, you could see the peaty bits subside three or four inches and spring up behind like a feather bed. But none of our trucks fell through. Indeed, it was the perfect smugglers' haunt of old-fashioned fiction; John Buchan, on whom I was brought up, might have invented it. We found the family who owned it – they lived in another more accessible part of Shetland – and rented it all – house, furniture, harbour, pier, and a huge but vague extent of heather, cliffs and shore – for £3 a week. And the Post Office put up, I think, seven miles of new poles to give us a telephone.

I lived at Lunna all through that winter, and at intervals after that, and I always loved it. It was on the east coast of Shetland, the right side for Norway, but the house faced west, across a narrow isthmus towards the Shetland hills. It was most easily loved, of course, on calm sunny days, which were rare; but I loved it too when horizontal rain or snow was driving in across the isthmus from right to left or left to right, and even when the wind reached hurricane level, force 12, and stately columns of sea spray marched up and over the hills and the solid stone house shuddered and the gusts raised the slates on the roof and slammed them down again with a noise like a herd of animals stampeding from end to end. But forty or fifty other men had to live with me there, and to tell the truth not many of them liked it. Most lived in places in Norway that were equally remote, but being so far from home they needed urban delights from time to time and we had to take them in trucks for a night out in Lerwick, where Bob often had to rescue them from the police the morning after.

All the men and boats arrived there together one evening late in August: six very good boats that we had chosen, with endless advice from Norwegians, from the hundreds that came in from Norway that summer bringing refugees; and about forty-five men who had been recruited in London as civilian volunteers, mostly fishermen but some merchant seamen. They had been told they could choose their own skippers from among themselves, and so they did – and only once made a mistake, when they chose a man who failed in what they expected of a skipper, whereupon they instantly deposed him and would have no more to do with him.

At first they were dressed in whatever old clothes they had. Later, we procured Norwegian naval uniforms for them, because it was thought that if they were captured in uniform they would have a better chance of being treated as prisoners of war, and not shot as spies. They expressed their democracy by insisting that they should all have the same uniform, skippers and the rest; and they expressed their dislike of any sort of discipline by not wearing the whole of the uniform at once – either uniform trousers and a civilian top, or the other way round. In fact, I do not think the uniform made much difference. Some in uniform were shot, and some in civilian clothes were only imprisoned. Not many were captured, however. It was not their job to fight, but to make their landings in secret, which above all meant avoiding a fight; if they were caught they fought to the death or sometimes escaped overland.

Before we were settled at Lunna, London was on to us to start operations, and early in September the first boat was ready. She was called *Aksel*, and was typical of the best sort of Norwegian fishing boat, which is built around Alesund: sixty-five feet long, with the crew's cabin forward, the skipper's cabin aft, a capacious hold in the middle, and a single-cylinder, semi-diesel engine. This is the simplest kind of engine ever built, with only three major moving parts – an engine which with luck will run non-stop for months, and makes a very loud and solemn tonk-tonk-tonk from its exhaust pipe – a nostalgic sound to anyone who knows the Norwegian coast. *Aksel*'s skipper at that moment was a young fisherman called August Naeroy, who had a crew of five. The first job was as simple as any: to land a messenger just north of Bergen who was to get in touch with a party of ex-army officers who were starting up a sabotage cell in the city, give them some money and tell them we had a cargo of eight tons of weapons and explosives ready to send to them. We were to pick him up a week later.

That was the first time I had been mixed up with fitting out an SOE agent, and like most people I started with an innocent enjoyment. That soon gave way to admiration for the agents' courage, combined with a cynical belief that most of the gear they were given might have been invented by grown-up schoolboys playing at spies. Who, for just one example, thought of giving this man a stock of cigarettes specially manufactured by Players with no name on the paper but which instantly identified themselves as British at the first puff of smoke? And why did I spend a whole day unsoldering a very big tin of Norwegian tobacco, stuffing it full of banknotes and soldering it up again? Nevertheless, off he went to the enemy-occupied country, and it was an emotional moment for all of us when

Aksel tonk-tonked out of Lunna in the dark, and sounded the V-sign on her siren.

She might have been back in three days, but by the evening of the fourth day there was no sign of her. Bob and I grew anxious. So many things might have gone wrong. She might have infringed some German regulation (they were always changing them), or run into a watchpost we had not yet recorded; the men from Bergen might have been arrested or, most likely of all, I might have forgotten or neglected something essential. Bob went down to the RAF station at the airfield and asked them to have a look, and they willingly diverted two Blenheims to search her track. One of the pilots said he had sighted her, still off Norway, and the crew had waved to him. That cheered us up for a moment; but when we came to think of it, it was far from conclusive. He had not seen the registration number painted on her bows (a false one which I had painted) and the crew of any Norwegian fishing boat would have waved to a British aircraft out at sea. But next day they sent another aircraft, and that one reported her halfway home, and going strong. And after a week I heard her engine coming in to Lunna.

When she came round the corner of the bay, she was decorated with heather and boughs of birch. That did not look like a sign of distress, and indeed she had not been in any distress at all. August told me they had waited all day offshore in the fishing zone the Germans permitted. The weather was clear but nobody took any notice of them, so when it was dark they went in to their rendezvous, where they met not only the right men but also the local girls, who welcomed them rightly as heroes and came on board for a feast of white bread and real coffee, and told them there was a dance the next evening in the village. So they waited for the dance, and then waited another day just because they were enjoying themselves. That taught me never to worry unless I had something definite to worry about – which God knows, as the winter came on, was often enough.

For me, the loneliness of Lunna was a double blessing; hardly anyone ever came to bother me there, and I was left to run the place in the only way I knew. Bob came, of course, from time to time, and I was always very glad to see him – somebody I could talk to without any secrets or reservations, somebody who laughed at the same jokes and who always believed, whatever happened, that I was doing my best and doing it reasonably well. Only once in the whole of that winter did I see a naval officer. One of the boats was grounded at the head of the pier, and I was standing underneath it up to my knees in the sea, wearing seaboots and a fisherman's trousers and sweater. I have forgotten what I was doing there – probably caulking a seam, with my hair full of anti-fouling paint. 'Ovart,' said the Norwegian who was with me, 'how long is it since you saw an admiral?'

'A long time,' I said. 'I keep clear of them.'

'Well, don't look now,' he said, 'but there's one behind you.'

So I looked, and there was: a large British admiral, who shouted in the loud voice we use for talking to foreigners: 'Can you tell me where I can find a naval officer called Howarth?'

It took a bit of explaining; naval officers seldom do what I was doing, or dress as I was dressed. When he was convinced, he said, 'I hear you have a sort of private navy here. D'you mind if I have a look?' I asked him on board the boat.

There was quite a lot to show him, especially the boat's guns. Our boats' first line of defence was always to look innocent, and hitherto they had been armed only with hand-held machine guns, which sometimes did more damage to the crew than anybody else. But I had just designed, and we had made, some hidden mountings for stripped Lewis guns. They were in oil drums, ostentatiously lashed to the gunwales, a common sight in fishing boats. But these drums had the tops neatly sawn off. A determined tug pulled off the tops and the twin guns, ready loaded, sprang up to the firing position – they had a counterweight in the hold underneath. The drums were lined with concrete and a steel shield unfolded as the guns came up, which gave the gunner at least some feeling of protection. I must say these mountings worked very well. They were never detected, and were often used in action. But some of the skippers, I knew, wanted something heavier too – specifically, half-inch Colts.

I also wanted the Admiral to meet the skipper, a man called Bard Grotle – roughly pronounced Board Grotley. He was one of our most successful skippers, though he did not look it: a tall, handsome, Viking sort of young man, with a twinkle in his bright blue eyes, who was especially allergic to uniform. He sometimes wore parts of it, but always, whatever he was doing, he wore a battered and filthy Trilby hat on his curly blonde hair, and we all liked him very much. I once asked him if he slept in his hat. 'Of course,' he said, 'then when I get up I'm ready dressed for dinner.' He never did get up until dinner-time unless he had to.

So I called down to his cabin that we had a visitor, and he came up, tousled and wearing his hat. I had never seen him surprised before.

'My God,' he said, 'what's he? A big shot, eh? Ovart, he can get us Colts.'

'Better ask him,' I said.

'*Du*, Admiral,' Bard shouted (he always shouted), 'we want Colts. Must have Colts. Them Lewises is fine for aircraft, but Colts shoot holes in them damned Jerry trawlers. You get us Colts, eh? You know, half-inch. Machine guns. Tat-tat-tat.'

I rescued the Admiral when I thought it was time, and took him up to the house. I wanted to give him a drink, but all we had was a bottle of Norwegian brandy, made of potatoes. He sipped it decorously, and I managed to go to the telephone to ask Mitchell if this was a genuine admiral. It was. 'Nice surprise for you,' Bob said. 'More of a surprise for him,' I said. 'He's met Bård.'

'Splendid. Give him the works.'

He was a very good admiral, I thought, and explaining things to him cleared up my own mind on what I was doing and why. I do not remember exactly what I said. I told him you cannot *tell* fishermen what to do, you have to persuade them; they are brought up to be independent. And these fishermen in particular were entirely on their own when they were at sea or in Norway. So neither Mitchell nor I, nor anyone else, could *tell* them to do a particular operation, or how to do it. We could only consult the skippers and suggest how it might be done, and if they did not like it they had to be free to say so.

In practice, Mitchell and I filtered London's requests and did not pass them on unless we could think of a way of doing them with tolerable risk, and the few times we disagreed with the skippers was when we thought they were willing to risk too much. And of course we all learned from experience. Picking people up, for example, was always more risky than landing them, because the party waiting for a pick-up might have been captured or tracked; and when we had to make a pick-up it was always safer for the people on shore to make their own way to the outer islands than for our boats to go right into the fjords.

Life was made more difficult, especially for me at the sharpish end of things at Lunna, because I was never allowed to go with them. Nobody would have expected Mitchell to go, because he was not a sailor, but I was, and naval officers are expected to share in dangers. I proposed it to London sometimes, but there were unanswerable arguments against it. I took care to know as little as possible about events in Norway, but I could not help knowing too much: enough to break up many good organizations and send many good men to the firing squad. Nobody was trusted to keep his secrets if the Gestapo really got to work on him, and I certainly could not trust myself.

Furthermore, our crews sometimes had to escape overland, mixing with the local people, and when I heard their stories I knew they could not have done it with an Englishman who spoke Norwegian with an obvious English accent, as I did. I knew they would have taken me, but it was simply not on. So it was my job, not entirely enviable, to stay in safety at Lunna and patiently get the crews everything they wanted or thought they wanted, starting with the best possible boats and all the hoard of information we collected about the German defences, then to see them off and then to wait, day after day and night after night, for them to come back, which was always anxious and sometimes tragic, because sometimes they did not come back at all.

At the time I was perfectly certain I was doing it in the best way, but now, more than forty years later, I am not so sure. Was it perhaps that I subconsciously tailored the job to suit my own shortcomings? Was I really lacking in Officer-Like Qualities, lacking the guts to put my foot down and make unpopular decisions? I don't really think so, but I suspect myself.

However, that excellent Admiral agreed with me. 'Most extraordinary set-up I ever saw,' he said – we must have been talking for hours. 'And you seem to have chosen the most difficult way to run it. But I do understand. I think it's the only way. Bård, for example. Excellent fellow, I took to him greatly. Now you tell me he cons that boat around in enemy waters and thinks nothing of it. That's all we ask of a naval captain. You can't put a man like that under discipline as a rating as soon as he comes ashore. It would break his spirit, and that's what matters. You'd have a mutiny on your hands too, and that wouldn't get the job done. No, self-discipline, willingness, enthusiasm, that's what you must depend on. To hell with spit and polish. Now, is there anything I can do for you? What about some navy rum for a start?' He looked at his half-empty glass.

'Rum would be better,' I said. 'I couldn't keep it here, though; it'd need an armed guard. Mitchell could lock it up in Lerwick.'

'And what about these Colts; is that a good idea?'

'I think it is, sir, if I can think of a way of hiding them on board. And I've got some ideas. I always try to get them everything they want, if it's reasonable. And if it's not, I have to explain why not. It's their job to keep out of trouble, but they can't always. The least predictable troubles at present are aircraft at sea and armed trawlers in the fjords. It would be a comfort to think they might see off a trawler.'

'Well, I'll see what I can do,' he said. 'Anything else?'

'There will be,' I said. 'They're always thinking of something new, and so am I. Sooner or later, for one thing, there's going to be an emergency at sea — either aircraft or weather — and then we shall wish we had some simple sort of ship-to-shore radio.'

'A bit difficult,' he said. 'But you certainly ought to have it. Would you use your organization or ours?'

'I don't know, sir. That's more Mitchell's job.'

'I'll talk to him, and fix something.'

'Rum, Colts, radio,' he said as he got into his car. 'When you come to think of anything else, just send me a signal. Dammit, you young fellows have all the fun.'

I had found my cap by then and I managed a salute, and meant it.

The three things arrived with miraculous speed, plus an expert to teach men we chose from the crews to use the radio, and an arrangement to pass their signals through the fleet's monitoring station. I was kept happy for a while disguising a Colt as a harpoon gun on the bows of each boat, and another on a special dwarf mounting which we made in the net pond on the stern, where it could be hidden under fishing nets. With two Colts, four Lewises and a gun held in the hands of any spare enthusiast the boats still looked innocent, but could throw up a very respectable display of tracer if they had to.

I think the lowest ebb of our fortunes was at the end of October. For the first two months, we had been running three times as many crossings as we had been led to expect, and the meagre shore staff was exhausted – Mitchell and I and the faithful and extremely English sergeants. One boat had been ambushed and captured – the crew were not shot, we learned later, but imprisoned; another, called *Nordsjön*, 'North Sea', with a crew of seven, was three weeks overdue; and we had just had our first death: in a fight against aircraft at sea, the very young man who was standing at the wheel was killed, and on a calm frosty morning we buried him in the little old churchyard below the house. Thirteen of the forty-odd men were captured, killed or missing, and on the same day we had a visitation from some army staff officers from the headquarters in London.

Bob Mitchell and I did not enjoy those visits. They were never a happy occasion like the Admiral's. Luckily, they were rare. Some of those men understood what we were up against but others, we thought, never understood it at all; for one thing, they were never there in a storm, and you have to see a Shetland storm to believe it. They were interested in our superficial appearance. I was ticked off because the house at Lunna and the crews and I were untidy. I think if any of them had asked me, I would have said we could not go on. We could either keep the house tidy or run trips to Norway, but not both; and I doubted too if we ought to ask more crews to sail, at least until we knew what had happened to the boat that was missing.

But Bob was more tactful, and the crews' courage, it turned out, had not faltered in the least. At the very gloomiest moment, when Bob and I were walking up from the fresh grave to the house, one man came and told him he had taken a fancy to a boat called the *Olaf*, the smallest we had in reserve. Could he fit her out and skipper her himself?

'Certainly,' Bob said. 'If you can find a crew.'

'I've done that already,' he said.

That was a man called Per Blystad, or Pete. He had not long arrived, and he was much better educated than most of the men – a civil engineer, I think. He did fit out the *Olaf*, adding many inventions of his own, and made several crossings in her; he would have become a great skipper, but he was captured, by sheer bad luck, on an operation he had devised himself, and the Germans imprisoned him, then shot him.

Meanwhile, he brought a ray of hope that dismal morning, and at dusk that same afternoon I heard the sound I had listened for for so long, the tonk-tonk of a Norwegian engine coming in from the sea. I and a lot of other people ran down to the pier.

'It can't be the *Nordsjön*,' I said to Bob. 'She'd be out of fuel long ago.'

'But nobody else is out,' he said.

The boat came round the corner of the bay. We saw the masts first, then the bow. 'It's not one of ours,' I said, 'but it must be our men. Who else knows the way in here?'

And it was. But as she came to the pier there were only five men on deck, not seven. The skipper and one other man were missing.

They told me their story sleepily that night. They had been driven ashore in a gale and shipwrecked, and their skipper and the other man had abandoned the rest on an island. They deposed him then and there and chose another, Leif Larsen. Larsen led them 250 miles across the fjords and mountains to a place he knew, where he successfully stole the new boat, which was called *Arthur*.

Leif became the most amazingly skilful, brave and successful of all our skippers. He survived through it all, and he was the man who won more British naval medals than anyone else has ever had: the Conspicuous Gallantry Medal, the DSM and bar, the DSC and the DSO. He would have got the VC too, but he could not because he was a foreigner.

The next day, when the staff officers were safely in their plane, Bob rang me: 'Well, sod the lot,' he said inelegantly. 'Relax, David. Go on as you are. Be yourself. It's *status quo ante*, and they promised me all the army trucks and drivers we want.'

So the trucks and cars and drivers began to arrive. Bob and I were also joined by another officer, a major of Royal Marines whom people knew as Arthur Rogers (Rogers was not his name at all, but he adopted it because his wife was Norwegian and her family were still in Oslo). A few months later, Bob was promoted and recalled to London. For some time, Arthur and I did not know which of us was to be made CO of the base. When Bob told me it was Arthur I had a moment's disappointment, but I soon admitted to myself it was right. The only thing I knew I was good at was keeping the boats in good condition, and keeping the crews contented, and sharing with the skippers the practical problems of pilotage for each expedition. Those made much more than a full-time job, they were what I liked doing, and somebody had to do them. In every other way, Arthur was a much better officer than I was. I still had the doubt, ever growing, as to whether I could be tough with anyone, and I did not want to have to try. I would never have liked to be ordered about, so I did not want to order anyone else about. I always missed Bob with his idiosyncratic sense of humour, but we settled down happily again, Arthur mainly at Flemington and Lerwick (as Bob had been), and I mainly at Lunna with the crews.

Most of them could be intensely irritating, and living alone with them at Lunna it was sometimes a strain to be sympathetic. But one had to make allowances. Norwegian fishermen were rather helpless ashore in a foreign country, and I was the man who had to bandage their minor hurts, soothe their wounded feelings, put them to bed when they were drunk and revive them next day, write the reports of their journeys, and persuade them at least to help me to do unpopular jobs ashore. If you do all those things for a gang of men, you probably come to hate them or love them, and on the whole, most of the time, I loved them, which was just as well; but it was also what made it so hard when they vanished.

We nearly always heard what had happened when they did not come back, either through broken German codes or through rumours on the coast. I think only one boat vanished with no explanation at all. But often the explanations were not complete, and one of those was the fate of Bård Grotle, the man the Admiral had liked. Bård had taken over the *Aksel* and was on his way back from a landing in the far north, on the Arctic circle nine hundred miles away, when one morning we got a signal on his radio: only five groups. The first four gave a position two hundred miles north of Shetland, the last said simply 'Send help'. Two of our boats set off at once but it was twenty-four hours' steaming for them so we asked the navy to send a fast motor torpedo boat, and asked the RAF for aircraft. A Catalina aircraft and the MTB were in the area that afternoon, but saw nothing. It was not rough for our fishing boats, but too rough for the MTB, which had to limp back in the night. Next day more Catalinas were sent and one of them found her: *Aksel* just afloat with her gunwales awash and the crew in their lifeboat and a rubber raft. Our fishing boats should not have been far away but visibility was poor and the aircraft could not find them; and the sea was too rough for it to come down and take off again. While they watched her just before dark, the *Aksel* sank.

We had not asked the Admiral for help because the navy had no other ships in Shetland, but when he heard what had happened a destroyer came up flat out from Scapa Flow to Bård's position. The search went on for three more days, but the men in the boat were never seen again.

It was awful to have to admit that Bård was dead, that the laughter we knew so well was silenced and the blue eyes sightless. Some of the men refused to admit it, and believed for weeks, against all reason, that he had rowed to Norway and would turn up again. Yet we never knew what sank the *Aksel*. She might possibly have hit some massive wreckage half-submerged, or, less likely, a floating mine that was still alive; or a German aircraft might have dropped a lucky bomb or a depth-charge which blew the bottom out of her. But if so, we would have expected to hear a German signal. Whatever it was, it was so sudden that she had time to send only the shortest signal, and to send it only once. I still dream of that moment, when, I suppose, the lifeboat foundered, and Bård knew his luck had run out and he was drowning. So it was with many friends that winter. We had started with forty-five men, and we lost forty-two. We finished with sixty because there were always willing volunteers.

It was not all disaster, however; far from it. We ran the fishing boats for two winters, made over eighty successful crossings to Norway, landed nearly a hundred agents and 250 tons of weapons and ammunition and I don't know how many radio transmitters. We also rescued some hundreds of people who were all more or less in trouble with the Gestapo. Most important of all, perhaps, we were a link with the outside world which did a lot to keep the hopes of Norwegians alive. They always knew that if they were in a very desperate state, there was a chance they could 'take the Shetland Bus'.

In the summer between those two winters, the summer of 1942, we moved our main base to the village of Scalloway, keeping Lunna for a few extra-secret operations. We had chosen Lunna at the beginning so that only very few Shetlanders, and nobody else, would see what we were doing. But those few always walked past Lunna with their eyes averted and had been so discreet that we gave up worrying. Besides, after that first winter, everyone in Norway knew what we were doing and the Germans knew it too. So the only thing that still had to be kept secret was the exact place in Norway where each boat was going. Only the skipper, the cipher staff, Arthur and I had to know that, and it was a secret as easy to keep in a village as anywhere else.

Personally, I missed the remoteness and beauty of Lunna, but Scalloway was a friendly little place, and much more practical; and at least, if I ever had nothing to do, I could walk on the hills all round, each with its marvellous seascape, or take myself out alone in a small boat to uninhabited islands, and choose a site for a hut and day-dream endlessly of hermits. The move did not make any difference to our curious status. It still remained a do-it-yourself operation, what the Admiral (not I) had called a private navy. We began to get what I especially needed: very good Norwegian shipwrights, and engineers from the factory in Norway that made those remarkable engines. We invaded and more or less took over an old-established local engineering workshop, and installed the shipwrights' tools and machinery in a disused fish store. We built ourselves a slipway out of bits and pieces – an engine out of a wrecked Norwegian boat, a winch that we found on the top of a hill in Fair Isle, and rails discarded from some kind of tramway in Aberdeen. We heard the army had brought up a big water tower from Scotland and then found they did not need it, so we persuaded them to lose it, and we cut it all up and welded it together again to make ourselves a 150-foot pier. I loved doing that sort of thing, though the first time we hauled a boat up on to the slipway I could hardly bear to watch, having designed it all on the basis of school mathematics.

Soon there was no job we could not do on a fishing boat, except foundry work. It was Per Blystad who found a way out of that. When we needed large castings, say cylinder heads, which were impossibly expensive to make in England, he ordered them from the German-run factory, brought us the bill, and then went back to pay for them and collect them. Some pedants said that could land us in gaol for trading with the enemy, but we liked breaking silly laws.

The voyages grew more dangerous all the time, partly because we goaded the Germans into making a vast and expensive system of coastal defences, and partly – perhaps mainly – because like all the countries the Germans occupied, Norway ran short of oil, so that big fishing boats had to stop fishing. Robbed of their merit of disguise there was no real point in our using fishing boats, and we all simultaneously began to want warships.

That was not easy. What we needed was very unusual: boats faster than the armed trawlers the Germans used in defence – doing, say, 15 knots; seaworthy enough for hurricanes; armed to the teeth yet quiet; and small enough to put in to fishing village harbours in the dark and lie alongside their quays. I knew the navy, for all its magnificence, had nothing with all those qualities, and I could not imagine anyhow that the Admiralty would give us British warships without British crews. Yet our own crews could do the job in Norway better than anyone. With two years' experience, they knew the coastline – not only geographically, they personally knew hundreds of trustworthy Norwegians who lived on the islands, the few who were not trustworthy, and scores of safe houses, barns and caves for hiding themselves or their cargoes of arms. But there was a snag. Whatever ship they had, they absolutely refused to join a navy, not ours and even less their own Norwegian navy. They insisted on remaining buccaneers.

Leif Larsen in particular did not want to be a naval officer. We had many good skippers, and Leif – who had been chosen by his crew marooned on an island and had led them overland and successfully stolen the *Arthur* – was always our Francis

Drake. He had a genuinely Drake-like genius for remaining calm in the most desperate tight corners, discerning the only conceivable way out of them for himself and his crew, and taking it. He had been hove-to in a hurricane for a week. He had stood, unscratched, while his wheelhouse was shot to small pieces all round him and all his crew except two were badly wounded, and then had rowed them for six days, not to the nearest land but to the nearest he thought they could escape from. He had talked his way through the German controls right into the German fleet anchorage at Trondheim, towing two special torpedoes under water with six English submariners hidden in a double bulkhead – my masterpiece of disguise and of his cold-blooded courage. I greatly admired his genuine bravery, and his equally genuine humility. I was often with him in company that ranged from his own crown prince to the humblest of Shetlanders, and he was always himself with them all, quiet, soft-spoken and self-effacing. I am glad to say he was a good friend of mine.

It went without saying in our gang that if we could get a warship, Leif would be its skipper. But a warship would have to carry naval cyphers and recognition signals which were only issued to officers and Leif was adamant: he would not go on an officers' training course. Indeed it would have been ludicrous to send him on the sort of course I had done. He and I made a private bargain: if I could find a warship, he would be skipper and I would go along with him just to provide the gold braid. I thought London might stand for that, but luckily we did not have to try.

I searched through the Admiralty lists in London and travelled around in England and Scotland looking at minesweepers (too slow), MTBs (not seaworthy), fishery protection ships (too big), large motor yachts (unreliable) and even, I remember, an ice-breaker; but there was absolutely nothing in Britain that would do. Summer was passing, and we began to think we would have to give up and Norway would have to be cut off again.

Suddenly in August somebody – I do not know who – pressed the right button. Admiral Harold R. Stark, Commander-in-Chief of the US Naval Forces in Europe, heard of our problem and said (I was told), 'Send 'em two or three of our sub-chasers. Just the thing for the job.' Within days, three 110-foot US Navy sub-chasers left Miami for New York and were loaded on the decks of merchant ships, with their complete crews of three officers and twenty-three men each, and shipped to the Clyde. I went down there to meet them, followed a few days later by most of our crews. When our men came off the train I found the holiday atmosphere of the journey had been too much for them, and most, to put it the best way I can, were drunk as newts. Thank goodness it was dark. We had to march from the railway station to the American naval base. They had never marched before, and I think they did it as badly as they could, just to show they were not naval ratings. They looked like a crowd of football fans whose team had won an away match.

It was lucky they did not meet the American crews that night. To the Americans the whole of Britain was a 'combat zone', and they had come all the way from Miami to the Clyde believing they were some sort of suicide squad. Next morning our crews were quite different, as sober as bishops and desperately eager to show they could master these elegant, complex and unfamiliar ships, which looked like the chicks of destroyers. The Americans took the anti-climax well.

Sub-chasers could not have been a bigger change from fishing boats. They were twice as long and three times as fast – 22 knots – and they had every imaginable gadget and comfort for the crews: central heating, an oil-fired galley, refrigerators and ice-water fountains, wine lockers, hot and cold showers, electric toasters, three typewriters each, fur-lined boots and coats and a variety of funny hats. Each of them had two 1200 h.p. engines, the only ones of their kind in Europe. To be technical for a moment, they were 16-cylinder two-stroke supercharged diesels. They had been designed as diesel aircraft engines but were over-taken by jets and converted for boats by turning them up on end, with the crankshafts vertical and bevel gears at the bottom to drive electrically-operated variable pitch propellers. The engines and propellers were controlled from the helmsman's comfortable chair on the bridge. Each ship, I remember very well, had forty-two assorted electric motors for us to maintain, and each sea-going fishing boat engineer had thirty-two cylinders to look after instead of one.

I never doubted Admiral Stark was right: they were just the

thing for the job, marvellously reliable and perfectly seaworthy. I never doubted either that our crews could run them at sea and in Norway. I did doubt whether I and my little squad of Norwegian shipwrights and engineers could maintain them. But nobody else expressed the slightest doubt, so I kept my mouth shut and we proved we could, by doing it. We did more, we improved them. We took them to Scalloway after a week with the Americans, and it was a great day when we all steamed in line ahead and the whole village turned out to have a discreet look. Then, with no one to watch, we got to work. We extended our homemade slipway to haul them up, and fitted silencers, radar, electric logs, echo sounders, davits to hoist our dinghies and a forest of guns. They already had Bofors cannon in the bows. We added two twin Oerlikon cannon in power mountings amidships and a quick-firing two pounder aft – what the sailing navy would have called a stern-chaser; and for old times' sake we put two half-inch Colts on the upper bridge. With all that, they could not only outrun but outfight anything German they were likely to meet among the islands of Norway. The open sea, as ever, was empty of shipping, and when German aircraft sighted them out there they kept a respectful distance.

So the sub-chasers brought a host of fascinating technical problems, but they solved many more. The Norwegian navy gave up arguing about Leif and gave him a sub-lieutenant's uniform without any training course, and they did the same for one of the other skippers. To command the third ship, a Norwegian officer joined us. As for the British navy, I think they had always regarded us with a kind of amused admiration, and they went on doing the same. They always helped us when we asked for their help – for example, they gave us the guns and other gear – but even when we were running quite formidable warships in their ocean, they never claimed any say in what we did. In their eyes, we were still a private navy.

It needed a lot of skill to pilot the ships in the blacked-out fjords at night, but it was infinitely safer than it had been in fishing boats. During the last winter and a half of the war, we beat the number of successful fishing boat landings, and did it without a single casualty.

Of course it did not end as we had always half-expected, with a re-invasion of Norway or an armed rebellion, and for Norway's sake I am glad that never happened. What it did do was to hold down a German garrison of 284,000 men all through the invasion of France and Germany itself; and the surrender of that enormous force was accepted by Norwegians with weapons we had sent from Lunna or Scalloway.

In Shetland, it did end in the sort of way I might have expected. I don't think our gang of amiable buccaneers ever drank at sea, but on shore they were always ready to celebrate anything. In the morning of VE day, the crew of one sub-chaser, on the far side of the harbour, began their celebration by firing their Bofors gun. Hastening out, I saw the stream of shells landing on the hillside above, to the consternation of the sheep. Some were going over the top, to land heaven knows where. What worried me more was that one of the sub-chasers – it was Leif's – was on the slipway, and I knew its crew would follow the example. I did not know, nobody did, what would happen if you fired a Bofors on a boat that was propped up on dry land. It might have wrecked the whole thing. Worse, an old lady lived in a cottage across the road, about ten yards from the gun, and it would certainly have blown in her windows, perhaps have blown off her roof, possibly even given her a heart attack.

Sure enough, when I got there they were drunkenly loading the gun. 'Ovart, come and have a drink,' they shouted merrily. I knew them well, and knew it was useless to tell them to stop. The only possible thing was to out-drink them. I had never had a good head for drink, but those years had taught me all a barman's tricks and I stayed on my feet until they were far beyond remembering how to fire a gun. I saw them safely tucked up in their bunks, and then staggered home and put myself to bed, feeling very ill but also feeling, for once, that my qualities had been Officer-Like.

And as ever, when the time came to sail they were sober again. Some time that night we got Leif safely off the slipway, and all three sub-chasers sailed again for Norway. Openly at last, two of them went into Bergen and one into Alesund. They were the first Norwegian or British ships to reach Norway, and the rejoicing, I believe, was phenomenal.

Looking back from this very long distance in time, I think we did some good. We helped Norway a bit to win back its peace and pride. We helped a small but perceptible bit to push back the evil dominion of Nazism. Like anyone pitched into an active part of a war, we were left with friends to grieve for. But we certainly saved more lives than we destroyed, and that is the only bearable recollection one can have of war.

As for me, I think it does anyone good to have to cope with matters of life and death when he is young. I am sure it helped me not to exaggerate the importance of my own life, or my own death. But that does not go far to excuse the wickedness of war.

ELEVEN

Stuck in the Mud

That Shetland episode had offshoots, during the summers when we could not operate and were only busy getting ready for the next winter. I particularly remember one because it was so macabre, another because it is comic to look back on but was terrifying at the time, and a third because it seemed to me sheer lunacy.

The macabre one happened at a fishing village called Burghead, on the east coast of Scotland, where for a time we kept a subsidiary base, for boats and crews in reserve. An army captain was in charge of it, and one summer's day, with two Norwegians, he hired a small open sailing boat just for recreation, in the neighbouring village of Findhorn. They set off to sail it back to Burghead, about five miles away, and they disappeared. So I was sent there to find out what had happened, and to look after the base until somebody could decide what to do with it.

Three weeks went by. It was obvious, whatever had happened, that the boat and the three men were never coming back. Then the police in Findhorn rang me up and said a body had been found: could I come and identify it? 'Tis oot on the sand,' they said. So I drove there in a small van, and took with me the sergeant-major from the base, partly for company and partly because – though I knew the captain quite well – I only knew one of the missing Norwegians by sight.

Findhorn Sands are banks of sand and stones offshore which are covered at high tide and cut off as islands at low tide. It was early dusk when we got there, and the tide was rising. The body had been found by two fishermen, I was told, and they would row me out to see it and to bring it in.

That was all very well, but with nightfall heavy fog was coming

155

in from the sea, and the fishermen turned out to be identical twins, both of them deaf and dumb. Very soon, the harbour of Findhorn was invisible, and soon after I understood that the two mutes were not quite sure where they had seen the body, and were also disagreeing about where we were ourselves. They communed with each other in loud grunts, and pointed in opposite directions, and when one rowed ahead with determination the other dug his oar in and turned the boat round. There was no wind, the sea was still and, except for the grunts and the squeak of the oars and the tiny eddies as the tide came up among the seaweed, the place was dead quiet.

It was an experience I would not recommend to anyone, to be lost in Findhorn Sands looking for a very dead body, night coming on, the cold wet fog growing thicker, the tide rising, piloted in a rickety boat by two identical angry mutes who were lost and did not even have a compass. The sergeant-major's knees were visibly knocking together.

It was nearly dark when both the oarsmen began to point the same way, and confidently ran the boat aground. We clambered out. One of them led us stumbling through the seaweed and the other stayed with the boat; that at least showed a gleam of sense in their poor bewildered minds, because when we had gone twenty yards the boat was invisible.

Any corpse is a rather shocking mess after three weeks in the sea among the crabs and lobsters, but this was certainly the captain's. We carried it to the boat, still draped in seaweed, guided by wordless bellows from the man who had stayed to watch, and we tumbled it in and pushed off again. The feet were bare, which made me think the boat had sunk and he had tried to swim ashore, and landed perhaps on that island and thought he was safe; but when the tide rose the island vanished. That led to morbid thoughts of our own boat, which was decrepit, patched and overloaded. I have often been glad to see harbour, but never more than I was that night when torches loomed through the fog and we found two policemen waiting for us.

I thought the ordeal was over then, but there was more to come. I was the only one who had a van, and they moved the passenger seat and pushed the body in feet first through the door at the back. The smell inside the van was bad, and nobody volunteered to come with me. They told me the way to the mortuary: 'Ye canna miss it.' But I took a wrong turning in the dark and fog and blackout, and got lost in the maze of what seemed to be a housing estate. I saw nobody there except middle-aged ladies towing their children. You cannot stop in a housing estate with a mutilated corpse beside you and ask a harmless housewife the way to the morgue: at least, I didn't think you could. I drove around with my cargo a very long time indeed before I came back to the harbour where I had started and tried again.

The tragic part came later. The captain's wife turned up, and asked me if she could see his body. I had been shocked to see it, and I told her I thought she had better not. Heaven knows why that decision was left to me. I knew nothing about the psychology of wives, or the cosmetic jobs that undertakers do. Anyone else would have been better – a doctor, the local lawyer or minister, perhaps, or the police. But she seemed to take my advice quite willingly, and we gave him the best military funeral we could manage. In peace, there would have been an inquest, but not in war.

Then she began to insist, poor woman, that the man we had buried was not her husband. He was not drowned. I was mistaken, so was the sergeant-major, and nobody else who knew him had seen the body. Or, she said on second thoughts, we were both in a plot and deliberately lying to her. It was very wrong to tell cruel lies and to try to hide what she knew had really happened: a German submarine had come in and kidnapped him and taken him to Germany, and dumped the body I had seen.

Almost anything was possible in the kind of life we led, but not that. Yet I began, as usual, to doubt myself. Was it possible? What if the captain had been a double agent, a much cleverer man than I thought he was? Had he given a hint to his wife? Something depressingly similar had happened to me before. One of our boats from Lunna had been captured, and the signal that told me so was followed by another, 'Most Immediate', to say I must not tell anyone whatever. But the skipper's wife was at Lunna, helping in the house, and I had to hide what I knew for a fortnight, while she grew more anxious and tearful day by day. I hated it, but I did not know the source of the information and

I supposed many lives might depend on it, so I did as I was told.

This time, it was my own eyes that were being questioned. I had been perfectly certain it was the captain – but it had been the briefest possible glance, in the dusk and fog. If I had thought that anyone might doubt it, I would have dragged in other people to confirm what I had seen, but now it was too late. It is a disagreeable task to try to persuade a woman you have buried her husband when she refuses to believe it, and she went away after days of grim discussion still insisting that what she said was true, that the sergeant-major and I were fools or rogues. I hope it was a comfort to her.

The next of these episodes, the comic but frightening one, also happened in Scotland, but on the west coast, in a very obscure little sea loch called Loch A'Choire, between Oban and Fort William. Some government designer's office had come up with a plan for a one-man submarine called a Wellman, which had no originality or merit at all. In one off-season, I was told to plan a route for getting two or three of these machines into Bergen harbour to demolish a floating dock. I said I could not plan a route unless I had driven the submarine. The Admiralty agreed and sent me to Loch A'Choire where I found a large merchant ship flying the blue ensign of a fleet auxiliary. She was under a commander RN, and on deck she had a whole litter of the baby submarines. 'Howarth!' he said, as if I were a long lost friend. 'Thank God you've come. I can't say how pleased I am to see you.'

I think I was still a sub-lieutenant – perhaps a lieutenant by then – and this was a most unexpected greeting from a commander. He took me to the wardroom and gave me a double pink gin. 'Trouble is,' he went on, 'we sit up here playing with these things, but nobody tells us what they're for. I want to know what you Admiralty experts are going to do with them.'

I did try to tell him I was not an expert – I had never been in any sort of submarine – but he thought I was being mock-modest and did not believe me. It was difficult because I did know what the Admiralty was planning to use them for, but it was Top Secret and I had not been told if I could tell him.

'I've only come here, sir,' I said, 'to ask you if you can let me drive one.'

'Drive one?' he said. 'Nothing easier. Anyone can drive them. I'll tell the chief to have one ready for you in the morning, and you can drive it all day. But that doesn't solve my problem.'

A big diagram of the controls was pinned up on a bulkhead, and I studied it when he was not looking. There was what used to be called an aircraft joy-stick between the driver's knees. Forward to go down, back to go up and sideways to turn: it couldn't be anything else. A two-way switch for the electric motor, ahead and astern. Above one's head was a large lever which flooded the ballast tanks, and down on the right three small air valves. The front one was labelled 'Blow Tanks', and it did not say what the other two were for. There was a depth gauge and a compass. It all looked like a toy submarine, and I reckoned I could do it.

'Oh, there's one thing that diagram doesn't show,' he said when he saw me pondering. 'But you know, of course. The flooding cock. It floods the whole vessel, so you have to wait quite a long time till the pressure inside equals the pressure outside, and you can open the hatch and get out. In theory. But I'd rather you didn't do it unless you really want to. Nobody's tried it yet. And of course it means I lose a submarine.'

Next morning, soon after a cheerless dawn, a fatherly chief took me down to a wooden pontoon alongside, and there was my submarine ready. My impression was that it was about twenty feet long and two and a half in diameter, and it had a small turret with a hatch on top. 'What's your weight, sir?' the chief asked in a conversational way.

'About a hundred and forty pounds,' I said. I had not weighed myself for years, if ever.

'OK then, sir. Better give me your cap. There's not much room for a man of your height.'

I gave him the cap, and lowered myself carefully in. It was like getting into a very small single-seater sports car. I felt around, identifying the controls from the diagram.

'All aboard, sir? Nice day for a trip round the bay.' He clanged the hatch shut on top of me. It cut off all sound from the world outside, and most of the vision too. There was only a slit window about three inches high, and about six inches above the surface of the sea.

I supposed the first thing was to submerge – that is what a submarine is for – so I pulled the big lever above me to flood the tanks, heard the water gurgling in, and saw the outside surface creeping up the window, like being inside a bottle. It covered the window, and I had a glimpse of the surface from underneath, then of separate layers of water, the brown river water above and the green sea below. It was all vanishing above me, rather fast. In surprise, I looked at the depth gauge. It said twenty feet, and it was going round like the seconds hand of a clock. I had closed the big lever pretty fast, but it had made no difference. I started the motor and pulled the joy stick back, but that made no difference either. I thought of blowing the tanks and grabbed the small air valve – the front one, I remembered. It would not turn. Everything was getting dark, and soon it was pitch black and the only thing I could see was the depth gauge, which was luminous. It went right round to fifty feet, which was as far as it could go, and there it stuck. Rather later – I have no idea how long – there was a very slight jar and the damnable machine tilted down by the nose. It was on the bottom.

I think it was the abrupt transition that was most alarming, from the morning sunshine to the abysmal dark, and from the bustle of the ship's deck and the cheerful chief to such utter solitude and silence. Obviously, I had done something wrong, and I did not know what; but blowing the tanks was the way to undo it. Yet I could not turn the valve. I tried it anti-clockwise, the normal way, and then thought for a bit and tried it clockwise. I pushed it and pulled it: still no good. I could feel thin pipes at the back of it, and feel them bending when I put my strength to it, and I reasoned that if I broke it high pressure air would be released in the boat and would kill me very suddenly. Never mind, brute strength was the only way. I thought again, managed to kick off one of my shoes, and with the heel I hit the valve as hard as I could. Something gave way, there was a hiss of air. It took me a second to discover I was not dead: it was blowing the tanks. It went on hissing and then, a sinister sound, it began to bubble. That could only mean the tanks were empty, so I shut the valve – it shut quite easily. She had maximum buoyancy, and she had not moved. She was stuck in the mud.

I think it was the only time I have expected to die rather soon and not been able to think of anything to do about it. I felt claustrophobia rising like a physical lump inside me and said to myself – aloud, I think – 'If you keep calm, there must be a way out of this. If you don't, there isn't.' Oxygen was what I thought of most. How long would it last? Not long, I supposed; the space was very small. How long would it take them to find me? Much longer, I was sure, if they ever could. I tried to unstick her by rocking from side to side, then thought of the extra oxygen I was using. I felt for that flooding cock and found it, but was perfectly certain that even if I opened it and sat there while the water rose up to my neck, I would not be able to open the hatch, much less to come to the surface without escape gear. (I did not know how deep I was, except that it was deeper than the gauge was meant to go. In fact, I discovered later, I was seventy-two feet under.)

When I was satisfied there was nothing more I could do, I sat still and told myself I was not afraid of being dead, but only of the process of dying. It was nonsense, of course; I was afraid of both.

She came unstuck for no reason at all that I ever discovered. I felt nothing, only found that I could see again. It was getting lighter. The depth gauge gave a jerk and started to go down as fast as it had gone up. That gave me something new to worry about. Above me was a large merchant ship and several motor launches. What if I hit the bottom of the ship with an awful clang and dented my submarine and made it leak? Or if I just got stuck there under its bottom? I carefully let out some of the precious air in the tanks. She stopped going up, and went down again, right down into the darkness until I felt her on the mud for the second time. But I was beginning to get the hang of her, and by juggling with the big lever and the little valve I got her reasonably steady, at just about the level where there was a little light. And looking up and out I saw in front of me a perfectly enormous propeller. I very hastily switched on the motor, which worked a pygmy propeller and, remembering the compass course for the middle of the loch (I was quite proud of that), I motored out there until I was sure it must be all clear above. I pulled back the joystick and, with no little joy, I surfaced.

Looking round through the slit window, I saw the crew of the ship all staring down at the place where I had disappeared. My brain was not working very brightly by then, and I did not think until they told me that they had seen the great bubbles of air I had released, and thought I had made the fundamental mistake of blowing the tanks when their vents were open. They were waiting, with the detached excitement of fishermen, to see if my body came up with the bubbles. Among them, I saw the commander, looking rather pale and not at all pleased, as if his breakfast had disagreed with him.

I motored alongside, and the chief opened the hatch and let in a blessed dose of air. 'Thought you was a goner, sir,' he said, as cheerfully as ever. 'Thirty-five minutes you've been down there. That's a record, that is.' He was still holding my cap.

Well, I did work out an ingenious route into Bergen, and three intrepid men tried it, but all of them got lost and had to swim ashore. Having seen how little one could see from a Wellman's window, I was not at all surprised – only glad that all three escaped alive. They had been trained, of course, and had dived for weeks in Wellmans with a rope on – and had not made the mistake of guessing their weight and guessing it far too low.

The third of the episodes I specially remember, the lunatic one, was some time after the end of the war, and it was connected with Shetland only in that the Secret Service still knew me and sometimes called me in when they had a simple and ignominious job to be done. I have great respect for the British Secret Service. It used to be the most efficient in the world, and I hope it still is. But secrecy is habit-forming. People who grow addicted to it are sometimes inclined to be secretive when there is no need to be, and sometimes therefore do the simplest job in difficult and complicated ways. Flying balloons in a forest was a case in point.

It happened in Austria, when that unlucky country was still divided into four zones of occupation, Russian, British, American and French. I was despatched there without being told what I was going to do. Whatever it was, they said it had to be done in uniform. Naval uniform was no good, because Austria has no sea. I had to dress up as an army captain. I did not like that, because I was in fact an executive lieutenant-commander by then, while an army general service captain in his thirties, especially at the end of a long war, is labelled as one of life's failures. But I needed the money.

It is difficult to be disguised as an army officer if you are not one, and it was made more difficult because I had to fly to Vienna as a civilian and then change into uniform in a city I did not know, which was divided into four zones like Berlin and surrounded by a zone that was Russian. But my destination was not Vienna, it was Graz, far down to the south in Styria, and the only way to get there was by an army train through Russian territory.

So I slunk out of my hotel in the morning feeling conspicuously friendless, and took a taxi to the railway station. The platform was crowded with British soldiers, and a young subaltern greeted me respectfully: 'Ah, Captain Howarth, sir, you'll be O.C. Train.'

I nearly fell at the first fence. 'O.C. what?' I said.

'Train, sir.'

'What do I have to do?'

'Nothing much,' he said. 'I don't think you'll have any problems. The Russians will search the train, they always do. But they're no trouble really, unless you have some nitwit who has lost his pass. Then you'll have to put him on a charge, of course.'

All the day-long journey, that foreign train had a commanding officer who sat quaking in his first-class carriage. The Russians did search it, but it was not much of a search because none of them seemed to speak English and none of the passengers spoke Russian. They did not bring anyone in by the scruff of his neck, saying he had no pass. It was not the Russians I was scared of, it was the British soldiers. What if I made a mistake and gave myself away as a bogus officer? In those circumstances they could not do less, if they knew their duty, than get me arrested as a spy; and my true masters would not be pleased to have to get me out of that.

I felt safer in Graz, which was the headquarters of the British zone: it felt like one of those nursery games of Ludo when you are on the final straight and know that nobody can catch you up and jump on you from behind. But somebody could, and did. I had to report to the Colonel, who was in the officer's mess. A large moustached sergeant-major was at the entrance. 'Sorr' he shouted in a sergeant-major's best parade-ground voice, 'you are wearing your belt upside down.' So I was, and so I had been all through the journey – just what a second-class foreign spy would have done.

Outside that mess I had a narrow escape from a gaffe which was even worse. There was a table covered with belts and caps. I put two and two together and concluded that the army took off these accoutrements when they went into their mess. But I did not know, and nobody told me, and I was on the verge of going in, belt and all, with my cap under my arm, and then everyone would have known I was a sham.

It was in Graz that I heard what my job was. I have conveniently forgotten who told me, but the colonel knew about it and had chosen a sergeant to do the hard work and a section of soldiers to help. What I had to do, first of all, was to drive alone round that beautiful countryside to the east, near the Hungarian border and the Iron Curtain but not too near, finding glades in the forest where an army truck could get in but nobody was likely to see what it was doing. Then we had to go back in the dark to the glades I had chosen, any night when there was a westerly breeze, and blow up balloons with hydrogen to about eight feet in diameter, each with a sheaf of leaflets attached and a fuse which would let the leaflets go. It was all unspeakably secret, from the Russians and their allies, and from the Austrians too, and the rest of the British army.

The leaflets were in a language I did not even recognize. It was just as well I did not know what they said. My heart was not in it. My own war was over, and the cold war, I thought, was only a political quarrel. I liked the Austrians, and was quite prepared to like the Hungarians or Rumanians, or whoever the leaflets were addressed to. It was none of my business to be showering them with propaganda. But it seemed reasonably harmless, naughty rather than wicked, and I admit it was fun, not unlike that other nursery game Hide and Seek, or the more frightening version my family used to play, Murder in the Dark.

In this dark, in my chosen glades at night, I posted unwilling and timid sentries with orders to grab but not to shoot any prowlers; in this game we did not want any murders. The truck contained a hydrogen generator. You poured metal pellets into a liquid in a pressure container, screwed down the lid and took a pipe to the first balloon. The sergeant knew all about it, but it must have been invented by a chemist in the nineteenth or even the eighteenth century, and it was unbearably slow. It took all night to blow up two balloons, bearing about a thousand leaflets.

Those nights were long and cold and damp, but never dull. A forest at night, of course, is always full of noises – owls, invisible animals, falling branches, sudden mysterious commotions – and the noises kept us alert: which of the hoots of owls was a secret signal? Which of the crashes a posse of Austrian policemen, or a Hungarian border patrol, or, worst of all perhaps, a British platoon who would demand explanations I was not allowed to give them? Nobody we met could be a friend. Once in the depth of night a herd of large bodies came crashing through the trees towards us, pursued by forlorn cries of 'Halt' from the sentries. Perhaps they were deer, but they sounded like Waterloo. When they saw or scented us and our truck the herd divided in two and stampeded past us, some on each side, and crashed away into the forest beyond.

If the wind changed in the night, we had to give up. A balloon which landed in Austria, I had been told, was a disaster to avoid. So was a balloon which rose too slowly and got stuck in the trees. But with luck we got our two balloons away, and watched their glowing fuses vanishing into the sky as they started their journey over the Iron Curtain.

It was not difficult to think of better ways of doing it, if it had to be done. You could cram two inflated balloons under the canopy of an army truck, so you could blow them up in daylight and at leisure in the secluded army garage, and then drive out at night and let them go so quickly that it could be done almost anywhere except on a main road, and with much less risk of being seen. By using two or three trucks we increased our production to six or eight balloons a night. We could have done far more if we had used cylinders of compressed hydrogen instead of the primitive generator, but I was not encouraged in that. I think we were already doing far more than anyone had expected, and the whole plan had become an embarrassment to the clever fellow who had thought of it.

Thus it may have been a relief all round when after a couple of months it came to a sudden end through a leak: not a security leak but a hydrogen leak. I was called to an army telephone.

'One of your bloody things has come down,' said a voice which I knew. 'The police have got it at Hartberg' – which I knew very well was in Austria. 'There's a stinking row on. Better lay off until further notice. And remember, if anyone asks who did it, it wasn't us.'

The further notice never came. After waiting a week or two, I was allowed to go home, and get rid of another uniform. I did not know if I was in disgrace or not and I did not care very much. I had done what I was told to do, but done it a bit too well.

Flying balloons or sinking in submarines, however, were not my regular occupation when the war was over. When I was demobilized I went back to Shetland and set myself up as a master boatbuilder.

The BBC was embarrassingly kind. Throughout the war, I found, it had been making up my naval pay to what it would have been had I stayed in my job, and I was surprised to find I had over two thousand pounds in a bank in London which I had not known was there. They asked me to come back, and not only to the old job but to the job to which they thought I would have been promoted had I stayed. Would I be tempted, they asked, to be a regional programme director, or to be in at the rebirth of television?

Of course I was tempted, and I felt meanly ungrateful to say no, but after five years in wild northern places I could not bear going back to a city again and being cut off from the sea and boats and the beautiful desolate coasts. Financially, it was a fearful risk to put my two thousand pounds into buying equipment for a boatyard, but that was what I wanted.

I had been married for six months by then, but I was not being entirely selfish because my wife, who was only eighteen, had never been out of Shetland except on our honeymoon, when for the first time she encountered railway trains and both of us encountered flying bombs. I thought she would be happier if we stayed there, near her family, and so did she. But it was an anxious moment. The BBC gave me a final date to make up my mind. We came to the last day we might have written to them, and then to the last day we might have sent them a telegram, and on that day for the first time she felt our first baby moving. But we did not send the telegram, and never regretted it.

Designing and building boats is a pleasant act of creation. A good boat is a blend of science, craftsmanship and tradition, and more than most human artefacts it has a life and personality. On the building ways it is inert, merely a wooden structure, but the moment you launch it, it is born; it instantly comes alive like a new-hatched seabird.

It seemed there was a chance for this creation in Shetland at the end of the war. Shetlanders had been fishermen for centuries, and most of their big boats had been lost in the war, either senile and rotting on beaches from disuse or requisitioned by the navy and never returned. But no boats except open dinghies (some six-oared) had ever been built in the island; the fishermen bought the bigger ones second-hand in Scotland, and the newest of them were a generation out of date.

Goodness knows why I was so sure I could build the Shet-landers better boats than they had ever had; at that age, I thought I could do anything I really wanted to do. Most boatbuilders start with a long apprenticeship, and I had never built – much less designed – a boat at all. But at least I had learned from the most bitter experience in the war what was a seaworthy boat and what was not. And with the dregs of my maths and physics I could understand a nautical textbook and calculate simple things like stability, laden and unladen, and make the measured drawings in three projections which are called the lines, and the later drawings which determine whether intractable things like the engine and the bunks will actually fit. It is all far more fascinating than merely designing a house, where everything except the roof is either level or vertical and all the walls are at right-angles. In a boat, nothing is square or vertical or horizontal. Almost everything is curved in three dimensions, except the keel and the mast.

So I set to work to design a 65-foot boat from first principles, bowing to tradition only in the graceful curved stem which the Shetlanders had inherited in their small boats directly from the Vikings.

It was much more a problem to persuade any Shetland fishermen I could build it. At length I met a crew of five from an outlying island who wanted to put their life savings into a new boat, and a licensed grocer in Lerwick who had prospered in the war and was willing to lend them more money. My drawings did not mean much to them, but I also met a man called Bobby Walterson who had been a petty officer shipwright in the navy, and he skilfully made me a scale half-model of the hull – and also offered to become my foreman if the project got off the ground. That encouraged me greatly: he was a craftsman, and he approved. So did the advent of a boy called Davey Leask, who came and asked me to take him on as an apprentice.

Bobby's model was peered at from every angle, argued over and criticized, and caressed by scores of hardened hands. It was unlike other fishing boats, with leaner underwater lines and a finer entry. I promised it would be faster than any Scottish boat: it is an advantage, especially in herring fishing, to be first back to port.

The older fishermen did not believe it. 'She'll no carry,' they said, shaking their wise old heads, and meaning that she would float down by the head when she had a good cargo of fish; and I had to argue that it is the hull's shape above the waterline, not below it, that carries the cargo, while the shape below, by and large, determines her speed and what she will do in a sea.

It took those five men from the island weeks to make up their minds, and no wonder. To accept my opinion and reject their fathers' was an act of faith on their part, and the grocer's, and I have always been grateful to them. I offered to build the boat for six thousand pounds, which turned out to be far too cheap; but they deserved a bargain for daring to be first.

So I went and bought a circular saw and a bandsaw second-hand in Scotland, and the essential electric hand-tools; and oak trees and larches sawn into slabs, the oak in four-inch slabs for the frames and the larches in two-inch slabs for the planking, and two superb 8 × 7s of oak for the keel, and Douglas fir for the decks, and Norway spruce for the masts and spars, and I set up my workshop and yard in Scalloway, next door to the buildings we had occupied in the war and close to the engineering workshop that had done such good service then. Bobby and

Davey and I started from scratch by building our workbenches, and one at a time we were joined by four or five other Shetlanders who had been carpenters in the Merchant Navy.

It took us most of a year to build that first boat, from the heaps of lumber and the sacks of six-inch galvanized nails to the last coat of paint. The whole year was exciting for me, seeing my concept grow: first the keel and keelson and the stems, all with the meticulous scarph joints Bobby made; then the frames, the deckbeams, the planking. I did my best with the manual work, but all the others were more skilful at it than I was, and most of my work consisted of translating each careful curve from my drawings to the solid in full size – and of course in procuring the materials, paying the wages and looking for future orders. She had to be built in the open air, there was no shed in Shetland anything like big enough, and it was not always easy to work in the gales of lashing rain or the driven snow – or under the eyes of so many critics. Standing on the foreshore of Scalloway, our creation was in full view from the village street, and people came from all over to watch and tell us, quite politely, we were doing it all wrong. They were not certain yet whether she would be a success or a historic disaster.

Then at last the day of her birth. We hopefully adorned her with flags. A huge crowd turned up for the launching (huge for Shetland). The ancient mariners firmly said she would float bottom up. Old sailors are the most conservative people in the world, and at their happiest forecasting a fiasco. My wife performed the ceremony in her best and probably only frock, broke the bottle of champagne, or something like champagne, named her *Enterprise*, and we knocked out the chocks and let her go.

What a moment. There are three comparable moments in a life: having your first baby (but that is an achievement of wives); launching your first boat; or seeing the first bound copy of your first book. The *Enterprise* stood a split second where she had stood so long, began to slide, met the sea gracefully, nodded her head to the audience and floated right way up. She was beautiful. Nobody cheered – Shetlanders do not cheer – but everyone clapped. I hurried down to the pier to make her fast, jumped aboard and felt her moving under my feet, alive; and the grocer, bless him, gave us all lunch and lots more of his champagne, all the seven builders, the engineers and blacksmiths from next door, the five new owners and all our wives.

There were plenty of orders after that. The *Enterprise* was the biggest boat we ever built, and – as I had promised the owners – the fastest boat in the Shetland or Scottish fleets. But we built many other fishing boats a little smaller, and passenger ferries for the outer islands, and sailing and motor yachts, some for the Shetland landlords and some for export to Scotland. I designed nearly all of them and each was different, a new creation, to suit the whims of its owners. Each had its launching ceremony and later its trial trip; usually fairly bibulous occasions.

That little boatyard was the centre of my life for several years, together with a bungalow I built for my wife and daughter and myself on top of a minor hill with a wonderful view of the village and the harbour, and the outer islands and the Atlantic Ocean. It was what I had wanted, and it was a happy time.

Once, my old friend Richard Dimbleby turned up there. He was rich and very famous by then, a visitor from the other world I had abandoned. He had finished his career as war correspondent, and television had scarcely begun again; he was filling in time with a weekly programme called *Down Your Way*, which came from a different place each week, and it was that which had brought him to Shetland. He was being lionized by the self-styled gentry in the town of Lerwick, but he came over to Scalloway to see us.

He sat in our kitchen as portly and cherubic as ever, but he looked bewildered, an impression I had never seen him give before. I do not think riches and fame had changed him. He was still as friendly as ever. But it seemed he could not bring himself to believe I had willingly chosen obscurity and rejected fame – or if not fame, at least authority in the BBC. I tried to tell him I liked building boats for fishermen, I liked living in working clothes, liked putting my feet up at a peat fire in my kitchen stove. But it was no good; I could see he thought I was wasting my life and the talents he thought I had. Dear Richard: he was a very good friend, but I had put a gulf between us. I think it cannot be avoided when one of a pair of friends becomes famous. The other cannot join the crowd of sycophants who crowd round famous people, and cannot use his old friendship to claim a special place. I know I have lost other friends in the same way, and I hope they know I did not want to, and still cherish the memory of them.

I think I saw Richard only once more. That was at the twenty-first birthday of his son, my godson David. It was the party of a successful father. The gifts were displayed on a table, except Richard's offering of a sports car which stood in the drive outside. Remembering my previous ill-chosen presents, I took six bottles of rather good sherry, which I thought could not be wrong – until I heard another guest, looking at the array, say 'Good Lord, who ever gave him *sherry*?' That party was memorable too for the very aged relation who had been chosen to propose the young man's health. He got up, stood there swaying a little for what seemed a long time, then he said 'Well, dammit. Forgotten what I was going to say,' and sat down again. It was the most successful after-dinner speech I ever heard.

Very gradually, I became aware in Shetland of a worm eating away my contentment. The boatyard was not making money, it was losing it. I could build boats all right, very good boats, but in all my training in mathematics nobody had mentioned double-entry bookkeeping, and I did not understand it. I ought to have remembered I was descended from Samuel Paget, who had gone bankrupt running his brewery. The Pagets had been more or less like that ever since, and so had the Howarths: successful bishops, surgeons and professors, but no businessmen except my brother, who was a chartered accountant. Samuel brewed good beer, and I built good boats, but both of us sold our products too cheaply.

By way of defence, I must say that costing a pint of beer ought to be easy, but costing a wooden boat is notoriously difficult. Buying a tree in a forest, you can never be sure how many planks or frames you will get out of it; and making a plank a craftsman may shape it and plane it and bevel it for days, and then have it split when he fastens it in place. But my initial mistake had no excuse. I was paid for the *Enterprise* in instalments of a thousand pounds; my clients brought them in cardboard boxes full of one pound notes which they insisted I should count. They came with one instalment, I recollect, when I was feeling very ill with glandular fever. We counted the notes on my bed, and I entered that instalment on the wrong side of my ledger.

So for years I thought I had broken even on the *Enterprise*, but I had not. The local chartered accountant who did my annual audit did not notice the mistake, and reported a profit. One of the local gentry who was said to be an accountant joined me as a partner, but he did not notice it either. It remained a puzzle to them and to me why there was never enough money in the bank, and as I used the *Enterprise* accounts as a basis for later estimates, the trouble grew worse and worse until worries about money drowned the pleasure of creating boats.

All that time – it was five years or so – I was labouring all day in the boatyard and sitting every evening writing *The Shetland Bus*. I did not mind the hard work; I was used to it and I liked it – my work was always a hobby – but it must have made life very dull for my wife. I never expected the book to be published, much less to make any money, but I finished it and sent it to a famous literary agent, who sent it back with the comment that it was not of public interest. So I put it away in a bottom drawer with my oldest clothes and tried to forget about it, and it stayed there a year.

Then I met a learned and charming man called Dr Mortimer Manson, who was editor and proprietor of one of the local papers. 'You know,' he said, 'you really ought to write a book about those wartime adventures.' 'I have,' I said; he asked if he could read it, and I dug it out of the drawer.

He must have read it all night, because he rang me up the next day and insisted I should send it to a publisher. Between us we chose the old-established house of Nelson; they published mainly Bibles and educational books, but they had issued a guidebook of Shetland, so we knew they had at least heard of the place. They fell on my book with vast enthusiasm, and did things with it that fill me with wonder now. That was long before anyone thought of the phrase to 'hype' a book, but *The Shetland Bus* was hyped. They spent thousands on advertising it, with a logo that every potential reader came to know, and I meanly hoped that literary agent knew he had missed a winner. Thirty years later it is still selling gently, and Nelson still send me small but welcome cheques for the work I did half a lifetime ago. I have a lot to be grateful for to Nelson, and to Dr Manson.

So it came about that I enjoyed the third of those moments of creation, when the first bound copy came in the mail, with its elegant and imaginative wrapper showing a fishing boat approaching a mountainous coast lit only by the aurora. It was delivered to me in the boatyard, and I dashed up the hill to the house to show it to my wife. As I said, I am ashamed of its literary pretensions now, but I still have that first copy and refuse to lend it to anyone.

It was a lucky coincidence, because the boatyard's affairs had got to the stage when I dreaded Fridays because I had to cash a cheque to pay the wages. I started moving the money I earned from the book from my own account to the boatyard's. I could not bring myself to close the yard and pay off the men who had worked so well and so willingly and always trusted my judgement. Bobby Walterson and Davey Leask had been there at the beginning and were still with me. It must always be difficult to stop a thing like that; there were always boats part-finished on the stocks. At last, to my great relief, Bobby took over what assets there were, with the help of the most human of the local gentry, a man we had built a motor yacht for. I very much hope they did well with it. I am told it still exists, not rashly building many boats but more wisely repairing them.

I set myself to pay off the yard's debts from the book's earnings. There was no legal obligation to do it because the yard had become a limited company when the partner joined me, but in Shetland moral obligations count more than legal ones, and I felt those as strongly as my great-grandfather James with his father's brewery. I think I paid all the genuine claims, but I was terribly ashamed it had to end that way, and felt my wife's large family must be ashamed of me too – though if they were they never said so.

Under that cloud of worry we left Shetland, which had been my home for eleven years and hers all her life, and we moved down to England, close to my parents. We had two daughters, no money and no plans.

TWELVE

Finmark

Building boats was delightful, but for me a bad way to make a living. The only other thing I thought I could do, without going back to city life, was to write. A great many people think they can write, and probably most of them could if they made a start. I was told it was impossible to make a living by writing books, which was discouraging but untrue. What is difficult is to make a steady, respectable, middle-class income: most writers make either far more than they deserve or, more often, far less. I spent nearly forty years writing books and made quite a lot of money, but I rashly gave most of it away and brought up six children on the rest, so that I ended almost as poor as I was when I started.

When I regret being poor, as I often do, I try to comfort myself with the thought that making money is not the only object of writing books. The prime object is to give pleasure to people who read them, and if you succeed in that, the money follows. It is no good writing anything that few people want to read; it is no good writing only to please yourself, or your friends, or even a limited class of people – scholars, say, or historians. To make a good living, you have to please people in millions, and not only in your own country but in America and other places too.

To do that, you need only two things: something to write about, and a knack of writing it. The subject may come entirely out of your head, which is fiction and makes you a novelist, or it may be fact from ancient or recent history, which for want of a real word is called non-fiction. For the knack, a more pretentious word is style. It is not just grammar. Bad grammar will annoy the readers you want to please; but grammar is a thing you can take liberties with, and once you have learned good grammar you can leave it to nature and forget it.

You can never forget good style. Prose needs a rhythm like verse, but a subtler rhythm, always changing. Each sentence ought to be balanced, so that it sounds right if it is read aloud; it should end before a reader runs out of breath. Above all, it should say exactly what it means, in the simplest way. So should a paragraph, which is a set of sentences strung together to express a train of thought. A writer should stop at the end of each paragraph he writes and ask himself, 'Is that what I was really trying to say? And have I said it as plainly as I can?' And, of course, 'Was it worth saying?' If one of the answers is no, he should go back and do it again.

I learned in the BBC Talks Department that being lucid was a writer's basic virtue, but if I had any training it went back beyond that, to the time when I failed to master what I was told in physics and the higher concepts of maths. I made a habit then, when I could not understand something, of simplifying it, and re-simplifying it and probably over-simplifying it, until I had something which was not the whole truth but was an idea I could understand. I believe better physicists and mathematicians play this trick; they make imaginary models of things that cannot be imagined, like quanta or the square root of minus one. And I think simplifying is a useful habit in writing. If you write down something you only half understand, you cannot expect your readers to understand it, or to enjoy trying. Of course there are thoughts and emotions the best of prose cannot compass, but if you cannot express them clearly, you had better leave them out. Nobody but you will know or care what you have discarded.

Yet some writers seem to like to write obscurely, as if they hope to seem more clever than they are. I doubt if that fools anybody. Robert Louis Stevenson was a master of stylish prose in my father's generation, and I love to quote him. 'In any narrative,' he wrote, 'there is only one way to be clever, and that is to be exact.'

However hard you try to maintain your style – and trying is most of the pleasure of writing English – you should never expect to be complimented on it, because good style, like other arts, should hide itself. If it becomes obtrusive, it is not good style but bad. The most you should hope for is to have someone say 'I like your books, they're so easy to read.' You should not hope he (or she) knows why they are easy, or how much hard work you have put into making them so.

I know this dour little sketch of the knack of writing is over-simplified. Fat books have been written on style. But I am not a professor, or an artist, or even a wit. I learned when I was very young, from my brother and a host of witty cousins, that I had no hope of ever being a wit, and from my children, when I was getting old, that I was not an artist. I just have to put up with it, and so do my patient readers, of whom, thank goodness, there are or have been a sufficient number of millions. Some of them, strangers all over the world, still write kindly to tell me my books have given them pleasure, and that is a writer's reward, whether he makes a lot of money or not.

Anyhow, this is not a text book, it is a narrative, as true as I can make it, or as I wish to make it. After *The Shetland Bus* I wrote two novels. One was a thriller. It was really rather bad, but it did well. The other was a straight romance, and I thought it was good, but it did badly. Both are forgotten now, and deserve it, but they taught me I was not about to make my fortune as a novelist.

Then one day in Oslo (it may have been when I gave that frightening lecture) I met Jan Baalsrud. I had known him briefly during the war, when he was one of the agents we landed in Norway. It was the most northerly landing and the longest fishing-boat voyage we ever made, to an island between Tromsö and the North Cape, a thousand miles from Shetland and three hundred beyond the Arctic Circle, and it came to grief. Our information up there was much more sparse than it was in the south, and the agents, of whom there were four, had been told of a shopkeeper who was thought to be reliable. His name was Hansen, a common name in Norway. They called at the shop in the night. But Hansen had sold it to another man, also called Hansen, and by the time they found out they had told the second Hansen they came from England. He was a most unusual Norwegian: he lost his nerve and reported them to the Germans.

They were attacked by a warship, and they blew up their own fishing boat, which had eight tons of explosive from Scalloway in its hold. In the fight that followed all except one of the agents and crew, eleven men in all, were either killed or wounded, captured and executed. Jan was the only survivor. He escaped in ice and snow across the sounds and islands and mountains to Sweden. It was only about eighty miles, but it took him two months, and when he recovered in a Swedish hospital he wrote a report. It reached us in Shetland, and I quoted it in *The Shetland Bus*.

The interesting thing about that report was that it said so little and left out so much. Through most of his escape, Jan had been half-conscious with concussion, snow-blindness, frostbite and gangrene. He did not know what had happened, could not remember exactly where he had been, and had never been told the names of the hundreds of people who had evidently risked their own lives to save him. One of the few things he did remember clearly was cutting off nine of his toes with a pocket knife, because they were gangrenous and there was nobody to do it for him.

When we met the second time, in Oslo ten years afterwards, I persuaded him to come to the far north with me and find the route he had taken and meet the people who had helped him, so that I could write the whole story. He was reluctant at first, because he felt guilty at being alive. He thought it had been his duty not to escape but to die, in order to put an end to the awful risks the brave local men, and their wives and children, were willingly running to save him. No single life was worth endangering so many. He had felt this at the time, I discovered later, and had tried to kill himself, and in logic he was right; but by the stage when he tried, his hands were too weak to cock his revolver, and he failed. It was still on his conscience.

Not many visitors went to the far north of Norway in the early 1950s when we were there, because it is frozen solid (except the sea) in autumn, winter and spring, and full of mosquitoes in summer. But it was easy enough to get there, so my journey was not adventurous. I enjoyed it. We went in the early spring, before the thaw; Jan's escape, from late March until early June, had been a race against the thaw and the midnight sun. At that time of year, the country he escaped across is very beautiful. 'Pity I was blind last time I was here,' he said one day when we stood among the spectacular snowy peaks and looked down on a glittering fjord. And, beauty apart, there was all the excitement of a detective story in finding out where he had been, and meeting the people who had got him out of each perilous situation, and seeing each bit of the story fall into place.

All those meetings were emotional. None of the people had known the whole story, only the bit of it they took part in, but I think they remembered that more vividly than anything else in their normally placid lives. They had last seen Jan when they passed him on from their own hiding-place to the next, sick, filthy, emaciated, agonized, with only the faintest flicker of life in him, but almost always with a sense of humour. Most of them had assumed he had died in the end, and they were excited and delighted to see him alive and well and human, and to learn that their supreme endeavours had not been wasted but had saved a life worth saving. It had never crossed their minds that he ought to have died, and, sitting talking to them night after night, I saw his haunting guilt being exorcized.

We went to the little island where the fight had been, and saw the sound that Jan had swum across, pushing aside the floating ice, to escape from that island where the Germans were on his tail; and met two small girls (grown up now) who had found him exhausted on the beach and taken him home as a sort of trophy to their mother. So from house to house and from island to island, each with its reminiscence, until we came to the hamlet of Furuflaten on the mainland, which had played an important part in the drama.

I should think the Furuflaten people remember me mainly for my incompetence on skis. I knew about mountains and mountaineering, but I had seldom had to ski and had never been told how to do it; while the Norwegians who live up there, of course, have to go on skis for eight months of the year whenever they go out of their doors. Their children can ski as soon as they can toddle, and none of them had met an adult who could not.

They wanted to take Jan and me five miles or so up a valley among the mountains called the Lyngen Alps, to see the ice-fall where he started an avalanche and fell three hundred feet, and the valley where he wandered day after day, concussed and snow-blind. They chose to go on a Sunday, and it was a fine sunny day so most of the village came too, children and all, and made it a picnic.

178

The bottom of that valley is all ups and downs, and covered by small scattered bushes. The bushes had confused Jan when he was blind, and his tracks, which they saw before the summer, had shown he walked round and round them, believing perhaps he was following somebody else's footsteps. The bushes confused me too although I could see them. Going up hill, I was all right, but going down I could not steer between them and constantly crashed. It is very difficult wearing skis to extract yourself from a prickly bush, and whenever I was entangled the smallest children, almost babies, whizzed past me howling with laughter. Luckily, I was laughing too; it was painful, but grotesquely funny.

We stayed in Furuflaten two or three weeks, until I knew the little place and its people well enough to understand how and why things had happened as they did: how Jan had stumbled, blind, lame and covered all over with ice, against the log wall of the wooden house of a man called Marius Grönwald (he never told Jan his name); and why Marius could not keep him hidden in the village, where a German garrison was billeted in the school and everybody knew everybody's business; and how Marius and his sister told her two small children they must keep the secret, even from their friends; and how he and she and two other men carried him down the frozen river bed, within a couple of yards of the school, to the shore of the fjord, and sailed him across to a tiny deserted shack on the other side.

I had known, of course, what the Germans usually did to a Norwegian village they suspected of doing what Furuflaten did; but this was my first insight into the personal problems of such a little place when it suddenly had a life-and-death secret within it. It was not a problem just of Jan's life or death, but of the life or death of the village. The Germans would have burned it down if the secret had leaked, shot everyone they thought had known it – women and children too – and deported the rest to concentration camps or at best left them homeless to work our their own survival.

But Marius, and in the end about a score of other Furuflaten people, gladly took the risk: gladly because they were ashamed they had never had a chance to oppose the German occupation, and this was a chance. Saying their innocent prayers, they thanked God for sending them the test.

Marius and three other men had gone across to the deserted shack to look after Jan whenever they were not prevented by German activities or storms, and the same four men sailed Jan and me across there. It was the last remnant of a burnt-out farm. None of them had been there in the ten years since their great adventure, and there was no sign that anyone else had been there. It was still full of wooden rubbish, whitened with age like bones, which they remembered and even Jan remembered when he saw it. Against one wall was the wooden bunk he had lain in for a fortnight.

There was no window in the shack, and they had hoped his eyes would recover in the darkness. His eyes did get better there, but his frostbitten feet got worse. He remained optimistic, but all the others knew he would never walk or ski to Sweden. He would have to be carried there, or hauled on a sledge.

The first lap of that journey was to get him up the steep mountain wall behind the shack. Jan and I made that climb with the men who had hauled or carried him up on a home-made sledge ten years before. Unburdened, it was a pleasant ice-and-snow climb, the sort of thing I had loved before the war. Hauling a helpless man, it had been a nightmare, for them and for him. In mountaineering accidents, it is not uncommon to carry an injured man down a mountain, but that is the only time I have heard of carrying a man up; and it was three thousand feet.

At the top they, and we, were on the great plateau of Finmark, the same plateau, but a more western part of it, that I had walked across on that summer holiday from the BBC. Then it had been an obstacle course of rivers, lakes and bogs; now, at the end of April, it was solid ice with thick fresh snow on top.

We carried our skis up the climb, and used them again on top. It was easier than the valley because there were no bushes, but I discovered another hazard of skiing with experts. This was a long expedition, and they had brought plenty of food and home-made brandy, but they were much faster than I was, especially down-hill, and every time they stopped to eat and drink I was far behind. When I caught up with them they were always cold and eager to start again, in case a blizzard came on. So I got no rest that day, and very little to eat, and no brandy.

But we found the self-same hole in the snow, just the size of a grave, where they had been forced to leave Jan because they had to be home before the Germans were stirring in the morning. It was in the lee of a boulder, where an eddy of the wind scooped it out the same every year. At that stage of the rescue a series of things went wrong, and they left him there much longer than they intended. I had noticed before that arctic people take little account of time, and none of them could tell me how long he had lain there, often buried by blizzards. But I worked it out most carefully. He was in that hole, and another similar one about a mile away, unable even to crawl, wet to the skin when the sun shone and frozen stiff when it did not, from 25 April until 22 May.

It is only about twenty-five miles from there across the plateau to the frontier of Sweden, but when you get there the border is marked simply by cairns on hill-tops miles apart, and it might be as far again on the other side before you find a house. Several parties of men tried to drag him there on the sledge and failed, beaten back by blizzards to where they had started. It would have been a dangerous journey even in peace, and none of my companions wanted to risk it when there was no more than a writer's inquisitiveness at stake. What was the point? they asked. There was nothing to see up there, the plateau was all the same, and there was nobody for me to talk to. I think they were oppressed, as I had been on my summer walk, by its barren, monotonous, intimidating emptiness. So that was the only part of Jan's escape route we did not try to follow, and I shall not tell here the unique means by which Jan crossed it in the end: if anyone wants to know, it is all in the book.

That was the first of my books I am not ashamed of. It is probably indexed in libraries under War Stories, but I liked it because it was an anti-war story. Jan always insisted he was not a hero: 'All I did was run away,' he said. I told him it can be heroic to run away, but I agreed with him who the real heroes were: not military men intent on glory, but the humblest of people impelled by nothing but charity. It was such a good story it could not have failed, but I read it again not long ago and thought I had made a worthy job of it. It sold enormously but it did not make me a fortune, only half a fortune, because I had offered to share any proceeds fifty-fifty with Jan. I could not have cut off my toes and he could not have written the book, so half-and-half was the only possible way to balance our contributions.

The only failure was the English title. I called it *We Die Alone*, which was an attempt to translate Pascal's seventeenth-century *pensée On Mourra Seul*. But when it came out in later editions in paperback I found the publishers, Collins, had changed it, without consulting me, to *Escape Alone*, which I thought undistinguished and boring. Billy Collins himself explained that you could not give your aged aunt a Christmas present called *We Die Alone*. 'But it's not a book for aged aunts,' I told him, too late. It still exists with both titles, *We Die Alone* on the hardbacks and *Escape Alone* on the paperbacks. I hope nobody has thought they were different books and bought them both.

THIRTEEN

Arctic Ethos

That book convinced me I could write non-fiction, and with luck make it pay. It also set a sort of pattern for my life for many years, a pattern of journeys. I developed a taste for travelling – not travelling for its own sake, but travelling with the purpose of finding out the truth of a story. By that time, in the 1950s, it was absurdly easy – merely expensive – to go anywhere in the world, and I was a generation too late to fulfil my father's ambition and be an explorer. But some of the journeys were mildly adventurous.

The first, after my expedition with Jan, took me much farther into the Arctic, which I was in love with. There were three reasons for that love affair. One was that parts of the Arctic are incomparably beautiful; another that it is the only part of the world where men of any nation live at peace with each other; and the third was that I had grown up with romantic stories of the great polar explorers, Amundsen, Peary, Scott, Nansen, Shackleton and, going much further back in time, Cook, Franklin and even Frobisher, Davis, Baffin and Willoughby. I do not count Hudson, who must have been a detestable man and got what he probably deserved in Hudson's Bay.

So a very brief report in a technical journal caught my eye and stirred up this latent affection. In the Second World War, it said, Greenland had formed an army of its own – two officers, one sergeant and six corporals, aided by six Eskimos who were non-combatant. They were ordered to patrol five hundred miles of the coast of north-east Greenland on dog sledges in case the Germans tried to make a landing there. The Germans did come and set up a weather station and the two parties reluctantly fought a war of their own. It lasted six months, with each side about the size of a football team. The most interesting episode was that one Danish corporal of the patrol was captured, and he and the German commander made a very long and apparently aimless journey with a single sledge and eight dogs, and on their return found their positions reversed: the Dane was the captor and the German the prisoner. What had happened to change them? The short report gave no explanation at all.

Greenland is a province of Denmark, and it was a Danish story, so I went to Copenhagen. There I met a man called Eske Brun, who had been Governor of Greenland throughout the war and had founded its miniature army. (When I met him, he liked to call himself General, and to explain that like all good generals he stayed five hundred miles behind the firing line.) I also met the leader of the patrol, Ib Poulsen, and all except two of his men, including Marius Jensen, the one who was captured. All of them were happy to tell me all they remembered. But the first thing I wanted was to go to north-east Greenland. I did not think I could write about it unless I had seen it, or write about a sledge patrol if I had never even tried to drive a team of dogs. But so far as I knew the Patrol's scene of action was still a place you could reach only by a full-sized polar expedition.

I was wrong. It was even easier to reach than most other places on the planet. Eske Brun told me that after the war the Danes had opened a lead mine there. It was a most unusual mine, only practical because the ore it produced was outstandingly pure. It was as far north as the seas are ever open. Ships could reach it for a few weeks in August every year, and in those weeks they brought out the whole year's production of ore. All the rest of the year it was serviced by long range aircraft which, with luck and good weather, landed on an airstrip on the ice. Eske Brun told the company I needed a lift, preferably a free one; and they told me they had a plane going the next week. If I could be at Prestwick airport in Scotland at the right time, there might be room in it, and they hoped to bring me back a few weeks later. All they wanted was what the army or navy used to call a blood chit, a document to say that if you get injured or killed it is nobody's fault but your own. I was always having to sign them in those days.

On the day they proposed, I took the ordinary commuters'

train from my home to London, with the city gentlemen in their bowler hats, flew from there to Prestwick and found a large four-engined Danish aircraft full of massive mining machinery with a few miners crouching in its midst. It took off after lunchtime, stopped for fuel and supper at Reykjavik in Iceland, and took off again in the night for the mine, another six hundred miles due north. It landed there about three o'clock in the morning, but in brilliant sunlight, and I stepped off into forty-five degrees of frost still wearing my city suit and a raincoat.

You could not see the mine from the airstrip. It was some miles up in the foothills of the 8500-foot peaks called the Stauning Alps, and almost all of it, including its living quarters, was underground, where it was not very warm but never excessively cold. The airstrip was on the shore of an immense fjord, King Oscar's Fjord, and there was nothing there except a row of snow-covered wooden huts which contained a weather station with – best of all – two dozen sledge dogs tethered to chains outside them. When the plane had gone and the last echoes of its alien noise had vanished among the mountains, the peace and stillness of the Arctic came back.

All the Danes of the Sledge Patrol had spoken about that seductive stillness, and I had glimpsed it myself in north Norway. Now I felt it in full, and began to understand that the arctic peace was the centre of the story, the explanation of the way they had all behaved; not only the Danes, but some of the Germans too, and especially the German commander.

In the Arctic in spring, nothing moves except the sky, and yourself, and your dogs and your companions if you have any. There is no water to ripple, no grass to blow in the breeze. 'With a blue sky above,' I wrote afterwards, 'and the diamond ice below, the place has a blazing brilliance of colour and clarity of outline which make more familiar scenes seem dingy and faded, and give the impression that this is how the new-made earth should have looked on the third morning of its creation: for the only colour which is absent is the green of life.'

I admit that was over-romantic; it was the Arctic at its best. In winter, of course, it is uncomfortable, dangerous and dark. The only people who travel around in it then are single-handed hunters with their teams of dogs. Each of them has his own territory, about sixty miles square, with a hunting station, a primitive but habitable hut somewhere in the middle of it, and much more primitive huts, perhaps only six feet square, scattered at intervals of a dozen miles. The hunters never expect to see anyone they do not know, but there is a very strong convention that every stranger is a friend. All humans are united against their harsh surroundings. Nothing in the Arctic, for example, is ever locked. On the contrary, if you rest in a hut, your own or somebody else's, you leave the fire laid ready in the stove before you go, and the paraffin lamp and a box of matches and whatever food you can possibly spare, just in case a stranger comes that way in need of shelter – perhaps in desperate need.

Most of the men of the Sledge Patrol were hunters; three were weather observers, but they also hunted and travelled when they could. When Eske Brun told them to patrol the coast and watch for Germans, they happily agreed. It meant they could carry on hunting, and be paid by the government too. None of them thought they would ever find a German, or that if they did he would not be as friendly as anyone else on the coast. So when one of them, eighty miles from anywhere, saw a footprint in the snow, he was amazed but not at all alarmed. He was more alarmed that night when a gang of men attacked his hut and succeeded in stealing his dogs and most of his clothes, a deed never heard of in the Arctic. He deduced they were Germans and that they had a ship frozen in close by, and he walked in his socks the eighty miles to the nearest weather station, to suggest they should send a signal to Eske Brun.

I had gone to the Arctic not only to see and feel the beautiful wilderness where this happened, but also in the hope of a glimpse of the life the hunters enjoyed. It was not that I wanted to hunt. I have no hunting instinct at all. When I was at school, I shot a snipe in an Irish bog and blew it to bits. I was so ashamed – such a tiny bird – that I have never shot at anything since except Germans who could shoot back, and I do not think it did them any harm.

When I asked, I learned that the dogs at the airstrip belonged to a couple of hunters, so I asked them to take me along. 'No problem,' they said, in Yankee accents; it was their favourite English phrase, nothing was any problem, but I think they also thought it was all a huge joke. They were going to the first hunting station up the fjord; it was called Ella Island and was fifty miles away. I did not think I would get as far as that, but I imagined I might ride on one of their two sledges. Not a bit of it, they lent me a sledge of my own, with a half-team of six dogs, and told me I needed only four words to drive them.

Of course a sledge dog can be trained in any language. These were used to Eskimo, in which the words for go, stop, right and left have very distinctive sounds evolved especially for dogs. Go is a sharp '*Ah,ah*', like the bark of a dog, stop is a long-drawn '*Ai,ai*'. Right is '*Illi,illi*', and left is '*Yu,yu*'. The only defect of these simple commands is that dogs have opinions of their own and take no notice of anything you tell them unless it happens to be what they want to do. That is not only my own experience. The most expert drivers have told me the same.

I got on all right when we were going over land, because there were drifts of fresh snow and the dogs sank in to their bellies and went at a reasonable speed. I even managed in heaving the sledge up and over the broken ice along the tidemark. But when we got out on the smooth sea-ice, disaster loomed. Dogs are said to be able to gallop at twenty-five miles an hour when they are excited at the beginning of a journey, and I believe it. I copied the hunters, skiing alongside the back end of the sledge with one hand gripping the raised handlebar and the other a ski-stick. I pathetically mewed '*Ai,ai*'. Nothing would stop those dogs. They were determined not to be left behind the other sledges, which they could see or scent ahead, and the drivers of those, I suspect, could no more slow down than I could.

I don't know how far I got before I fell over and the dogs went joyously on without me. It was farther than I expected – farther too than the hunters expected, I think. 'No problem if you loses your sledge,' they had said in their Danish Yankee. 'Your dogs is following ours whatever you says. You just goes home along your own tracks.'

I made several expeditions like that, all more or less abortive. If nothing else, I learned what it would be like if you could do it properly.

Coming back from one trip after losing my dogs again, I made a detour out on the sea-ice to look at an iceberg. The icebergs calve from the glaciers in summer and drift towards the sea, and some which have started late are frozen in again in the autumn and stay there as part of the scenery until the next summer sets them free. There was one just opposite the airstrip. There, the air is so clean and clear that everything looks much closer than it is. It looked like an hour's stroll to the other shore of the fjord, which has the ungainly name of Geographical Society Island, but it is really fifteen miles, and the iceberg was about halfway.

Skiing round it, I came upon a polar bear. I had an idea that no wild animal will attack you if you do not molest it or run away. It was only a theory because I had never then seen a large carnivorous animal except in a zoo; but I had a special sympathy for polar bears just because I had seen them in zoos, where of all animals they are the most tragic. In nature, they have a limitless cold domain. Shut in a concrete bear pit, intolerably hot, with nothing but a scummy green pond too small to swim in, they seem to go quietly mad. You can see it in their endless pacing; they put their feet down in the same places every time until they wear smooth pad marks in the concrete, and every time, as they approach the wall, the same stimulus reaches what is left of their brain and they stop in mid-stride and turn, and do it again, and again, and again, hour after hour, day after day, I presume until they die. I am told imprisoned mother bears eat their cubs and savage the mates they are locked in with, because in nature they meet only to mate, and spend the rest of their lives in solitude.

So meeting one in its own home ground, I stood still and spoke to it kindly, with remorse for what humans did. 'Hi, bear,' I said, and the rest of the conversation was equally inane: 'How are you? Nice to see you.' It is not easy to make small talk with a bear. It was shambling towards me when I saw it, and I was glad when it stopped, perhaps fifty yards away. We stood and looked at each other for rather a long time. I think it was more surprised than I was. After all, I had seen a bear before and knew what it was, and I doubt if it had ever seen a human, certainly not so suddenly and so close. After a while, I began to wonder what happened next in this scenario. Exit, pursued by a bear? I always thought it the funniest line in Shakespeare, but with all those miles of flat open ice behind me I couldn't see any dignified exit. 'Bear,' I said, 'I'm not going to run away, you'll have to.' It began to get visibly bored with the whole performance. It snorted, as if it didn't like the smell, and at last it seemed to shrug its shoulders and turned its back on me and sauntered off eastward, the way it had come. When it had gone, I went on round the iceberg.

Back at the weather station one of my hosts said sternly, 'Where have you been? Out on the sea-ice? Alone? And without a rifle? You must never do that. It's dangerous. Why, you might have met a bear.'

I do not remember much about the flight back to England, except that it started in brilliant sunshine in the middle of the night, and ended on Waterloo Station again in sooty rain in the rush hour, among the packed commuters and the dripping bowler hats.

So to Copenhagen again for more talks with the Danes, feeling now I knew at least what questions to ask them. Then I set about finding the German officer who had led the landing in Greenland and commanded the weather station and made that curious journey with his prisoner. The Danes knew he was a naval lieutenant called Herman Ritter, and told me they had liked him. I traced him to a super-tanker on the regular run between the Persian Gulf and northern Europe; he was its first officer. Sometimes it came into Southampton Water with its cargo, sometimes to the oil terminals of Holland or Germany. Wherever it docked, I contrived to be there, and Ritter and I had a series of conversations which lasted months.

He took a long time to decide he could trust me – not because we had been in opposite navies, but because he was still a frightened man. He was not afraid for himself, but afraid of the gangs of neo-Nazis who were still active in Germany, and of what he imagined they might do to his wife and daughter in revenge for what he had done, or failed to do, in Greenland. I did not know if the fear was justified, so I had to respect it.

As the story evolved, I also came to like Ritter and admire him: a tall, aquiline, greying man, much older than his Danish opponents, shy, ascetic and patently honest, who promised to tell me what had happened as he remembered it, and left me to judge it myself.

He had run his ship, a trawler, into a sheltered bay in the

autumn of 1941, and waited until she was frozen in and covered with snow, safe and invisible. All winter they had sent out their weather signals. But while the Danes were happily driving about the coast, the Germans shut in their ship were at war with themselves and miserable.

Ritter was a devout Austrian Catholic. Moreover, he had spent five years in Spitzbergen before the war, and had fallen in love, like so many others, with the arctic ethos. I never met anyone so driven by his conscience, or so confused by conflicts of loyalty. His first duty, he believed, was to God, and within that he felt a duty to preserve the arctic peace from the sacrilege of war. He had a duty too to the German navy, which had trusted him with his isolated command, and a duty to his crew. But among the crew was a ruthless Nazi faction whose instinct was to carry the war to the Arctic and kill the enemy, the Danish hunters, or smash up and burn their huts so that they would die for lack of shelter. He could not feel any duty to them, and they let him know that they had plans to report to their Party at home that he could not be trusted.

After the German base was discovered from the footprint in the snow, there was a series of encounters between the Germans and the Sledge Patrol, and Ritter was driven to actions he thought defied his duty to God. The worst was when the Germans laid an ambush for one of the hunters in his own hut, and one shot him dead (by mistake, he said) with a machine gun. Ritter blamed himself for a crime and a mortal sin. The hunter had every right to be there and the Germans had none. Next day, Marius Jensen fell into the same trap and was captured. It was then that Ritter felt he must sort out his conscience in peace and told Marius as an expert sledge driver to take him on a journey away from the German base.

That journey began with a military pretext. When the Germans knew their base had been detected they assumed the American air force would come to bomb it. So did the Danes. In fact, the nearest American base was 750 miles away, and they had no aircraft to spare for the job. But Ritter thought he might have to move his base, and ought to find a hunting station to which he could move it. He told Marius first to take him north, into the ultimate ice that reaches the Pole, and beyond.

But away from the base and its atmosphere of politics and ferocious enmity, so foreign to the Arctic, Ritter had a revelation he told me he had not expected. He saw the Arctic again unsullied, as it had been in his happy Spitzbergen years. Again, he was a free man in its barren beauty – its God-given beauty he would have said. Again he heard the ring of sledge runners on the ice and the clamour of well-trained dogs in the hands of an expert, the very sounds of freedom. He wanted to go on and on to the north and never come back. In that euphoria he quite forgot what he was looking for, and also forgot that Marius was his prisoner, not just his companion.

They did not speak much on their journey, even at night when the dogs were fed and the two men cooked and ate together in a hut or a tent, and slept within an arm's length of each other. Marius could easily have escaped by shooting Ritter in his sleep or simply by taking the sledge and Ritter's rifle and leaving him there to die. But neither ever dreamt he might do it.

That was the strange situation Ritter described to me, bit by bit, in the incongruous smell of crude oil in his austere cabin on the tanker, and at least once at his home in the hills of Austria; and nobody hearing it like that could have doubted that all his agonized self-questioning was genuine. If confirmation had been needed, Marius would have confirmed it; they had not met since it happened. Ritter was a very complex man but Marius was the opposite, a simple, straightforward farmer in Denmark when I met him. What had surprised him, he said, was that Ritter was not at all what he expected a German officer to be – neither harsh nor ruthless nor even efficient, but a vague and gentle person who wanted only to talk about his home and learn all he could about driving dogs. Under the arctic influence, both these dissimilar men rejected the brainwashing of war, refused to be enemies, and instead became friends.

Probably what Ritter needed most was an uncomplicated friend, and affection for Marius brought him back to his senses. If they went on farther north they would come to a point of no return, and he would not want to drag Marius beyond it, so he asked him to turn and go south, passing the base at a distance.

Down there were several hunting or weather stations, and Marius knew them well. First was Eskimoness, but the Germans had already burnt it. Then Mosquito Bay, an old Norwegian station which had been deserted a long time; then Ella Island, which was an active weather base; and finally Scoresby Sound, an Eskimo village, with something between a hundred and a hundred and fifty miles from each to the next.

They went first to Mosquito Bay. A day's march before they got there they both saw two recent sledge tracks and silently wondered who had made them. At the solitary hut there was smoke from the chimney and two dog teams tethered outside. Marius knew them, and cursed himself for leaving his escape too late. They were dogs the Germans had stolen. And the door was flung open by the leader of the Nazis, with a machine gun in his hand and three more Germans behind him.

The six men were shut in by a blizzard that night, and the Nazis' hatred of Ritter blew up to the verge of physical violence. Marius did not know what they were quarrelling about, because he did not speak German. What he wanted to know was what the Germans were doing down there, and where they thought they were going. Ritter answered that for him. 'These men want to go to Ella Island,' he said in Norwegian. 'They want to ask you the best way to go.'

Marius would never have said he was a quick thinker, but he thought very quickly then. There were (and still are) two feasible routes from Mosquito Bay to Ella, a long and slow but safer one by the inner fjords, or a short cut across the sea-ice. He told them to take the long one: the sea-ice so late in the year, he said (it was April) would be dangerous. Next day when the blizzard blew itself out the four Germans set off, and took the long way, as he had told them. As soon as they were out of sight Marius took Ritter's rifle and began to harness the dogs. Ritter asked him where he was going, and probably knew the answer. 'To Ella, the short way,' Marius said.

Alone, Marius drove very fast across the sea-ice he had said was dangerous, and covered the ninety miles to Ella without a stop. He took it for granted that the Germans, whose sledges were laden with machine guns and hand grenades, meant to burn the place or at least destroy the weather station, and anyone they found there would be killed or captured. He also thought, rightly, that when they found he had misled them and got there first with a warning, they would be furious.

But when he arrived, the place was empty. There was nobody to warn. He found a letter Poulson, the leader of the patrol, had left for him two days before. They had searched for him, it said, but had given it up, and on radio orders from Eske Brun they had all retreated south to Scoresby Sound. They would leave caches of food for himself and his dogs. There was a sketch map to show him where the caches would be.

So his escape route was all laid out for him. He did not take it. He went back by the way he had come, full speed again, to Mosquito Bay. He drove right round the hut two miles away counting the sledge tracks: three in and three out, including his own. The chimney was smoking. So Ritter was still there, and still alive and alone.

When Ritter saw him coming, it did not strike him as strange that a prisoner who had escaped should come back to the place he had escaped from. He was so tired, mentally and physically, that nothing would have surprised him. If he thought at all of the future, there were only two things he could have expected. Either the four Germans would come back, after escaping an ambush at Ella which they would think he and Marius had planned, and would shoot him there and then or take him under arrest to the base. Or nobody would come back, and he would die at Mosquito Bay, of scurvy if nothing else had killed him first. All Marius said when he came in was, 'Get your clothes on. We're going south.'

South they went. They had already travelled six hundred miles together, and it was three hundred more to Scoresby Sound. There was no darkness, it was only a fortnight more to the midnight sun, and they had to pass within sight of Ella Island. For the first ninety miles, Marius expected to meet the Germans coming in the opposite direction. But the Germans in fact were still at Ella Island. They were keeping a bad lookout, and did not see the sledge go past. In fifteen days Marius and Ritter reached Scoresby Sound and met the rest of the Sledge Patrol.

Inevitably, Poulson asked Marius why he had gone back to Mosquito Bay; it was a crazily dangerous thing to have done. Marius laughed and said, 'Because I knew you'd ask so many questions. I thought I'd better bring Ritter to answer them.' The story of what Marius had done reached the military people without a better answer, and Marius was given two medals, one British and one American — but for capturing Ritter, not for rescuing him.

There the matter rested, until I met Marius at his farm in Denmark after the war, and asked him the same question. He laughed again. 'I just went because I liked the man,' he said. 'We had come a long way together, and I was ashamed to have left him alone. But I couldn't explain that in wartime, and I still can't explain it to people who don't know the Arctic. You know Ritter, and you know a bit about the Arctic. You ought to understand.'

I think I did, and that was why I liked the story. The distorted morals of war broke down, and the morals of the Arctic won.

FOURTEEN

The Dalai Lama

Admiration for the Arctic and arctic people has always stuck with me, but after that Greenland journey my travels to investigate stories began to take me in the opposite direction, to hot countries instead of cold ones: to the backwoods of the Zambesi valley to meet the primitive tribe called Tonga whose villages and ancestral lands were being drowned in the lake behind the Kariba Dam; to the deserts of Arabia for a biography of King ibn Saud; to the tropical forest of Panama for its long buccaneering history; to Argentina and Uruguay for the fate of the German battleship *Von Spee*; and of course, between hot and cold, to all the countries of western Europe and a good many of the United States. Most of these trips had exciting or comic moments, but I am not going to write about them all. Now that travel is so easy, travellers' tales are boring, and many people have seen much more of the world than I have.

To me, though, the journeys all had a theme, and a central point in the theme — and certainly the most educational of the journeys — were my visits to the Dalai Lama of Tibet, the first in 1962 and the most recent in 1984.

Like most things in an author's life, my acquaintance with the Dalai Lama — or friendship, I think I may say — began by chance. When he was driven out of Tibet by the Chinese communists he decided to write his autobiography, although he was only in his mid-twenties. He wrote or dictated it in Tibetan, and it was translated, not very well, into English, and came into the hands of McGraw Hill, who were my American publishers at the time. They rang me up from New York and asked if I would go to India to see him, improve the English of his story, add some bits which he had left out — his rigorous education, for instance, which he did not think would interest western readers – and generally advise him how to put the story together. When I asked them why they had chosen me, they said they 'reckoned I was the kind of guy who could get along with a living Buddha'. I don't know what formidable sort of prelate they expected him to be, but that turned out to be the least of my worries. The Dalai Lama was very easy indeed to 'get along with', a charming, modest, humorous and highly intelligent young man.

That was the nearest I ever came to the role of ghost writer, and I do not think I would have done it for anyone else in the world. I did not expect to be specially impressed by him. But Tibet in its deliberate isolation had seemed a romantic place to many Englishmen. For me the romance went back to the first attempts to climb Mount Everest when I was a boy. Now, it had suffered a cruel invasion. I was not concerned by the politics of it; I think I thought Marxism was the best, maybe the only way to govern the vast peasant population of China. But the International Commission of Jurists had produced a damning report and found China guilty of genocide in Tibet. Evidently the Dalai Lama, the secular and spiritual leader of that country, had an important story to tell, and evidently he needed a little help in telling it, because he had never then travelled out of Tibet, except to China and India, and did not know much about the tastes of the western world. I wanted to help him if I could.

In his exile, he was living at a place called Dharmsala, a derelict ex-British army hill station, long deserted, which the government of India had lent him. To an Englishman, it was a beautiful but melancholy place. On a steep flank of a ridge of the Himalayan foothills, bungalows were scattered among the oak and rhodo-dendron forests. I suppose they had been inhabited by British officers and their memsahibs, but they were falling into ruin. Hidden in the woods was a stone-built gothic church with a graveyard where forgotten men lay buried far from home. I was told there was an English lord among them, and that two Christians were still living in the place; certainly somebody rang the church bell on Sunday mornings. There was also a crumbling hamlet called McLeod Ganj (who was McLeod, I wondered) with a large shop which was almost empty except for odds and ends of ghostly merchandise: a box of dusty briar pipes, for instance, though probably nobody within a hundred miles had smoked a briar pipe since Indian rule began, except me. The hillsides were crossed and re-crossed by bridle paths, hewn out when labour was cheap but now neglected, where memsahibs no doubt had taken decorous exercise on horseback, escorted by obsequious syces. It was all a relic of a time of British arrogance I did not like to think of.

But when I was there in 1962, its ambience had changed. The military pomp had vanished. Instead, it had an air of learning, gentleness and calm. There was an Indian army guard, but in the two and a half months I lived there I met nobody but Tibetan Buddhists, admirable people, infinitely patient, kind, jolly and full of fun, among them the Dalai Lama's cabinet, his mother and two sisters and his tutors, respected philosophers, all of whom had joined the flood of a hundred thousand refugees who had followed him out of Tibet.

Half a mile or so above the sepulchral hamlet, up a track too steep for anything but a mule or a jeep, was the largest bungalow. It must have been the general's, and that was where the Dalai Lama lived; but it was being eaten away by ants, and its red tin roof leaked so much in the monsoon that all the rooms had buckets to catch the drips.

My first impression was simply of friendliness. The Dalai Lama took both my hands in his, patted me on the arm – a gesture I came to know well – and led me to an armchair on his derelict verandah. He wore the robes, maroon, brown and yellow, of a monk. Later, when he came to know me better and there were no Tibetan visitors, he sometimes wore English sports clothes, but still in Buddhist colours – maroon shirt, brown slacks, yellow socks and suede shoes. Dressed like that, with his horn-rimmed glasses and his shorn head like a crew-cut, he might have come straight from any western university – except that whatever he wore, it was always immaculately clean and pressed, and he always looked as if he had just had a hot bath.

In the first few weeks, he always spoke to me in Tibetan through his interpreter, a young Sikkimese called Sonam Topgay Kazi. Then one morning Sonam was called away, and the Dalai Lama began to speak English, very shyly. Now, he speaks it fluently, but I think I was the first Englishman he had spoken it to, and he did it slowly, correctly and rather pedantically, because he had taught himself entirely out of books. In time he became more confident and relaxed and I could see he was beginning to think in English. But he used it only for ordinary conversation. For anything complicated he went back to Tibetan, which he spoke quickly and evidently forcefully, emphasizing what he said by gestures.

It was a strange privilege, and a unique one, to spend hours every day discussing his eventful life, his religion and his hopes for the future, with a young man some millions of people respected as royal and revered as divine. In spite of the open friendliness, I could never quite forget his status. Our sessions were often interrupted when his secretary, a monk called Khenchung Tara, came in to say that a party of pilgrims had arrived. I took myself off when that happened, thinking a foreigner would be an interference, but sometimes I hid where I could see without being seen. The pilgrims came mostly in groups of twenty or so, men, women and children – families I think – who must have walked for weeks or months in hope of a glimpse of him. They were moments of strong emotion. He went to the top of the steps of the verandah, with his boyish smile and graceful gestures of blessing. Men bowed to the ground before his presence, weeping, their faces set in expressions of ecstasy, crying out in a transport of religious joy. Girls held up their babies so that his glance might rest on them, or theirs on him. I don't remember that anyone spoke: they just cried. After a few minutes they were led away again, bemused by emotion, and each was given a single bead, a symbol of blessing, to form the first bead of a rosary one felt they would cherish till they died.

After the first of those visits the Dalai Lama said to me: 'They think I am a god. I think they are mistaken. But you know, our religion is founded on reason, not on faith, and everyone must interpret it within the limits of his own intellect. They are very simple people, so they interpret it in very simple ways, which they are perfectly entitled to do.'

'If you are not a god, what are you?' I said.

'I am a High Incarnate,' he said in English, and began to laugh. 'You look bewildered,' he continued. 'But you're not a simple person. Let me try to explain.' And he began then and there to tell me that all beings, human or animal, are reincarnations, working their way through a series of lives towards Buddhahood, the perfect enlightenment of Nirvana. In the end, they will all escape from the cycle of birth and death by achieving that perfect state. Many lifetimes ago he had achieved it, but he had chosen of his own will to be reborn, in order to help all other beings towards it.

And then we were off on a chase which was often repeated as I tried to follow him through the infinite convolutions of Buddhist thought. It often made him laugh, not at me for being so slow to follow, but at himself for saying things that were so obscure. I had to do my best, with the help of the interpreter, because he wanted to condense it all in his book. But we had to agree in the end that there was a limit to what I could understand or put into English, because the words simply do not exist in western languages to express many Buddhist concepts. Buddhist ethics are simple, and good by any standards, but its dogma and practices are very complex to a western mind.

Although it was often hard for me to follow him, I was always struck by the clarity of his thought, and always aware that what he was saying was crystal clear to Sonam, and to the secretary Khenchung Tara, if he happened to be there. I often had to ask him why he had taken some action in the past; and when I did he would look up at the ceiling for a second or two and then produce an answer that was orderly, logical and complete. And when Buddhist practice was not logical, he confessed it.

An obvious and simple lack of logic arose when I was dining with him and his staff of half a dozen. A fly would sometimes get in through the holes in the old screen doors. Everyone stopped eating while somebody caught the fly. They were adept at catching a fly in their cupped hands without hurting it; then whoever had got it would carefully carry it out of doors and let it go. 'Mathematically,' the Dalai Lama said, 'it is only reasonable to think that every animal and insect, in the course of its innumerable lives and ours, has been our best friend, our father or mother, or brother or sister. So we are bound to treat them with affection and respect.'

I didn't deny it, and he laughed and added 'I know what you will say with your logical mind. We eat meat. It's true, and we know we shouldn't. But in Tibet we had to eat animal fats and proteins, because the crops we could grow were so limited. So of course we thought of an excuse. Butchers have chosen to do what they do, although they know they will suffer for it in future lives. The rest of us see bits of an animal in a butcher's shop and tell ourselves it would be silly not to eat it when it is already dead. Its death would be wasted. I am told most religions have moments when logic wears thin. Do you agree?'

My own logic wore thin with rats. There was nowhere for guests to stay, and I lived in what had been the cookhouse. So did Sonam and Khenchung Tara. Its ceilings were full of holes, and the rats peered down at me in bed. Nobody would have thought for a moment of killing them, but everybody agreed they were a nuisance and was delighted one day when a mongoose got into the roof. There were three nights of mayhem above our heads while the mongoose demolished the rats, and then peace.

There was not much recreation at Dharmsala. The Dalai Lama worked non-stop at one thing or another, and everyone else seemed quite content to follow his example and think themselves on call at any time. But of course I could never see a mountain of any kind without wanting to climb it, and I was tempted by the ridge we lived on, if only to see what was on the other side. I proposed it to a few people, and the expedition grew to a major picnic, eight or ten Tibetans and me. The ridge was not a mountain by local standards but it was quite a height, eleven thousand feet I believe, and half way up there was a simple sort of shelter like an Alpine refuge, another relic perhaps of the British Raj.

From the Dalai Lama's portraits, I had never thought of him as a very athletic young man; he looked it more when he wore western clothes. But three hours was thought good time to reach the shelter; I did it in three myself. The Dalai Lama was said to have done it in two, and I have this much reason to believe it: the whole of his staff, I know, lived in mild trepidation of being invited to go up there with him. They rather pointedly did not suggest he should accompany us.

The Tibetans were like children when we reached the snow, which they had not seen since they escaped, except in the distance. They ate it and rolled in it, and threw snowballs at each other

The Dalai Lama around the time when I first met him.

Endless patience: the District Officer tries
to explain the Kariba Dam.

Tonga village as the flood rises.

Tonga girls before the move – and after.

Panama –
Caledonia Bay.

A Cuna Indian
and his granddaughter
pole me through
the moat dug
by Scotsmen in 1700.

Sailing my boat.

and at me. From the top, there was an endless fascinating vista of snow peaks and shadowed valleys across Kashmir to the frontier of Tibet. There was also, I remember, a stunningly beautiful and dirty shepherd boy wearing nothing but a sheep-skin, barefooted, driving his flock out of India through the snow towards an unimaginable destination. He did not speak to us in any of the languages we tried.

With us was a young man who had been in the Tibetan army, a rather primitive organization. He kindly carried our picnic in a rucksack, and sticking out of the top was an instrument like a flute, so I asked him for a tune. Standing up there looking out at his inaccessible home, I hoped for some beautiful melody to fit the scene, expressing the pain of exile. What he played was 'It's a long way to Tipperary'.

'Thank you very much,' I said through Sonam the interpreter. 'That's a British army song, you know.'

Sonam told him. 'No, no,' he relayed the reply. 'He says it's a very old Tibetan marching song.'

I had put my foot in it, and I should have known better. There was a logical explanation. Back in Edwardian times the then Dalai Lama had decided to modernize his army, and he invited three other armies, Japanese, Chinese and British, to train it. A British sergeant-major won the competition, and it was he who brought the Tibetan army up to date, including no doubt its military bands; or so British history says.

But who was I to argue with that young man? I always thought it was a British song, and he thought it was Tibetan, and for all I really knew he could have been right and our history could have been wrong; it often is. The Edwardian sergeant-major could have picked up the tune from the Tibetan army and brought it back to England, or to Ireland, and the words have the same significance in any language: 'It's a long, long journey back to Lhasa, But my heart's right there.' It expressed his feelings any-way, and thank goodness I had the sense not to argue. We British robbed many people in the past. We can at least leave them their songs.

I don't think I ever understood while I was there what an appallingly difficult job the Dalai Lama had to do from that forsaken bungalow. Perhaps then he only partly understood it himself, because he was still at the beginning of it. For twenty-five years now he has laboured to build a religious yet economically self-supporting community among the hundred thousand refugees who followed him. In this he has succeeded. He has created schools and craft workshops, communal farms and hospitals, saved the refugees from starvation and given them something to live for; a nucleus of Tibetan culture is assured. But even the refugees are divided. Most of them share his religious ideals, but the teenagers, like teenagers everywhere, are inclined to be more interested in politics than religion, and most interested of all in discos and the Beatles. In Tibet, among those who stayed behind, the divisions are far more acute.

The Chinese have done their best to destroy Tibetan religion and culture. They have wrecked huge monasteries, killed something like a million monks by the cruellest means, preached communist slogans, and above all taken Tibetan children to China to bring them up as communists. Most people would have said Tibet was hopelessly fragmented, and its ancient civilization could never be revived.

After those twenty-five years, there are beginning to be signs that it will be. If it is, it will be due to what the Dalai Lama practises and preaches: universal kindness and compassion.

His first ambition when I was there was to travel in the west, to learn about western religious philosophy and technology, the foundations of material prosperity. These had been completely lacking in Tibet, although he himself knew a surprising amount about science, which he had taught himself – like his English – out of books. One day, seeing my camera, he grieved over its dustiness (everything was dusty at Dharmsala) and he took it away, took it all to pieces, cleaned it inside and out and put it together again. He also took watches to pieces, at first to find out how they worked and later to mend them when they did not work. He was a keen photographer and had movie equipment too, and I don't doubt he now has video and computers, and takes them to pieces. I came home in the middle of my stay at Dharmsala and asked him if there was anything I could bring back from England. He said he would like some more books on science, and when I asked him what sort of science he said, as my eight-year-old son might have said, 'Oh, you know, sending rockets to the moon and all that sort of thing.' I heard years later, when he was in America, that he had visited some NASA control centre, and I could imagine he longed to take that to pieces too, and find out how it worked and put it together again. He would have succeeded, I'm sure.

In those early days I tried to persuade him not to be in a hurry to travel. He was too innocent to know what he would be up against, and I did not know if he would survive the west – the press conferences, the television interviews, the cranks and debunkers, the comparison with bogus eastern gurus, all the unavoidable assaults on dignity and innocence. He would lose his aura of mystery, and I did not know what he had to put in its place. In fact, he did put off going for eleven years, whether through my advice I do not know. Then he went, with success.

He has been to Russia, given lecture tours in America and met all the Christian leaders of Europe – the Pope, the Archbishops of Canterbury and Westminster, the Moderator of the Church of Scotland – and has been greeted with equal honour and affection by them all, which is no small achievement in itself. When I last met him, he was in England, and he asked me to lunch with him alone in the Deanery of Westminster, where he was staying as a guest of the Dean. He had not changed very much from the young man I had known. He patted my arm again and led me by both hands to a room the Dean had lent him, and said how happy he was to meet an old friend.

He is a well-known international figure now, and has won the hearts of the most unexpected people. He seems to have done it by transparent honesty and goodness. Nobody, however cynical or suspicious, can suspect him of guile. The only thing he preaches is the oldest and simplest of religious messages, love and compassion for all beings, especially your enemies; and he does it without any dogmatic strings attached, without trying to convert anyone to Buddhism – much better, he says, to stick to whatever faith, if any, you were brought up with.

One wonders how far mere goodness can go in the modern political world. Can you disarm your political opponents by loving them, by taking a step beyond Gandhi's passive resistance? It remains to be seen, but nobody yet has found any other way of doing it. He has been talking lately of going back to Tibet in 1985. If he does, it will be the sternest test of what he stands for. Most Tibetans will flock to follow him again, to the extent that the Chinese will have to admit they have failed. So they will be tempted to bury him secretly in a Chinese gaol. He knows that he may be the last Dalai Lama, and he has prepared for it by drafting a democratic constitution, in which, he says, the most important thing is that the Tibetans should be able to get rid of him if they ever want to. But he hopes not to give them any reason to want to. I think he intends himself to choose the child he will be reborn in. There is no doctrine to stop him doing that, and it would free him for the rest of his present life from power and wealth and allow him to be an ordinary monk – 'the monk Tenzin Gyatso‘, he says, which is his name. All he wants for himself is to pursue his monastic studies in quiet obscurity. On the other hand, if he leaves it until he dies the Chinese will announce they have discovered his reincarnation in a Chinese communist boy, no Tibetan will accept it and the succession will vanish in warlike argument. Recently I read a sermon he preached to Tibetans in Delhi. It ended, 'If there is anything you like in what I have said, fine. If not, no problem. All you have to do is reject it. You must not accept anything just because it was said by somebody called the Dalai Lama. Accept it only if it seems reasonable to you, and of benefit to you in your spiritual life.' It seems to me the most ruthless enemy will be hard pressed to find a weapon to counter that.

I am lucky to have met him when he was young and to have known him so long. He never made me a Buddhist, but he would not have wanted to. He did make me a better man, more patient and tolerant and kinder than I was.

FIFTEEN

The Tonga

I have been lucky in my modest travels to meet men and women of many different religions, perhaps because that was fundamentally what I was looking for: Eskimos who are purely and simply Christian and whose every action is guided by the Sermon on the Mount; animists in the African bush and the jungles of Central America; Hindus and Buddhists in India; Mohammedans in Pakistan and the desert of Arabia; and of course a variety of Christians, Jews and pagans at home, in Europe and in America. I do not often talk to them about beliefs, I only listen, and meet good men and bad among them all; but I think the goodness is more conspicuous in some, especially Buddhists, as I have mentioned, and Eskimos.

What took me to central Africa was the Kariba Dam. An American magazine offered me what seemed a lot of money to go there and write about it, so I did. It was half finished then – a very large dam, a very long way from anywhere, designed to produce enough hydro-electric power for the whole of Rhodesia, and incidentally to create the biggest man-made lake in the world. But I soon got tired of millions of tons of concrete, and wondered what was happening farther up the Zambezi River, where the enormous lake was quickly rising.

At first, the only people I could find who took any interest in that were the game rangers; they were concerned about the animals left on islands which were getting smaller by the day and in the end would vanish. The rangers were capturing all the animals they could, doping them and releasing them again on the mainland, and I went out with them many times in their motor boats to watch.

I must say it was very exciting if you had never lived for long in the African bush and were not used to animals. It reminded me of deep sea fishing; you never knew – or at least I never knew – what you were going to catch. The valley had been thickly forested elephant, lion and rhino country, and the rangers would catch anything. But I think they had a good idea what was left on each island before they landed on it to round up the survivors. They must have known, if only to take the appropriate gear.

Approaching those islands was hair-raising to a seaman. Crossing the open lake was pleasant; the sun blazed down, but there was a breeze, and it was very much cooler than the dam itself, which is in a gorge. (It was said that if you had a mug of tea down in the gorge – some people did – it was no good waiting for it to cool before you drank it, it just got hotter and hotter.) But as the boat got nearer the islands you had to navigate among twigs and then branches sticking out of the water – the topmost boughs of drowned trees, still standing. Nearer, you were among the trunks of the trees, all dead. It is an odd sensation to be steering a boat half way up the trees of a forest, especially when those trees have snakes, trying to escape the waters, in their branches. The passage of the boats shook them off, and the rangers jumped overboard and wrestled with them, swimming, and got most of them on board and into boxes. As it grew shallower, you were ploughing a channel through a thick mat of weeds, water hyacinth I believe. I never saw the shoreline, but the junior animal catchers sounded with poles and jumped in when it was waist deep, and towed the boat with its clogged propellors until there was more or less solid ground beneath it.

They waded ashore with a very large net and quantities of worn-out nylon stockings, and they strung up the net about ten feet high in the branches right across the island. Then they all went round by boat to the farthest point of the island, leaving me, usually alone, behind the net. I was reasonably agile in those days and I had signed the usual blood chit, but they didn't trust me on the business side of the net when they started to drive the animals towards it.

Most of the animals they caught while I was with them were impala, large and very beautiful antelopes. Normally they are perfectly harmless. But I heard them coming, crashing through the undergrowth, before I saw them. I didn't know what they were and it was quite exciting enough.

On the first day, the first thing I saw was a family of warthogs, father and mother and three children, which had got under the net and came charging at me in single file, their tails straight up in the air like periscopes. I don't know if frightened warthogs are dangerous, but they look it and I did not want to find out, so like a coward I stood behind a solitary tree which had the defect of being much thinner than I was, and they raced past it, only glancing at me with blood-shot eyes. Then the impala were there, all round and above me, scores or hundreds, fleeing in terror with incredible leaps. A few got through or even over the net, charged past me and vanished beyond; but most in mid-leap caught their feet in the net and crashed struggling to the ground. The rangers, black and white, all shouting, came running behind and jumped on the animals, wrestled with them, subdued them by sheer strength and tied their legs together with the nylon stockings, which were supposed not to injure them because they were soft. When they were quiet enough a senior ranger, or the doctor from the clinic in Kariba, came with a hypodermic syringe and gave them a shot of something that stopped their struggles; then they were carried to the boats and dumped on board. I don't know if they were unconscious or only paralyzed, but their staring eyes bore expressions of terror and despair. Some started to move again in the boat and were given a second shot.

On the mainland they were carried ashore and laid out in rows, their legs were untied and when they began to come round they tottered to their feet and staggered away, quite lost and disorientated, to look for somewhere to hide.

The world's press got hold of this story in the end, and gave it huge publicity and a ridiculous name, Operation Noah. I refused to write anything about it because I had secretly come to believe it was futile. The rangers were not to blame. Their hearts were in the job, they cheerfully put up with discomfort and danger and were as gentle as they could be – though that was not very gentle. But in my own mind I questioned whether their good intentions could really repair any of the damage done by that man-made flood. Would it not have been better to leave the animals to work out their own salvation if they could? No doubt more would have drowned or starved, but the survivors would have been healthy, not traumatized, and the balance of nature would have settled down again.

Some things struck me as absurd. Why risk your life to rescue poisonous snakes – except perhaps to prove to yourself that you can? Or baboons? The rangers rescued baboons even though they were classed as vermin and the government paid a bounty of half-a-crown for a baboon's tail, eight tails to a pound. That was good money; an African labourer on the dam worked for sixty hours to earn a pound. Even the harmless impala were part of the diet of African tribes, and I was told each landing place was surrounded at a discreet distance by a ring of native hunters, who gladly knocked off the impala before they recovered. And some animals had much more sense than they were given credit for, and were quite able to look after themselves. I heard – though it was only a secondhand story – that another party of rangers, halfway up the lake, had doped two elephants on an island and towed them with enormous labour and ingenuity to the mainland. When the elephants woke up, they waded into the water and swam back to the island, and some weeks later, when they were good and ready, they swam to the mainland again.

One day in the boat we passed a drowning village, round thatched huts with the water up to their eaves. 'What about the people?' I asked someone in the boat.

'What people?' he said. 'Oh, you mean the Tonga? I dunno what happens to them. They don't come under the Game Department.'

I don't mean to suggest that nobody cared about the Tonga. Some people did, but very few people in the cities knew anything much about them. They were a small and humble tribe, about 50,000 of them, and they lived in that valley and nowhere else. But not only did they not come under the Game Department, they came under two quite separate departments, indeed two separate governments. I began to think I had missed the real story of Kariba, so had the journalists. It was not the technical marvels of the concrete, and not the animals, but the people who had lived in the valley before the flood; and I went back to Africa several times to see what was happening to them.

At the time, I did not wonder why I took such an interest in the Tonga. It started with my annoyance that the newsmen who were making such a fuss about the animals seldom mentioned the humans who also had to be rescued. And when I began to meet the Tonga I found they were very likeable humans, courteous, gentle, cheerful and easy-going. I liked them a lot more than I liked some white Rhodesians. But, looking back, the main reason was that I had never before met a simple tribe at the very moment of its first head-on encounter with civilization. Those moments happen all over the world these days, and they are always full of drama, and nearly always tragic.

When I was first there, you could meet the Tonga in both stages, before and after the encounter. Before it, they were much the same as when Livingstone found them, a hundred years before. The men had taken to wearing tattered shorts, but they still carried spears; the women wore sticks or porcupine quills through their noses and not much else. When they were about fourteen, their top front teeth were broken off by holding an axe against them and hitting it hard with the back of another axe. Nobody knew why: it was just the fashion, and it is often hard to find reasons for fashions.

So the first superficial effect of the encounter was more evident among the women than the men. When the government came and moved their villages they met a few people from other tribes and, toothless and naked, they felt conspicuous and foolish. Traders got among them, and easily convinced them they needed cotton frocks and headsquares and sandals. I must admit it seemed to me an improvement. Wearing the frocks they had chosen, some of the Tonga teenagers – still young enough to have their teeth – looked quite charming, and even more cheerful and twinkle-eyed than before.

But frocks cost money, and they had to extract the money from the men; and as the men had always used goats as currency, they had no money and had to take temporary jobs, road-building or working in cities or on European farms along the railway eighty miles to the north.

On maps, the Zambezi River was the boundary between Northern and Southern Rhodesia. Both had been British colonies, but the South was in the process of declaring its own independence, while the North had not yet begun. Both governments knew the Tonga would have to be moved from the land they were living on before the British came, but they had quite different methods of doing it. In the South, under the government in Salisbury, the tribe could be ordered to move by law, and police or even troops could be used to see that they did it. But the North was still governed by the Colonial Office in London, which was still wedded to the ideal of government by consent, and it had no legal power to order anyone to move.

The river had never been any sort of boundary to the Tonga. About half the tribe lived on the south side of it and half on the north. Villages near it were neighbours, and people often crossed it in canoes to borrow things, or to visit girl-friends on the other side, or simply to go to parties when somebody over there had brewed some beer. Each government planned to move its own people away from the river, an unimaginable distance into the hills, never to be seen again.

My instinctive sympathy was with the northern method, the old-fashioned colonial ideal, so in my later visits I spent most time on the northern side. But I can't entirely have neglected the southern side, because I remember flying in a very small aircraft the 150 miles up the southern shore of the lake to see the man who was in charge of the Tonga there. I could not forget that flight, because the pilot insisted on flying among the tree-tops, looking for elephants. He found a big herd in the end, and flew round and round it to give me a better look, which caused a stampede and was against the game laws, and anyhow made me airsick. I felt like stampeding too.

When he landed me, safe and rather ill, at the only airstrip near that end of the lake, I found the man in charge. He was a sympathetic character who had lived among the Tonga for years, and was fond of them and sorry for them. He told me he governed them by Valley Law, which he defined as one quarter law and three quarters common sense. But he was moving them in the southern way, by force of law and without much explanation of what was happening. 'Remember, they've never even made a cart on wheels,' he said. 'How can you hope to explain to them about hydro-electric power? It would only confuse them. I tell them

I'm sorry, but they have got to move because the government says so. They understand that all right. They don't like it, of course, but we find them enough land clear of the flood, and they'll settle down there in the end. You'll see, it's the kindest way.'

Nevertheless, the people like him on the other side, having no legal powers, had to do it by patient explanation and persuasion. That task, which nobody could envy, fell mainly to five British administrators – the District Commissioner and four District Officers who were his juniors – and the very few Tonga (I met only two) who spoke English. The first explanations were semantic. There were no words in the Tongan language which meant anything like dam, generator, turbine, cable, electricity, power, so the English words had to be used, and in the end they crept into the Tongan language; but they were only words, and gave the Tonga no mental image of the things they described.

Among all the uncomprehending questions the Tonga asked, there were two that those five men began to dread: What is the use of the dam? Why do people want electricity?

They had to say the dam would help to bring prosperity to the country, which meant more schools and hospitals and roads and factories and houses. It would create more jobs, and better-paid jobs. But the Tonga had never had any of those things or consciously wanted them, except the half-dozen mission schools which were already established in the valley. Least of all did they want to be wage earners in mines or city factories. All they wanted was to be left where they were, and to live as they had lived for as long as they could remember. Perhaps the only honest answer to those questions was that for the Tonga and most other rural Africans, as far ahead as anyone could foresee, the Kariba Dam was no possible use whatever.

On the colonial side, I attached myself to the District Commissioner or one of the District Officers – when I could without getting in their way. With the DC, I attended meetings of the Tonga Native Authority, which was an embryo parliament and the court of law. With the DOs I did my best to keep up on their marathon tours of the Tonga villages. There were several places where you could get a Landrover down to the floor of the valley, or to the advancing edge of the lake; but it was their professional pride to walk, very fast in spite of the staggering heat, usually with only a single attendant, a messenger who was a Tonga. They never carried any sort of weapon or seemed to take any notice of lions, elephants, and other alarming creatures. They were supposed to carry snake-bite outfits, but they often forgot. It was partly tradition; DOs since the earliest days of the colonies had always walked on their tours. Also, they explained to me, you could meet the Tonga as man to man only if you travelled as they travelled. It certainly worked. When the DO walked into a village, unheralded and unguarded, everyone was plainly glad to see him and greeted him as a friend. The village headman sent his wives to bring stools, the only symbols of authority, one for the DO and one for himself, and also one for me. I did not deserve one, and I don't think the headmen ever quite discovered what I was there for, but any foreigner brought by the DO was an honoured guest. The rest of the village gathered round and sat on the ground, and the day's discussion began, the DO breaking off now and again to tell me what was going on.

Mostly it was routine. The people were telling him everything that had happened since his last visit; the minor crimes, the crops, the weddings and funerals. It struck me how few events there were in a Tongan village. But inevitably the discussion came back to the single great event, the impending move, and I began to understand that the Tongas' fear of the move was mainly spiritual.

When these encounters happen, between an elementary tribe and civilization, the first things to get trampled underfoot are the religious beliefs of the tribe. I had read in the newspapers that the Tonga believed in a serpent-god who lived in the river and would knock down the white man's wall. But like so much city opinion, that was rubbish, and underrated the Tonga. They loved the river, but only in the sense that seafaring people love the sea. The river was much the most important feature of their physical surroundings. Every year in the rains it brought down a load of silt which made its banks fertile, and often the crop they grew in the silt was all that saved the Tonga from starvation. The river's flow seemed as eternal and immutable as the rising and setting of the sun, and to talk of stopping it seemed impossible and wrong.

They had only a vague idea of a supreme god. It may have been a relic of the sermons Livingstone preached when he passed that way in 1855, or perhaps an emanation from the half-dozen mission schools, which each had a small circle of nominal Christianity around it. But that god had not much effect on their daily lives; they were content with the thought that nobody could possibly know the wishes of a god like that, so it was no good praying to him.

What they did believe in strongly was the human soul. When a person died his soul was inherited by somebody living, who also inherited the dead person's husband or wives and children; and the soul went on existing, real but invisible, not inside the inheritor but close behind his back. Nearly all the Tonga went about with one or two disembodied souls behind them, and the souls had wishes, needs and opinions of their own. After two or three generations, the individual souls were forgotten and were thought to have joined the vague company of the ancient dead. On the whole, the souls were conservative and hated change, and it was not only the living Tonga but the souls who had to be persuaded to accept the idea of the dam.

The only people in direct communion with the souls were priests or diviners called Sikatongo. The Sikatongo were saintly men who also controlled and prophesied rain, and were therefore in charge of seed corn and planting. They performed their ceremonies in shrines, and this made them doubly conservative. They were certain the souls would be resentful and angry at the great change of moving to other lands, and they also feared that, if their shrines were flooded and drowned, they would not be able to move them and would lose their power over the rain.

Hearing of all this in those little groups of huts, so isolated and wild among the forests, I had no inclination to laugh at the Tonga for their beliefs, as the city people did. They seemed to me to be as worthy of respect as other religions are.

Patience nearly succeeded. There were seven chiefdoms on that northern side of the valley. Two of them, far up the valley, did not have to move because their lands were above the estimated flood-line. For four, new land had been found so that each would have to move the shortest possible distance. That left one, the

213

domain of a chief called Chipepo, for whom there was simply not enough room in the valley. Chipepo had about seven thousand people. Two thousand of them could be fitted in, but the other five thousand had to move over a hundred miles, right out of the valley and down again to a district called Lupitu, which in fact was downstream of the dam. The chief agreed, reluctantly, but others, especially the Sikatongo, could not bring themselves to imagine going so far. The discussions swung forwards and backwards. On one day, a whole group of villages would agree, then in the night they would change their minds and refuse to listen. Ancient arguments, disproved months or years before, were dragged out again: that the river would push down the dam or flow round the ends of it, that it was all a government plot to steal the Tongas' land and give it to European farmers, that if the Tonga were strong and refused to move, then the government would be weak and abandon the whole idea.

The DO responsible for Chipepo's people was a young Scotsman called Alex Smith. He knew those people better than anyone, he liked them and they had always trusted him. Now he became aware that somebody else, some politician, was getting among them and arguing against him, telling them things that were quite untrue but were what they wanted to hear. Village headmen, people he had known for years, said they were not allowed to speak to him now, but some of them showed him cards which they said they had had to buy for three shillings and sixpence each. They could not read them, and thought they were something the government was selling, a kind of talisman: if they bought them, they had been told, they would not have to move. In fact they were, or purported to be, membership cards of the African National Congress.

Generally, Congress was a respectable institution. Its aim was to protect Africans against exploitation, and since the laws of Northern Rhodesia had been conscientiously drawn up with just the same aim, the government had no quarrel with it. Possibly, if anyone had spoken up for the Tonga at the very beginning, the Kariba Dam might have been judged unfair to them, but everyone had agreed, the Government, the Chiefs, the Tongas' own parliament, even Chief Chipepo himself – everyone except a few young Tonga who were taking the chance to collect

three-and-sixpences. The urban slogans of African nationalism –
'One Man One Vote' – began to appear on notices nailed to
trees. But it was much too late. Everyone who had any worldly
experience knew that the governments had already spent tens of
millions of pounds on the dam, and the protests of Chipepo's
remaining five thousand people were not going to stop it now.

This was the last straw for Alex Smith. He began to feel that
all his months of patient labour had failed. Against that sort
of unreasoning opposition, he could not persuade the rest of
Chipepo's people to move a hundred miles. Nor could anyone
else. It could not be done without the weight of law behind it
and, much though he hated the idea, he knew he had to ask for
police to enforce the move.

His request went up and up through the hierarchy of the colonial
administration and a series of more and more senior officers came
down to his lonely camp, close to the river, to see for themselves.
Nobody blamed him, except himself, but it was clear the government would not change the law of the land to make those five
thousand people move. At last, somebody discovered that the
Native Authority, the Tongas' parliament, had a constitutional
right to ban Congress from Tonga land, and also to request the
government to send police. That seemed to be a way out. But even
then, the Governor refused to agree before he also had come down
to have a look, and to judge if Alex was right.

The next scene in the camp was one of fantasy. The Governor
came in his full dress white uniform and plumed hat, and he
brought his military brass band. He spoke to Alex before he came
to the village. 'Do you think you and I could speak to these
people alone?' Alex hesitated. The peaceful Tonga were behaving
as they never had since the Matabele Wars of the nineteenth
century, doing war dances with bloodthirsty cries and gestures,
and marching with spears in imitation of the armed police. Until
the last two days he had never believed the Tonga would do him
any harm. Now he could not be sure for himself, and less so for
the Governor. 'Well, let's try it and see,' the Governor said, and
when they came to the first groups of Tonga spearmen he stopped
his car, walked into the middle of the nearest group and said:
'Greetings. I am the Governor, I have been told that something
is troubling your hearts and I have come to find out what it is.'

His boldness enabled him, in the next two days, to have long formal meetings with the Tonga, but it did not solve the problem; they refused the order he gave in the name of the Queen. Convinced that everything short of force had been tried, he approved the plans of the police.

Next day, therefore, when the Governor had gone, there was a battle. There were thought to be 500 Tonga with spears, and 160 police with tear gas, shotguns and a few rifles. There was never any doubt who would win. The police had orders not to hurt any Tonga unless they had to. In the end, eight Tonga were killed and thirty-five wounded, and the police carried the wounded to a doctor who had been hastily called, with an ambulance, from the hospital a hundred miles away.

It was a small affair really, but not for Alex. He watched it with horror, blaming himself. But the blame went much further back than him, to the decision to build a dam at Kariba. There had been an alternative then, another place where only one thousand instead of fifty thousand Africans would have had to move. If the choice had not fallen on Kariba, or if the Tonga had been more worldly-wise, if Congress had not interfered, or if the government had been quicker to take the powers it needed – then, eight harmless men would not have been lying dead.

SIXTEEN

Successes and a Failure

The successes were several more books. The failure was marriage.

The books I wrote in the 1960s brought me and my family the usual material marks of prosperity – a very large house, a good many acres in the 'green belt' of London, two or three cars, a modest yacht and so forth – things I did not value very much even then and now would not value at all, except the yacht. Yet it all went awry, because I could not make the marriage last a lifetime.

It had lasted a long time already. We had twenty contented years, but then five or six when I knew with growing horror that it was going to end. I never told anyone my own views of what went wrong, and I don't intend to start now. It was simply one of those awful moments in life when there are only two roads you can take – three if you count suicide – and both of them, or all three, seem equally wrong.

We did not blame each other. I think it would be fair to say we were victims of an aspect of marriage that is too often overlooked. When the church's marriage vows were drafted, the average length of life was thirty to thirty-five years. Even at the beginning of this century, it was only forty-five years, and in 1940 it was sixty years. Now in England it is seventy-two, and still rising. The person you want to marry when you are young may have become quite a different person twenty or thirty years later, and you are very lucky if this is the person you would choose to grow old with in the twenty or thirty more years you can now expect to live. The vows are not suited to lives so long, and they have become a heavier burden for each generation.

I don't say this to excuse my own failure. It *was* a failure, the one I most regret in my life – although it ended in happiness for me, and I hope in the long run for my wife too. I only mention it because my children, who wanted me to write this book, knew how important that event had been for me and said I couldn't just leave it out. Separating is a very miserable business, even now when it is so common, and I can only say we did it as decently as we knew how. The children have always been equally welcome to either of us, and I think they love us equally too.

Enough of all that. Writing books was a holiday from domestic disaster, but I began to change the kind of books I wrote. What the trade calls real books, or 'reading books', are written for royalties, a percentage, usually 10% to 15%, of the retail price of copies sold. So they are always a gamble. The publisher will guarantee you a minimum total royalty, paid while you are doing the work, on the basis of a synopsis or just an idea. The longer you have done it successfully, the bigger the guarantee grows. But it is hardly enough to live on, even with a separate guarantee from America. The gamble is whether you ever get more than that minimum, and that is balanced by the hope that the book will 'take off' and pay you handsomely.

But if you need to make a quick buck (and I did need it then, to begin life again) you start to write things for a fixed fee, which is bigger than the guarantee but much less than a great success. That made me take on the job of writing the text for several 'coffee-table' books: one about Arab dhows, which meant going to Arabia for a second time; two naval histories for Time-Life Books, one on dreadnoughts and one on the seventeenth-century Dutch wars, which took me only as far as Amsterdam and the Time-Life offices in Alexandria, Virginia; and one for Marks & Spencer, rather shamefully titled *Great Sea Battles*, which I wrote without leaving my study. In my 'real' books also, I found myself driven to writing about battles – not because I like battles, I don't, but because people like reading about them. So I wrote books about Waterloo, Trafalgar, the Spanish Armada, D-Day, 1066, and the Greek War of Independence.

After all that, people naturally began to think I was a historian. But I am not, and I would rather confess it than wait to be found out. Nobody ever taught me any history after I was thirteen, when I managed to get out of it because I was frightened of the history master, a sarcastic old devil who was convinced that if you looked sleepy in his lessons it showed you were wicked and lazy, and not that he made his subject so deadly boring. After that, I had no interest in history until I was nearly fifty. Coming to it so late, I wondered if you can trust it, if it is really true, and how any historian can be dogmatic. Of course this suspicion is nothing new: Thomas Carlyle, no less, once said history was a great dust-heap, and on another occasion, 'History is a distillation of rumour.' And some of the greatest of modern philosophical historians, people I now have the greatest respect for, have argued the question whether any historical fact has reality.

The trouble is that all history, or nearly all, comes from ancient documents which happen to be preserved in archives or libraries or attics, and whether they have been preserved or not is a matter of chance. At best, these documents were written by eye-witnesses of events or, more likely in ages when few people were literate, were written down from the stories the eye-witnesses told. But historians can see the events only at secondhand, through the eyes of the writers of the documents; and the writers were only human, they had prejudices of their own, their memories perhaps were faulty, or they had an axe to grind or a natural inclination to make a good story better. These frailties are often difficult to detect.

And what of the documents which are lost? For every one that has survived through the centuries, one would suppose that scores or hundreds have disappeared, through fire or damp, or being eaten by mice, or written in ink that faded, or just being thrown out with the junk. Would these lost documents perhaps have contradicted the ones that remained? We can never know, and the chances are they would.

About battles, the interesting thing to my mind is not the tactics or strategy, much less the politics; it is what the men caught up in them thought of it all. From this point of view, Waterloo is the best of battles, because it was the first great land battle in which a fair proportion of soldiers were literate, so that there are scores of eye-witness accounts of what happened. Some men wrote reminiscences long afterwards, and some wrote letters home the next morning, to reassure their mums. The question remains, to what extent are they true? Do they tell what happened, or what ought to have happened, or what their writers thought had happened? Or indeed, when they are used in history books, what the historian thought ought to have happened?

I suppose even the most philosophical historians would agree that there really was a fight outside Brussels on a Sunday afternoon in 1815. But what more can we know about the Battle of Waterloo? The traditional way of describing a battle is with maps, with neat little rectangles on them representing regiments of infantry or cavalry, and arrows to show their movements. This is a matter of intellectual interest, but it obviously does not have much link with reality. It bears no relation to the human experience of a battle: nobody who was there saw things in anything like those terms. Most of them did not know where they were, much less where other regiments were, or what was really going on.

Surely history, whatever else it is, should be a record of human experience. I imagine the first feeling of the average man at Waterloo was, 'My God, this is a battle, and I'm in the middle of it, and that fellow is going to kill me unless I kill him first.' And the natural human reaction was to get the hell out of it. It is said that ten thousand men of Wellington's army ran away, or marched away. Bad soldiers perhaps, but common-sense human beings. What kept the majority there were the concepts of martial glory and regimental pride which all armies drill into their men; and, most of all perhaps, the fear of seeming afraid. The first idea of men who found that they were still alive that evening was that they had a splendid story to dine out on, or a story that would earn them free drinks in pubs for the rest of their lives. Even in the morning-after letters, one can see the story-telling beginning to form, and the myths beginning to grow. They were not telling the story for historians, they were telling it for their friends and families and making the best of it – and who is to blame them? Our legacy from that Sunday afternoon is a mass of personal stories, all subjective, all more or less revealing the teller in the light he wanted to be seen in, all more or less tinged with that human tendency to make a good story better. And all written by men whose memories were more or less clouded by shock, who at the moments they were trying to recollect had been half blinded by gun smoke, half deafened by noise, and either half paralyzed by fright or elated by dreams of glory.

Then what happens to those stories? There is a second stage

which removes them further from factual reality. The historians get at them. I can't speak for all the other historians of Waterloo, but I know what I did: I made my own selection from the stories, with the deliberate intention again of making a good tale. So I chose accounts which illustrated different parts of the battle and could be woven together to make a coherent picture of the whole. It was an arbitary choice, but the alternative was to try to put everything in. That was done a few years after the battle by a captain who recorded every movement of every regiment, and finished up with the dullest account of a battle I have ever read. Yet undeniably this act of making it comprehensible, a readable story, does remove it one degree further from reality. Nobody who was there could comprehend it as a whole; not even the Duke, much less the Emperor or Marshal Ney, and least of all the ordinary soldiers.

Many readers of my book on Waterloo kindly said it made them feel as if they were there, which pleased me because that was what I wanted to do. But if I became conceited, I had only to remember an evening in Brussels. I was asked to a reception at the Musée de l'Armée, and an English lady I was with decided I ought to meet some of the top brass of the museum – the librarian, I think. She introduced me to him: 'May I present Mr David Howarth, who wrote that splendid book about Waterloo?' 'Ah, Mr Howarth,' the great man said, as if meeting me was his life's ambition, and I glowed with pride. 'And you are the author of that book about Waterloo? Now, let me see – which one was it? We have thirty thousand here.' Ah well, they had thirty thousand and one after that, but plenty of people whose judgement was good said mine was the most exciting.

After *Waterloo*, I went much further back into history and wrote a book on the year 1066. Of course there were fewer contemporary accounts of what happened that year, but I was surprised when I started researching to find how many there were. I found ten that were written within living memory of the events, and ten more within a hundred years.

They provided a good example of a lost document. The two first accounts of the Battle of Hastings were written by a French bishop, who was highly critical of his allies the Normans; and by William the Conqueror's chaplain, who regarded Duke William as a super-human hero who never made a mistake or did any wrong, a sort of medieval Batman. The French bishop's account was the earliest, probably finished in 1067. Several chronicles mentioned its existence, but then it vanished and the Norman chaplain's version, written two or three years later, became so to speak the official account, though his prejudice is absurd. For 760 years it remained the basis of all histories of the battle. Then, in 1826, an extraordinary document was found in the Royal Library in Brussels. It was in Latin verse, which was not unusual; the extraordinary thing was that it was beautifully written in such tiny script that each line was less than an inch long. This turned out to be a very early copy of the French bishop's lost account – and in many important details it totally contradicted the accepted Norman version. After all those centuries historians had to rethink the history of the battle. And one wonders of course how many more old documents remain to be found, and perhaps to undermine that bit of established history.

I think I have read all the early accounts of 1066 that are known to exist. Many much better scholars have done the same. But each of them, using the same sources, would have produced a different history of the year. The early chroniclers were monks or clergymen who were bound to draw moral conclusions whatever happened, and most of them were writing for patrons who expected their own opinions to be confirmed. So it is difficult to separate the history from the preaching. As Carlyle said, it is distillation of rumour, and the further back in history you go, the vaguer the rumours become and the more important the distillation. History so long ago is largely the creation of historians.

Some of those battle books did very well, but none took me on distant journeys, and the last trip I made beyond civilization was to the jungle of Panama. I went there twice, the first time to write about the four centuries of turbulent history which lie there half buried among the tree roots, and the second time to make a television film of it. The first time I was alone, and I did not enjoy it much. I never liked travelling alone; it limits what you dare to do.

That first time the journey began in the Panamanian Consulate somewhere in the East End of London, where I had to apply for a visa, taking a letter from my bank to declare that I was solvent.

My bank is the Bank of Scotland, correct and formal as only the Scots can be, and the letter they wrote began, 'Gentlemen: Mr Howarth is a valued client . . .' and so on. In the Consulate's outer office I found a busty blonde lady, whom I took to be a receptionist. She looked at my letter. It reduced her to helpless laughter. 'Well, whaddya know,' she cried with peals of mirth, 'I been called many things in my life but never a "gentleman".' For she *was* the Panamanian Consul. It was an auspicious beginning.

Panama in those days was not a happy place, because the Canal Zone in effect was a colony of the United States, and it cut a swathe about ten miles wide right across the country from sea to sea, enclosed on each side by an unclimbable ten-foot fence. Inside everything was tidy and wealthy like a prosperous American suburb, and the Panamanians were not allowed in without a pass. Outside it was jungle, except where Panama City abutted on the fence, and there the elegant houses, the swimming pools and shaven lawns of the Zone stood face to face with the slum tenements of the city. The Panamanians resented the Americans and the Americans despised the Panamanians, and shortly before I was there, enmity had broken out in riots. Few people, inside or outside the fence, knew the Canal Zone had been created in the first few years of this century, not by rapacious Americans but by an unbelievably devious Frenchman called Bunau-Varilla, who knew nothing at all about international law but wrote the Canal Treaty alone in his hotel bedroom in Washington and tricked both governments into signing it.

It is always easier to sympathize with underdogs, so I lived outside the fence with the Panamanians and made most of my journeys in the jungle, and especially along the 250 miles of Caribbean coast to the east of the canal, the coast of Darien. It is a beautiful place, but hot, wet and unhealthy. I do not know anywhere else in the world that has such a long, eventful history and yet in the end has returned to primeval peace. There, abominable crimes were committed in the name of Christianity, and dreadful cruelties perpetrated in the greed for gold; and there still are the ancient Spanish fortresses of Nombre de Dios and Portobello, their roofless treasure houses and cathedrals wreathed in steaming jungle, and their cannons lying in rows where they fell when their wooden carriages rotted away two hundred years ago. There also, much farther east, is the site of the idealistic Scottish colony of 1699, doomed from its beginning. It is still called Caledonia Bay, though nobody who lives there now knows why, but I could not find any relics except the mound where the Scots built the fort they called St Andrew's, and the moat they dug to defend it. The moat is choked by mangroves now, but an old Indian who knew where it was – but not what it was – poled me along it with his grand-daughter in a dug-out canoe.

The only people who do live there now, or anywhere on that coast, are a gentle tribe of Indians called the Cuna. They build their villages of round huts with walls of bamboo and roofs of palm leaves on coral islands, out of the way of snakes and vampire bats, and they fish from canoes and plant meagre crops of maize and bananas on the mainland; and when a baby is born they plant six coconuts, which grow as it grows and provide it in later life with nuts to trade with the schooners which sometimes come across from Colombia. It is a contraband trade, but nobody cares. Their simple life is much the same now as it was before Columbus came that way in 1502, and they are some of the few lucky people in the modern world who seem perfectly content. Of course no sophisticated person could join them, but living a short time with them gives you an uneasy feeling that this is how mankind was meant to live.

All along the coast of Darien, hills loom above, covered to their tops by writhing jungle, and it was here, very close to Caledonia Bay, that the Spanish adventurer Balboa was told by a Cuna boy that there was another ocean beyond the hills, and marched across and found it. Balboa was a much better man than most of the Spanish commanders, but he was unlucky; he ended by being ceremonially strangled in the main square of a city he had founded and named Acla (this has disappeared so completely now that nobody knows exactly where it was). Bad luck followed him after his death, in some of the best-known lines of English verse, which attribute his moment of triumph to somebody else. It was not stout Cortez but Balboa who, in 1513,

'. . . star'd at the Pacific – and all his men
Look'd at each other with a wild surmise –
Silent, upon a peak in Darien.'

Nobody seems to know why Keats got it wrong, but Cortez, the conqueror of Mexico, saw the Pacific only years afterwards, and never went to Darien in his life.

You can still walk inland and begin to climb the hills where Balboa did, or anywhere else you choose, and I did it several times, but I never penetrated very far alone – just far enough to marvel that Balboa and his men did it all in armour and helmets, leather breeches, woollen stockings and boots. No wonder many collapsed with heat stroke. The jungle has not changed at all since then, and is still a daunting place and breathlessly hot. You know innumerable living things are watching you in the twilight under the trees. But they are not dangerous, except the snakes – and those only if you tread on them. True to tradition, the vampire bats do suck your blood if you sleep soundly, but it does you no damage unless they have rabies. Nor do mosquito bites if you have guarded yourself against yellow fever and malaria. The rest are mostly the harmless oddities of creation: tapirs, armadillos, sloths, anteaters, porcupines, iguanas, tortoises, and insects of formidable size. But the jungle stinks of decay. It is so virile, its life is so prolific, that death can be seen more plainly than usual as part of a cycle. The struggle for life is shown in every twist of the plants which grope and cling and thrust themselves up to the light. Everywhere are those which have failed or are clearly doomed to fail, to die and rot and feed the roots of those which have succeeded. The value you put on your own spark of life seems exaggerated. You know that if you lay down and died the jungle would instantly begin to convert you into humus. On the spot where you fell it would grow just a fraction taller, and you would have fulfilled your natural function. Nevertheless, the most serious risk in the jungle is not getting eaten and turned into manure; it is simply getting lost, which is easy when you cannot see where you are going.

On one of my solitary apprehensive walks, I suddenly found I was standing on cobblestones. I followed them, and found it was the ghostliest of all the ancient relics: the Spanish trail from Panama to Nombre de Dios. Guided by Indians, the Spaniards hacked through the jungle a path fifty miles long and at its best nine feet wide, just enough for two laden trains of mules to pass each other, scraping the undergrowth on either side. By 1535 or thereabouts it had the imposing name of El Camino Real, the Royal Road, and for centuries it was the only permitted crossing of the Isthmus, the most important highway in the Spanish Empire. Along this muddy wandering track came all the silver of Bolivia, the golden loot of the Incas, the pearls of the Pacific islands, to be collected by the fleets of galleons on the Caribbean side – the wealth which funded, among all else, the Inquisition and the Spanish Armada. This was the scene of Drake's first successful ambush, and of his final failure when he tried to march an army along it to Panama. And long stretches of it are still there if you can find them – not easy to follow, because they are blocked by fallen trees, their holes full of ants and tarantulas, which you have to climb over or crawl under or make a way round – not even easy to see unless you kick away the leaf mould which covers the cobbles. But there it is, an amazing survival, and struggling along it now alone in the silence and half-darkness you can feel the fears of the Spaniards, the hostile run-away slaves, the Elizabethan marauders, the buccaneers of Henry Morgan shouting to keep their spirits up, and the forty-niners hell-bent for California – and all of them lying down to die in their thousands of yellow fever and malaria in the steaming woods.

Reason told me it was possible to live off the jungle, if you knew how; there is another tribe of Indians, the Chocos, who never come out of it. I did not intend to try, but I thought I ought to know, so I asked the US Air Force, who had a Tropic Survival School in the Canal Zone. They were very kind, and happy I think to meet an enthusiast. 'No trouble at all,' they said. 'Check in here at 06.00 tomorrow, and we'll take you in a chopper, and drop you in the jungle, and you can walk out.'

I was not feeling very brave at six o'clock the next morning. It sounded too much like a practical joke. Drop me in the jungle? With a parachute, I supposed. And walk out? How? I did not have a compass, and compasses are useless in the jungle anyway. But I did not ask any questions, and of course they made it as easy as a picnic. The helicopter thundered low over the trees. I had flown over the jungle several times, and knew that what you see below looks quite unbroken and solid; but the surface you see is only the canopy of the trees, and the ground is hundreds of feet below that. The most experienced airman begins to think of a forced landing in the topmost branches, and the insoluble problem, if he happens to survive the crash, of climbing down to the ground far underneath. But the Americans had made a clearing, about the size of a tennis court, and the pilot slowly and carefully lowered the chopper into it. I was glad that one other man got out of it with me before it roared vertically up again between the trees, and left us there.

The first thing we did was to clear the clearing again: saplings grow fifteen feet in a season, and nobody seemed to have been there since the year before. Then we started to walk. The man they sent with me turned out to be a Panamanian Indian who had somehow got into the US air force, and he knew all I wanted to know. As we walked, chopping a trail here and there with machetes, he told me which fruit and nuts you could eat raw, and which young shoots of palms and ferns – and which, about half I suppose, were poisonous. He taught me to recognize the water vine, which provides a cool clean drink if you chop off a yard of it, and demonstrated which of the gargantuan spiders had poisonous bites, and which of the thorny bushes brought you out in a rash. He even lit a fire. Everything on the floor of the jungle is soaking wet, but with luck, if you pull on the creepers which hang everywhere like bell-ropes in a church, a shower of dry sticks falls on you from far above.

I have no idea where we were, or how far we walked, but it was not very far. In the evening we came to a river where two soldiers met us in a dug-out canoe with an outboard motor, and we zoomed downstream until we came to a road with a jeep on it.

It was only a day trip, but that excellent man made me feel I could cope with the jungle if I had to – except for the problem of getting lost, and there is no answer to that except to go with an Indian born and bred there.

After that visit, I wrote the book which was called *Panama* in the United States and *The Golden Isthmus* in Britain: a history which began with Columbus and ended with the plan, in favour at the time, to blast out a new canal with nuclear explosives – a plan that was luckily abandoned when the Americans discovered how dangerous it would be. The next year I went again to make the television documentary of the same history. That time I was not alone, and it was much more fun. I was with a producer-cameraman called Robert Cundy, who had done a lot of that sort of thing in Mexico, and his assistant, a Chelsea-type girl called Ginny. If Ginny and I had met in Chelsea I would not have dared to speak to her, but she was a splendid companion in a jungle, and so was Bob. She did the sound recording and kept the shot-lists and things, carried more than her share of the gear, and found time to wash my shirts – I needed a clean one every time I was on camera. She looked alluring in shorts and a T-shirt, but her undress shocked the Cuna, whose ladies are pretty but prudish.

In Panama City we had been told the Cuna would not have visitors in their territory at night. They had not seemed to mind when I was there alone, and I thought they could be persuaded. To that end, I had to make a speech to their Parliament. It met in a very large hut, and seemed to be a democratic assembly. The top men – the cabinet, one might say – lay in hammocks, rocking themselves with one foot on the ground. The rest, hundreds of men and women and their children, sat on benches. I think everyone in the tribe was an MP. When I was called I told them what we wanted to do, and tried to assure them we were sympathetic and could be trusted. Bob put what I said, or something like it, into Spanish, and a Cuna who spoke Spanish put it into Cuna. Then they had a debate. A lot of people seemed to ask questions. But in the end the head man of all, the *cacique*, said their country was our country, we could go anywhere with our cameras, and we could sleep in his village. He lent us a hut, and feasted us on lobsters and cooked bananas, both together. The only thing he asked us not to do was take pictures of the women, unless they said we could.

That was no problem at all. Where ancient voyagers took beads and looking glasses, modern ones take a polaroid camera, and as soon as the women discovered what it was they crowded round with their babies for the instant photographs. The children were enchanting, and an awful nuisance. They followed us in droves, always laughing in delight as if we were the funniest things they had ever seen – and I suppose we were, since they did not have much entertainment. There is no such thing as privacy in a Cuna village, except in the dark, because all the bamboo walls have wide chinks in them. In the evenings we needed a lamp – I to learn my lines for next day, Ginny to write up her lists, and Bob to tinker with his camera – and there was always a sparkling brown eye at every chink and ripples of laughter outside whenever any of us did anything. Once I got fed up and shouted to them, rudely but not angrily, to go away. They picked up words instantly, but usually got the vowels wrong. 'Bogger uff,' they shouted in unison, delighted. I was ashamed that was the only English they knew. 'You're just having a jolly good giggle,' I shouted back, and they made a chorus of it: 'Jilly god googgle. Jully gid goggle.' Cowardly, I abandoned my script and blew the light out, and just as well, because I then did the silliest and easiest thing you can do in a Cuna hut: I sat down again in the hammock provided for me, and fell out of it backwards with my feet in the air. If they had seen that, they would still be laughing now.

All three of us loved the Cuna, and the village, and everywhere else they took us on their coast. But for one day while we were there, civilization caught up with us. A huge cruise liner came in from the Caribbean, anchored off in the bay and landed crowds of tourists from New York. Poor things, they were utterly bewildered, and they never saw the village as it really was. The Cuna had given us all we asked for, and never asked for anything in exchange. But on that day, they turned mercenary. Huts became shops where the Cuna women sold the embroidered blouses called *molas*, and posed for photographs for a fee. The most popular picture was of mothers bathing their babies. Tin tubs were brought out and – though the Cuna are very clean people – the babies were bathed more on that day than in the rest of their lives. I had got in the habit of going around with bare feet because the Cuna did, but when the tourists found I could speak English they assumed I was a guide. 'What country are we in? Panama? Well, that's ours, isn't it? But don't try to tell me people live here. This place is not real, it's built for us by the cruise company. Well, I'll say they made a good job of it.'

That was an American cruise, but I had been on the receiving end of German and British cruises, in Greek villages and Lappish fjords, for example, and I think the same thing happens everywhere. The advent of a cruise transforms the places it goes to, so that passengers never see anywhere as it really is. In Lapland, Lapps had a special trick. A crowd of them met the cruise liners to pose with their reindeer for photographs at one dollar a time, and sold their souvenirs; then the liner moved on, and the Lapps bundled themselves into trucks and drove at full speed to the next anchorage; nobody seemed to notice it was the same Lapps and the same mangy reindeer everywhere. I never wanted to go on a cruise.

We three went to many other places in Panama, both inside the Canal Zone and outside; all the places I had been to the first time, and many others. Together, we ventured farther into the jungle. Alone, when nobody in the world had any idea where I was, I had worried about simple things like breaking a leg. Now, we even camped in the jungle. Not that we lived entirely on its questionable fruits. Among many other goodies, Bob had brought a tinned Christmas pudding from Fortnum and Mason, which we saved up gloating for weeks until we thought we were in the remotest place we would ever reach; then we lit a fire by pulling on the bell-ropes and boiled it. It was delicious.

All in all, it was probably an amateurish film we made. It was the first I had performed in. But the BBC thought well of it and showed it three times – an unusual accolade – and asked me to make some more, which I did, years later, when I had some authority as a naval historian.

While I was writing about battles, I plodded round dozens of battlefields: Waterloo, Normandy, Cadiz, Hastings and Stamford Bridge, and the west coast of Ireland where the Armada came to grief. Meanwhile, I took comfort in sailing my boat. I had always wanted a boat of my own since I was in Ireland before the war, but I could not afford it before the 1960s. To please me it had to be a boat my family and I could live in for our holidays, a boat I could imagine I might sail round the world if I ever had the time and energy. In the end, it was a compromise – the biggest boat you could legally tow on a trailer on the road – a new but modest family six-tonner, twenty-six feet in length overall. That is a plan I commend to anyone who wants to voyage beyond his own home waters, but does not have money to burn. I owned the same boat for fifteen years, and we all spent our holidays in it; we towed it with a Landrover to the west of Scotland, the Baltic, the south of France and the Adriatic, and sailed it far and often in Corsica, Italy, Yugoslavia and Greece. On the road, we carried a ladder to climb aboard it, and lived in it like a trailer caravan. It became a central part of all our lives.

I have never discovered anything better than sailing to cut yourself off from the world and all its worries. But many people, to my mind, spoil it for themselves by racing, either in dinghies or in vastly expensive ocean racers. I never had any competitive spirit, least of all in sailing. In the boat, I never wanted to get anywhere more quickly than anyone else. On the contrary, the essence of sailing ought to be contentment in going slowly, at the speed at which everyone used to go before the age of motors. So one can forget the eternal competition of life ashore. In a boat, you decide where you want to go, but it does not matter in the least when you get there, tonight or tomorrow or next week. You do not live by the clock or the calendar, but by the tides or winds; and if you have an unexpected night at sea, that is a special pleasure of its own – the phosphorescence in your wake and bow-wave, the green and red navigation lights which colour the sails, the dimmed light on the compass, the friendly flashing of lighthouses in the distance, the lights of steamers and Christmas tree illuminations of passenger ships, each bringing a minor problem of keeping out of the way.

Some people, normally kind and gentle, also spoil it for themselves and their companions by a change of character when they are in charge of a boat. They bellow orders in what they think is the language of a Nelsonian bo'sun, and get angry when their wives or children do not know what they are on about. Even the sight of a boat is enough to start some of them off. I once offered to help a man's wife and daughter, under his direction, to drag his dinghy across his back garden. We could have picked it up and carried it, but no: it had to be done properly on his words of command. 'Man the tackle,' he shouted, correctly pronouncing it 'taykel'. 'Now, bowse away . . . Check her. Belay hauling. Pay out handsomely. Handsomely, I said, Pamela. Fend off the port quarter, Pauline. Make all fast for a full-do. Pamela, what sort of knot is that? Use the painter with a clove hitch.' And so on, until everyone was in surly confusion.

My technique, I like to think, was the opposite, and the nicest compliment I had was from a boy who spent a day with us crossing the estuary of the Thames. 'I never really liked sailing before,' he said, 'but I love it in your boat. Nobody shouts at me, and nothing ever seems to happen suddenly.' That is how it should be. In a cruising boat, nobody should ever have to shout, and nothing should happen suddenly. It's the job of the person in charge to know what is going to happen, and to tell everyone calmly in plain English what he intends to do about it. So they all come to enjoy it. My family all did, anyhow, and became confident enough to take the boat abroad for their own holidays with their own friends. My most blissful recollections of being middle-aged all have a background of warm seas, strange harbours and surprisingly accurate landfalls.

Of course it all came to an end, like everything human. I grew too old, my elder girls started having babies, it became too expensive and the most charming coasts, year by year, were more and more over-crowded. Our last few voyages, unlike all the others, were a series of minor disasters which made me decide I could not do it any more.

That was in 1980 and 1981. We took the boat to the Mediterranean again, not this time by road but by the canals and west coast of France. My elder son sailed across the Channel from the Isle of Wight to the Channel Islands, and part of the way through the Brittany Canal. My new wife and I and my two step-children met him somewhere near Rennes to find the engine had several fatal diseases which none of us could cure, at least, not with French mechanics. So I spent all that summer holiday head-down in the engine compartment, my wife shopping and cooking and handing me tools and the poor children not even able to enjoy the Pernod and Muscadet.

Next summer my son and stepson and I tried again, and put the engine together. It worked, but only very slowly. However, once clear of the Canal we could sail, and we set off down the somewhat notorious Biscay coast, able to make about one knot ahead with the engine and nothing astern.

It made it more exciting, almost as exciting as it must have been when the English wine-ships coasted down there in the fifteenth century, to fetch their cargoes of claret from the Isle of Oléron. On the second evening, a monstrous squall was approaching across the sea, so I headed for a narrow tidal creek which was shown on the chart. When we found it, it was blocked by a new sea-wall. There was one narrow entrance, and inside a forest of masts – a brand new marina. We went in with a rising wind astern; there was nowhere else to go. It was full of glossy yachts – no room to turn and tack out again – and (it seemed to me) thousands of elegant Frenchmen in yachting caps and women drinking apéritifs outside a club house and eagerly awaiting a maritime disaster. I saw one empty space, and only one. The boys dropped the sails exactly on the split second it was needed without a word from me, I turned a tight circle to take the way off, and we glided into the space and made fast, pretending we always preferred to come into harbour under full sail. It was not difficult, of course, but it was risky and very ostentatious. I don't think I was feeling particularly British but, after all, this was the southern edge of Quiberon Bay, where we beat the French in a famous battle of seamanship in 1759.

That marina had one great asset, a mechanic who instantly knew what was wrong with our Swedish engine. In about half-an-hour he had it going full speed, and all that summer and the next it ran like a clock whenever we needed it. We went down the rest of that coast, up the river Gironde, past the villages whose names read like a wine list, through the ancient Canal du Midi, out into the Mediterranean through the Camargue, and along the French Riviera as far as San Remo, the first harbour in Italy.

I have always disliked the French Riviera since I first drove along it fifty years ago: a naturally beautiful coast, but ruined by ostentatious wealth, a string of ugly towns, and a main railway right along the foreshore. That year it was worse than ever. All its harbours were packed with costly motor-cruisers and a few huge ketches which never hoisted a sail; so that we, always the smallest and scruffiest boat in sight, had to anchor off and row ashore to go shopping. And I was saddened, the next summer, to find that the north coast of Italy had gone the same way. Portofino, for example. Portofino used to be a delightful little harbour, a wide piazza and steep hills all round like a Roman theatre. Now the only road into it was blocked every day by cars which could not get in or out, and every evening the harbour was jammed with those motor cruisers, which look as seaworthy as wedding cakes. There we met a kind and charming American called Bob. He lived in a small catamaran, and seemed to be an unofficial harbour-master. He despised the motor cruisers as much as I did. I had been in the habit of calling them bird traps, because their only visible function was not to go to sea but to lie stern-on to the quays displaying vases of gladioli and ice buckets of champagne to ensnare the nubile girls who stroll round Mediterranean harbours in bikinis. Bob more simply called them stinkpots: they fill the harbours with blue exhaust smoke. The first evening in Portofino we all watched one trying to come stern first to the quay. Its owner stood on its topmost bridge roaring his two huge engines ahead and astern and bellowing to his crew of paid hands and assorted females, who rushed round the decks waving fenders. 'My God!' Bob said. 'It takes more than an economic miracle to make a seaman.'

We had an ambitious plan to sail right round the south of Italy and so back to the Adriatic and the Ionian Sea, which had always been my favourite of all cruising grounds. It was there that we had found so many beautiful and empty places to anchor; there that we had spent so many exhilarating days and peaceful nights; there that we all had recollections of the most intense happiness that I think life can offer; there that I had wanted to die because life was so perfect. But it didn't work out, ever again. The next winter, we laid up the boat in a reputable yard near Portoferraio in the island of Elba, and when we came back in the spring, all its gear had been stolen: six sails, the warps and running rigging, the dinghy, the sets of charts, the tools and gas bottles, the compass and echo sounder, even one of the anchors. Nothing was left except the bare mast and spars, the engine and the main anchor, which was visibly stowed on deck and – the meanest trick of all – had its chain sawn off just inside the chain pipe. It was impossible to fit it all out again in Italy, and we had to decide to bring the pathetic remnants back to England by road. I spent a miserable winter arguing with the insurance company. They paid up in the end, but by then I had lost heart, and I sold her. I always knew that when I had to part with the boat, my only toy, I would suddenly grow a lot older; and I did.

SEVENTEEN

Hora mortis nostrae

My publisher – the same one for thirty years – has often told me books must not have a down-beat ending. I propose to defy him for once. The end of the story of anyone's life is death, and he would certainly say that is down-beat. I don't agree. Old age may be down-beat, but death is not unless it is premature. The death of an old man is timely.

My wise and admirable grandfather, the surgeon, wrote about death, anticipating his own; I have said he was not good at titles, but for that essay he chose the tidy Latin phrase I have borrowed. Death, he had observed, was like anaesthesia, and he had a lot of experience of both, of seeing people die and giving and receiving anaesthetics – he himself had thirteen major operations. He knew what it was like to see or feel consciousness being annihilated bit by bit (it was a slow process in his time, of chloroform or ether or gas). Anaesthesia could 'slip, in a moment, without a break, into death'. You could say it differed from death only if you came back to life, and in itself it was devoid of pain or pleasure.

Yet he did look forward to death in some ways: the restfulness of not existing, the end of struggle and apprehension, of the whole charade of screwing up one's courage, waiting, pretending not to be nervous, behaving nicely. The only thing he regretted was leaving his wife. He quoted an even earlier doctor, William Hunter, whose last remark was, 'If I had strength enough to hold a pen, I would write how easy and pleasant a thing it is to die.' But the comparison with anaesthesia, he knew, did not give the slightest clue to a psychic quality in death, or any sort of hope that it was something some part of you might survive. Only philosophy, not observation, could pretend to do that, and philosophers lived 'in an air too thin for ordinary people'.

There were three quarters of a century between us, but our conclusions were the same. Both of us, I suppose, were relics of nineteenth-century materialism, and I expect to be laughed at for being so naïve, but it can't be helped, that is the way my brain works when it is working at all. It is a result of being brought up as a physicist in the 1920s.

I sit here now, still writing on and off, in a hut in my garden. Almost everyone I know is younger than I am, but almost everything I see from my window is much older – it has a permanence far beyond an ephemeral human life. The cottage where I have finished up is very small and humble and is said to be four hundred years old, though I don't know how anyone can be sure. It was probably built by a forester or a charcoal-burner for himself and his family, because in the sixteenth century this bit of England, the remains of the Saxon forest of Andredeswald, was iron-founding country, and the charcoal from its oaks was used to smelt the ore. Guns that fought the Armada were cast in the parish; there is still a Gun Farm and a Gun Lane and a Gun Wood. My garden also is ancient, like the cottage, but it is large. My oaks must be descended, acorn to acorn, from the oaks that grew here before the Norman Conquest, and the stream that flows through the garden now was flowing the same in its valley when the whole place was part of King Edward the Confessor's hunting estates, and the gentry splashed through it on horseback with the new-fangled bows and arrows, intent on deer, or perhaps tried to jump it and fell in. I like to think of the lowly English people who have been born and lived and died happily here, and loved the place as I do, and I do not want anything more than to be one of them. I still plant forest trees which somebody else will enjoy when they are grown.

I am not sorry for myself; self-pity is not endearing. On the contrary, I know I am lucky. You cannot count it as bad luck to be old. It means only that you have had a good ration of life, and it is better on the whole to have it safely in the past where you can remember it, disappointing though it may be, rather than in the future, where you cannot foresee it. I am certainly lucky to have a kind wife who is loving by nature, and a host of descendants, closely united and not too far away: four children, two step-children, three children-in-law and four grandchildren so far. In my imagining of old age, I used to be a patriarch, dispensing words of wisdom to all my children. I have not often bored them with words of wisdom, but I have had some moments of patriarchy. One was my seventieth birthday, when the whole lot of them turned up in a convoy of cars, the front one flying an enormous Union Jack, all hooting their horns and bringing among many other things a birthday cake with trick candles you could not blow out. It was a beautiful summer's day and we laid lunch on tables on the lawn, and it was all enhanced by an American I had never seen before who turned up as if on cue at the sound of champagne corks in the forest and proved to be a fan of mine who had come a long way in the hope of meeting me. That impressed the children more than anything I could have said. They thought only pop stars had fans.

Superficially, what you most regret in growing old are the things you used to do with pleasure but cannot do any more. I shall never climb another mountain, not even the Matterhorn, which I have wanted to climb since I was too young to try. I shall never see the arctic ice again, nor the tropical jungle, nor probably a coral island. I shall never come out of harbour again and set a compass course for somewhere beyond the horizon, or find my way in to an empty anchorage in the cool of the evening where the hot scent of herbs comes off the land. I shall never play the solo part in a great romantic piano concerto – not that I ever did, but I always supposed it was the height of human ecstasy.

The first thing I gave up was appearing on television. I had not done it very often, but when I did I loved it – especially travelling with a producer and his assistant and a camera crew, all patient kind professionals. I admit I also enjoyed the astonishing momentary fame it brings. For a week or two, everyone you meet says, 'Saw you on the telly.' Then for a few more weeks, 'Didn't I see you on the telly not long ago?' Then it degenerates: 'Haven't I seen you somewhere?' Then everyone forgets it. Not many people remember authors' names, unless they are popular novelists, but they feel they ought to. So they are embarrassed if they meet them. 'What do you do?' kind ladies ask at parties. 'I write books.' 'Oh.' A long silence. 'Ought I to have read them?'

You can do without the physical pleasures. What is more difficult is a failing brain. That is insidious. You cannot be sure when it began to fail, or, as it proceeds, how quickly it is getting worse. You are aware or half aware that your brain is not so clear, so logical and ordered, as you think it used to be; but you know that when it gets one stage or two stages worse, you will not be aware of what is missing. You ask yourself if it was ever as clear as you thought it was. I have always known – well, not always but for a very long time – that my brainiest thoughts are the platitudes of cleverer men. But have all my thoughts been platitudes? They certainly are now. However, an author has one comfort: he did create books, pure products of his mind, and people did enjoy reading them, and not even professional critics complained they were platitudinous at the time. What is more, they still exist.

I said at the beginning of this story that when I was young I had no need to imagine life after death. I still have no need, when death seems rather close. In a Buddhist's Nirvana, time stops and leaves you in a static state of bliss where nothing happens, there are no events to measure the passage of time, and the chain of cause and effect comes suddenly to an end. So far as I know, the Middle Eastern religions do not express this concept of time that stops, though it is trivial to a physicist and is easy to imagine now, when all of us can see movies which can simulate time that not only stops but goes faster or slower, or backwards. Eternal life, going on and on for ever in time that passes, is an unbearable idea. It was fit perhaps for medieval serfs who were content to furnish their heaven with pearly gates and streets paved with gold and a ready supply of harps, but it is impossible now.

I am not a Buddhist, but to me their idea is more congenial. When I die, I expect to stop and let time for living people go ticking on without me, leaving me behind in a static present. This is not a faith, not much more than a form of words, but whatever stories you tell yourself about what happens to you after you die, nothing, after all, can be more comforting than nothing. If anything consciously happens to me when I am dead, I shall be as mad as a good Buddhist would be if he died and found he was in a Christian purgatory.

That raises the question of when and how to die. In any previous age I would have been content to leave it to nature, though nature may give you a way of dying which is more painful, disgusting or alarming than it need be, not only for you but for your family too. Perhaps nature will get there first. But I firmly think you should be free to end your own life when you have had enough of it, without being marked as depressed, eccentric, sinful, miserable or mad. The Biblical span of three score years and ten was about right; a little too short perhaps, but not much. Most people in their seventies begin this down-beat trip towards senility, and any wise person will avoid becoming senile if he can.

Modern doctors have confused the whole issue by finding how to prolong a life that nature would have ended, and insisting that their archaic oath compels them to do it whether the owner of the life wants it prolonged or not. And lawyers confuse it further. Suicide is not against the law, but the law makes it as difficult as it can by forbidding anyone to help you, or even to tell you the best and tidiest way to do it. Doctors tempt you with offers of a few more years of unnatural life, lawyers try to prevent you doing what common sense tells you is right, and if you listen to both, you will certainly end as a nuisance to your family. I emphatically do not want to be kept alive by a machine, however clever that is, and I do not want – worst of all things – to finish up in a geriatric ward. My wife, bless her, understands this very well, but for fear of the law I cannot ask even her to help me when the time comes. It has not quite come yet. I still enjoy the last few dregs of life. But I am getting tired, I have had nearly enough of a good thing, and I could do with a rest. The thing I am most afraid of now is leaving it too late and living too long.

Having written this, perhaps I shall still be sitting here, looking out of the window and trying to flog a worn-out brain towards coherence when I am eighty. It doesn't seem likely or desirable, and if it happens the last laugh will be on me.

As for the wise words I imagined I would offer my children, I have forgotten them all except one. They do not need that one, and it is very far from being wisdom of my own. It is simply: be kind. Kindness has many names, love, compassion, charity – call it what you like, they all mean the same. It is the quality that encompasses all virtue. Christ said it of course: 'Love thy neighbour.' St Paul said it many times: 'And now abideth faith, hope, and charity, these three; but the greatest of these is charity.' The Beatles said it, echoing St Paul: 'All you need is love.' And the Dalai Lama on his different foundation says it too, not claiming it as a Buddhist virtue, but as the essence of all religions. You can live a good and happy life without faith, which is the antithesis of reason, and you do not need hope unless you first have fear; but you cannot do without charity. I would not make a good preacher, because that is all I would want to say: do what you like, and if it is truly done in kindness, if it does harm to nobody and preferably good to somebody, who will dare to say it is wrong? If I wanted to pad out my sermon a little, and give it a slightly Christian slant, I might offer my congregation (all thirteen of them) one of my favourite quotations. It was in an unexpected place – in a letter Sir William Hamilton sent to Emma, before he married her. 'The whole art,' he wrote, 'is really to live all the days of our life; and not, with anxious care, disturb the sweetest hour that life affords – which is, the present. Admire the Creator, and all his work, to us incomprehensible; do all the good you can upon earth; and take the chance of Eternity without dismay.' Poor Emma – she seldom managed to follow his instructions. I have not been very successful either. But I have enjoyed trying.